# THE LICENSING BUSINESS HANDBOOK

How to make money, protect trademarks, extend product lines, enhance merchandising, control use of images, and more, by licensing characters, teams, celebrities, events, trademarks, fashion, likenesses, designs & logos!

## *By Karen Raugust*

EXECUTIVE EDITOR,
THE LICENSING LETTER

EPM COMMUNICATIONS, INC.

Library of Congress Cataloging-in-Publication Data

Raugust, Karen, 1960-
The Licensing Business Handbook: How to make money, protect trademarks, extend product lines, enhance merchandising, control use of images, and more, by licensing characters, teams, celebrities, events, trademarks, fashion, likenesses, designs & logos / Karen Raugust
p. cm.
Includes bibliographical references and index.
ISBN 1-885747-00-4
1. Marketing. 2. Entertainment. 3. Sports. 4. Fashion. 5. Trademarks. I. Title.

THE LICENSING BUSINESS HANDBOOK
# TABLE OF CONTENTS

# THE LICENSING BUSINESS HANDBOOK
# **LIST OF FIGURES**

# INTRODUCTION

The licensing business has come of age over the last decade. Total retail sales of licensed products in the U.S. and Canada, according to *The Licensing Letter*, have tripled from $20.6 billion to $70 billion in the 13 years from 1982 to 1994, while another $31.2 billion in licensed merchandise is sold each year overseas. As a result of this growth, the media — consumer as well as trade — has increasingly begun to cover licensing as a subject of interest to the general public. No more is licensing simply the domain of a few "licensing companies."

When people think of licensing, they usually focus on sports or entertainment. But there's a lot more to the licensing business than that. Most shoppers probably don't know (or care) that much of the branded merchandise they purchase is licensed. Fashion labels ranging from Sasson, Bonjour and Ocean Pacific to Perry Ellis and Pierre Cardin are virtually 100% licensed, and many other fashion brands license at least some of their products to other manufacturers.

In corporate America, licensing programs range from Coca-Cola collectibles based on nostalgic advertising images to videogames starring the 7-Up Spot and Frito-Lay's Chester Cheetah. By far the greatest portion of corporate trademark licensing is, again, "invisible," in the form of brand extension. Oreo cake frosting, Western Union home and office communications products, Dr. Scholl's footwear — all are licensed.

Notice that this book uses the term "licensing business" rather than "licensing industry." There is a reason for that. While many people refer to it as an industry, licensing is really a marketing tool that crosses over many industries — apparel manufacturing, professional sports, museums, publishing, entertainment and so on. Practitioners from all of these industries increasingly recognize that licensing is a marketing tool, and one that is being used in ever more sophisticated ways.

The licensing community includes a diverse group of companies from the largest entertainment studios to sole proprietors marketing a single licensed product from their home offices. This book was written to provide concrete information on the basics of licensing for everyone from manufacturers to property owners, from one-person companies to large corporations, from neophytes to those with more experience. It serves as an overview and introduction to the business, and also as a handy reference for those seeking answers to specific licensing-related questions.

It is impossible to offer an all-encompassing step-by-step method of launching a licensing program. Every effort differs in its objectives, target audience and property characteristics. Therefore, *The Licensing Business Handbook* provides a systematic approach that allows readers to develop their own licensing strategies. It illustrates the mechanics required to enter into a licensing deal, and outlines the key issues that should be considered for any licensing program. While there is no single correct way to approach a licensing effort, there are a number of questions that should be asked and resolved.

Toward that end, Part I offers an overview of licensing — what it is, how it has evolved over the years, how the business works and who the players are. Part II illustrates potential strategies for those just getting into licensing. One chapter looks at the subject from the point of view of the property owner (licensor), while another takes the licensee's (manufacturer's) perspective.

Part III examines the details of licensing, including how compensation is structured, what provisions are contained in a licensing contract, how to legally protect a property, how to best prevent infringement, what factors to consider when launching an international program and how promotions are developed.

Finally, the book includes a glossary of licensing terms and a list of answers to more than 30 frequently asked questions about licensing.

*The Licensing Business Handbook* is based on the knowledge of a vast network of licensing professionals, as gleaned in interviews, at conventions and seminars, through research and consulting, and in informal conversations. These professionals have created successful businesses through their effective use of the licensing techniques you will learn about in this book. *The Licensing Business Handbook* will allow you to acquire the tools you need to make licensing work for you.

# PART 1:
# HOW THE BUSINESS WORKS

# CHAPTER 1

# WHAT IS LICENSING?

Licensing is the process of leasing various rights to a legally protected (that is, trademarked or copyrighted) entity. The entity — known as the PROPERTY — could be a name, a graphic, a logo, a likeness, a saying, a signature or a combination of several of these elements. The rights to a given property are granted for a specific purpose (usually for a product or products to be sold in retail stores), for a defined geographic area, and for a limited time, in return for payment.

## TERMS & DEFINITIONS

The owner of a property is known as the LICENSOR, while the renter of the rights (usually a manufacturer) is called the LICENSEE.

The basic component of payment is the ROYALTY, which is generally a percentage of the wholesale price of every product sold. A guaranteed minimum royalty payment, or a GUARANTEE, is usually required — regardless of sales levels — and a percentage of that guarantee is normally paid up front as an ADVANCE. (See Chapter 7 for more on royalties and related issues).

While this book focuses primarily on merchandise licensing, a property can be licensed for many other, non-product purposes, as well. Examples include premiums, fast-food or packaged goods promotions, and television or print advertising. Many properties are licensed for entertainment vehicles, such as films, television series and live performances. For example, the rights to create films and television series based on the Teenage Mutant Ninja Turtles, which originated as comic book characters, are licensed by the Turtles' licensing agent, Surge Licensing.

The types of properties available for licensing vary widely. Babe Ruth's name, signature and likeness are licensed for collectible baseballs; the Coca-Cola name and logos are authorized for tin containers; the Peanuts characters are found on children's apparel; the World Wildlife Fund logo is licensed for ties; the artist Mary Engelbreit's name and designs grace dinnerware; the likeness of the musician Elvis Presley is found on pre-paid telephone calling cards; and so on.

## A BRIEF HISTORY OF LICENSED PRODUCT MERCHANDISING

Merchandising began more than a century ago. In the 1800s, for example, certain characters — such as the British puppets Punch and Judy in the 1880s (for banks and other products) and Palmer Cox's Brownies (for blocks and games by Horsman) — were translated into products. Merchandise endorsed by celebrities and royalty also existed.

The first Peter Rabbit toy, based on the book character by Beatrix Potter, was created in 1903. Merchandise such as banks and other products based on trademarks were also marketed in the early 1900s, based on properties such as Ford, Chevrolet, Pepsi, Dr. Pepper and Campbell's. Characters were also merchandised during this period, including Sunbonnet Babies, book characters introduced in 1902. The comic strip Buster Brown, with toys and games manufactured by Selchow & Righter and Steiff, and Amos and Andy, for which Marx manufactured toys, are additional examples.

Beginning in 1910, celebrities such as Charlie Chaplin were merchandised for dolls; the first Kewpie doll (based on drawings featured in *Ladies' Home Journal*) was marketed in 1911; trademarks such as Mr. Peanut were the basis of merchandise; and designers began to come into their own, led by Coco Chanel. (Not all designer merchandise is licensed; some designers operate in-house manufacturing facilities or source the products directly, and as a result license very few outside companies.)

In the 1920s, film stars and characters, as well as comic strip properties, were licensed. Walt Disney's first license was granted for a school notebook, based on Mickey Mouse after his 1928 debut in *Steamboat Willie*. Disney earned $300 on the deal. The Green Hornet, film star Tom Mix, Little Orphan Annie and child movie star Baby Peggy were other properties associated with merchandise during this decade.

Licensing really took off in the 1930s, with celebrities, comic strips and film and radio stars major property types. Corporate trademarks also had some activity in calendars, collectibles, banks and so on. Comic strip and film characters, including Betty Boop, Popeye and Felix the Cat, were extensively merchandised. The Batman comic was launched; the Lone Ranger, Mutt & Jeff, Dick Tracy, ventriloquist dummy Charlie McCarthy and Jack Armstrong All-American Boy were all merchandised. Celebrities with merchandising activity during the 1920s included Babe Ruth, Shirley Temple, the Dionne Quintuplets, Jane Withers, Sonja Henie, Gene Autry and Roy Rogers.

Comic strips, films and radio shows remained strong in the 1940s, with Bugs Bunny, Casper the Friendly Ghost, Terrytoons, Tom & Jerry and Woody Woodpecker all coming into their own. Fashion designers such as Pierre Balmain and Christian Dior set up shop in the 1940s, and corporate logos such as Borden's Elsie the Cow were the subject of merchandising. Other properties during this decade included Captain Marvel, Captain Midnight and Fibber McGee & Molly.

Several fashion designers became prevalent in the 1950s, including Pierre Cardin, Oleg Cassini, Givenchy and Valentino. Footwear designer Charles Jourdan was a licensor and a licensee, signing an agreement with Christian Dior in 1959. Publishing properties ranging from Betsy McCall to the Bobbsy Twins were merchandised in the 1950s, and trading card companies associated themselves with athletes from baseball and hockey. Cosmetic company Revlon authorized a Miss Revlon doll. TV properties also began licensing during this decade; entertainment-based properties active in the 1950s included Shari Lewis, Rin Tin Tin, Emmett Kelly, Huckleberry Hound, John Wayne, Davy Crockett, Hopalong Cassidy and Howdy Doody. In fact, these properties could be lucrative — Davy Crockett generated $300 million in retail sales of licensed merchandise, while Hopalong Cassidy rang up $70 million at retail. The first Peanuts book came out in 1952, and the first Snoopy licensed product, a plastic figurine, was authorized in 1958.

The 1960s were characterized by several TV-based licensing programs, ranging from "The Flintstones," "Rocky and Bullwinkle" and "Yogi Bear" to "Dr. Kildare," "Daniel Boone" and "As the World Turns." Alvin and the Chipmunks and *The Sound of Music* were also merchandised, and "Sesame Street" went on the air in 1969. The NFL began an organized licensing program in the early 1960s, being the first sports league to do so on a systematic basis. The Beatles and Twiggy were among the celebrities with licensing activity, and a number of fashion designers set up shop, including Liz Claiborne, Laura Ashley, Adolfo, Geoffrey Beene, Oscar de la Renta, Anne Klein and Ralph Lauren.

In the 1970s, the Pink Panther had 250 licensees, and a Rocky & Bullwinkle shop, one of the first such dedicated retailers, was opened in Hollywood by creator Jay Ward. The Muppets went on the air in 1972, and Holly Hobbie was licensed as a doll to Knickerbocker in 1974. The first collegiate licensing agreements were put into place during this decade. Designers who set up shop in the '70s include Giorgio Armani, Bill Blass and Claude Montana. Entertainment properties ranging from *Planet of the Apes* to "The Six Million Dollar Man" to "Mork & Mindy" were associated with licensed products. Many observers point to the licensing program surrounding the movie *Star Wars*, released in 1977, as the start of the "licensing business" as we know it today. That $2.5+ billion program, driven by toy licensee Kenner, demonstrated the upside of licensing; people began to enter licensing as a career.

The 1980s were characterized by the very rapid growth of the licensing business, building on the *Star Wars* phenomenon. Toy properties that went on the air as television programs were prevalent, including He-Man, My Little Pony and G.I. Joe. The Smurfs, which began as a comic in Belgium in 1957, debuted as a U.S. TV series in 1981 and generated $1 billion in retail merchandise sales, while another toy property, the Cabbage Patch Kids, dominated in the mid-1980s. Other entertainment properties in the '80s included Roger Rabbit, "ALF," "Thundercats," "Dynasty" and *Ghostbusters*. Several properties springing from corporate advertising also made a splash during this decade, including the California Raisins, Wendy's slogan "Where's the Beef?" and Budweiser's party animal, Spuds McKenzie. The late '80s also witnessed the beginning of the rise of sports licensing, with the major leagues and colleges becoming more aggressive about licensing and customers demonstrating a seemingly insatiable demand.

The 1990s are witnessing the maturation of the licensing business, including the first-ever annual declines in total sales of licensed merchandise, as well as a recession in the decade's early years. Still, several hit entertainment properties have emerged, including several animated Disney films, singing group The New Kids on the Block, the television show "The Simpsons," the Teenage Mutant Ninja Turtles, PBS properties including "Thomas the Tank Engine" and "Barney & Friends," "Beverly Hills 90210" and "The Mighty Morphin Power Rangers." More and more properties, in sports (e.g. minor leagues and auto racing), trademarks (e.g. cosmetics and sporting goods brands) and all other property types, are entering the licensing business.

*Figure 1* *(page 7)* shows total retail sales of licensed merchandise in the U.S. and Canada since 1982. *Figure 2* *(page 8)* illustrates retail sales figures for a variety of properties of different types. These numbers are all associated with successful properties and should not be taken as the overall norm; they do, however, indicate the great sales potential a licensed property can have.

## BENEFITS AND RISKS OF LICENSING

Many observers view licensing as an industry. In fact, it is a marketing tool that can be effectively utilized across many diverse industries. If embarked upon in a common-sense, realistic way, licensing can benefit both licensees and licensors. It can also be risky for both parties, however.

### BENEFITS TO LICENSORS

To the property owner, the money that accrues as a result of licensing is definitely a plus. The relative importance of this benefit depends, however, on what type of property is involved. Royalty revenues are of relatively little importance to a licensor of corporate trademarks, for example — the revenues from PepsiCo's core food and beverage businesses dwarf the incidental licensing revenues from "Diet Pepsi Uh-Huh" t-shirts, Chester Cheetah videogames and other licensed merchandise associated with its properties. Corporate trademark owners would not initiate a licensing program if it were not profitable, and the licensed lines often form an ancillary profit center, but in most cases revenue generation is not the primary reason for the effort.

On the other hand, licensing revenues will play a major role for an entertainment property. Up-front licensing fees (advances) are often put toward the TV show's or film's production expenses; in some cases, there would be no entertainment vehicle without the promise of licensing revenues to help pay for its creation.

In addition to the financial benefits, licensed products can effectively help market the property. San Jose Sharks caps and Chicago Bulls jerseys in department stores, fan shops, mass merchants and elsewhere help create and maintain consumer awareness toward the sports leagues (in this case, the National Hockey League and the National Basketball Association, respectively). Shoppers can also be sports fans and therefore potential ticket buyers. Similarly, *Jurassic Park* toys, apparel and gifts, seen at retail in 1993, helped to market the film to consumers, many of whom are moviegoers. Nonprofit organizations also use licensed products to create awareness for their missions, in addition to relying on the ancillary revenues this merchandise can provide.

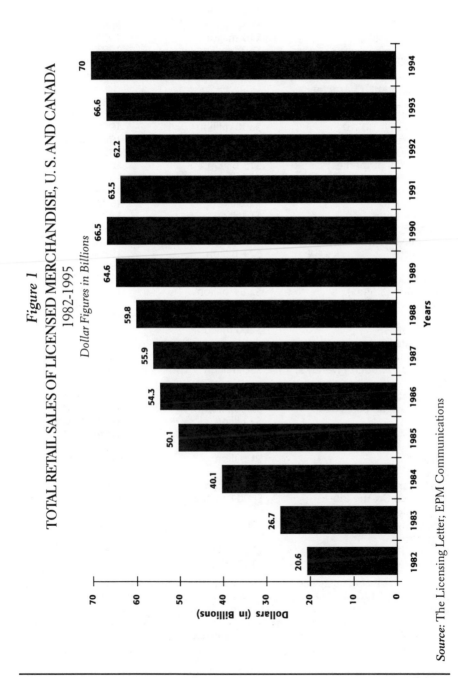

*Figure 1*
TOTAL RETAIL SALES OF LICENSED MERCHANDISE, U. S. AND CANADA
1982-1995
*Dollar Figures in Billions*

*Source:* The Licensing Letter; EPM Communications

## Figure 2
## SALES OF LICENSED MERCHANDISE FOR SELECTED PROPERTIES

| PROPERTY | SALES | TIME PERIOD |
|---|---|---|
| **Fashion** | | |
| B.U.M. Equipment | $140 million | 1993 |
| Bill Blass | $650 million | annually |
| Bob Timberlake | $70 million | 1994 |
| Gear | $400 million | 1993 |
| Perry Ellis | $800 million | annually |
| Pierre Cardin | $700 million | annually |
| **Entertainment/Character** | | |
| Alvin and the Chipmunks | $300 million | 1982-1994 |
| Batman | $2 billion | 1989-1994 |
| Beverly Hills 90210 | $500 million | 1990-1993 |
| Cabbage Patch | $4+ billion | 1983-1994 |
| Care Bears | $1.4 billion | 1983-1988 |
| Disney (all properties) | $15 billion | annually |
| E.T. | $1 billion | 1982-1983 |
| Flintstones (film + classic) | $1 billion | 1994 |
| Jurassic Park | $1 billion | 1993 |
| Looney Tunes | $1 billion | 1993 |
| Marvel | $200 million | 1993 |
| Sesame Street | $750-$800 million | annually |
| Simpsons | $2+ billion | 1989-1994 |
| Smurfs | $1+ billion | 1983-1984 |
| Star Trek | $1 billion | 1966-1994 |
| Star Wars (3 films) | $2.6+ billion | 1978-1983 |
| Strawberry Shortcake | $1.1 billion | 1980-1984 |
| Teenage Mutant Ninja Turtles | $5+ billion | 1987-1994 |
| Ultraman | $200 million | annually |
| **Corporate** | | |
| California Raisins | $500 million | 1986-1987 |
| Where's the Beef? (Wendy's) | $80 million | 1984 |
| **Sports** | | |
| Collegiate | $2 billion | fiscal 1994* |
| Major League Baseball | $2.5 billion | fiscal 1994* |
| NBA | $2 billion | fiscal 1994* |
| NFL | $3 billion | fiscal 1994* |
| NFL Players Association | $600 million | fiscal 1994* |
| NHL | $1 billion | fiscal 1994* |
| **Music** | | |
| Elvis stamp | $40 million | 1994 |
| New Kids On The Block | $800+ million | 1990 |
| **Art/Design** | | |
| Mary Engelbreit | $80 million | 1994 |
| **Publishing** | | |
| Beatrix Potter | $250 million | annually |
| Berenstain Bears | $100 million | annually |

*Note*: Figures include only licensed merchandise, not merchandise produced in-house or under contract, except for Disney, which includes all retail products. Figures are worldwide unless noted with an asterisk (*); asterixed entries denote domestic figures.

These are all successful properties and should not be taken as the norm for all properties. Annual sales figures may be higher or lower in any given year.

*Sources*: Various published reports, company information, interviews, TLL estimates

For corporate trademarks and fashion labels, licensing is a way to extend a company's product line to areas where the licensor itself does not have manufacturing or marketing expertise or existing distribution channels. Cosmetics marketer Revlon's expertise lies in cosmetics, fragrances and other personal care products. The Revlon brand is appropriate, however, for other health- and beauty-related merchandise, such as hair accessories, hair brushes, cosmetic kits and hair dryers. Revlon, as a cosmetics marketer, does not have expertise in manufacturing hair dryers. And while some hair dryers may be sold in cosmetics areas at department stores, where Revlon is accustomed to selling its products, other distribution channels, such as electronics departments, are unfamiliar to the company. Therefore, it makes sense for Revlon to enter appropriate product categories through licensing, which it has done.

In addition, licensing may be an effective means for a corporate marketer to test a new product category in a relatively risk-free way. If the category proves successful after a test period, the licensor can then set up an in-house operation to continue the product line. This large investment becomes less risky, since there are now some assurances that the line will sell.

Similarly, a company can often test or expand its brand internationally through licensing as well. Using a local licensee may be preferable to exporting, given cultural and business differences. In addition, licensing in initial stages could lessen the risk to the licensor monetarily, particularly if the product line needs to be altered for international consumption (perhaps even requiring several versions for different regions).

For some corporate brands, licensing can be more cost-effective than in-house manufacturing, even for core product lines. Generra, a men's apparel brand introduced in 1980, found in 1993 that its licensed lines — accessories and some apparel categories — were more profitable than the core apparel items that it manufactured in-house. As a result, Generra transformed into a full-time licensor, concentrating on marketing the brand while leaving the manufacturing to its licensees. Other fashion brands that became full-time licensors after a period of financial difficulties include Sasson, J.G. Hook and Ocean Pacific. If a potential licensor's royalties from a licensed product line would exceed its profit margins from an in-house operation to manufacture the same products, then licensing is an attractive alternative.

Another important reason to set up a licensing operation, particularly for licensors of corporate brands, is to strengthen existing trademarks. Trademark rights arise from the actual use of the mark or registration of the mark with the Patent and Trademark Office — signaling intent to use — in various classifications of goods (e.g. class 25, clothing, footwear and headgear). Licensing helps strengthen a trademark by expanding its use to products outside the licensor's core categories, particularly those in other classifications of goods where the mark is not necessarily registered. (Registration provides the most complete protection of a trademark, but use is the main criteria to establish that mark.)

For example, Harley-Davidson, the motorcycle company, would not want a manufacturer to begin distributing Harley-Davidson lollipops, even if it has no intention of entering the lollipop business itself. The unauthorized Harley lollipop would imply an endorsement from the licensor, thus potentially hurting its hard-earned brand image. In this hypothetical example, Harley-Davidson may not have registered its trademark for food products, but its other trademark registrations and its exploitation and policing of its marks in various categories (some through licensing), demonstrate to the courts that the company is serious about protecting its trademarks. (See Chapter 8 for more on trademark registration.)

A note on the use of the words "trademark" and "brand" throughout this book: "Corporate Trademarks" is one of the property types used by *The Licensing Letter*. It comprises corporate logos and brands that are available for licensing (see Chapter 2 for details). That usage — which is employed to distinguish a corporate trademark owner from licensors of other types of properties — is different from the legal meaning of the word "trademark," discussed above. Licensors from all property types own legally protected trademarks in this latter sense. In addition, the word "brand" is occasionally used to refer to a property if it — no matter what its source — is perceived as a brand by consumers and licensed as such by its licensor. (This concept will be discussed later in this chapter). Again, a brand in this sense does not necessarily originate in the Corporate Trademark property type. These differences should be clear given the context in which they are used.

A corporate trademark licensor can also use licensing to help relaunch a brand, or to reposition a brand within the marketplace. For example, if a property targeted primarily toward teenagers is being repositioned as a younger children's property, the availability of licensed products appropriate for that age group would be one effective way to achieve this. Licensing should not be the primary tool for this effort, but can be one effective component of an overall marketing plan.

In some cases, licensing can also provide an outlet for the licensor's products or by-products. This is true, for example, with food licensors that extend their lines into other food products. Nabisco supplies Oreos to Pillsbury for a line of licensed Oreo-flavored cake frosting and snack bars. Similarly, Jim Beam brand whiskey is licensed for charcoal briquets that use by-products from the whiskey-distilling process as an ingredient.

Licensing also offers a brand a better opportunity to cross-merchandise products and make a bigger impact at retail, because it gives the brand a wider product selection across more product categories. This is particularly important for home furnishings designers and brands, where cross-merchandising at retail is a major factor behind the best-selling lines, but it also holds true for other licensors, including fashion, other types of trademarks, artists and even characters.

Finally, for some property types, most notably art and artists, licensing is beneficial in that it allows the artist to maintain control over his or her images. The alternative to licensing is to sell those designs outright to manufacturers of gifts, domestics, tabletop items and so on. Selling a design outright to a manufacturer of bedspreads, for example, may lead to uses of the work in ways or on products of which the artist does not approve. However, if he or she sold the rights, the artist has no control over how the design is used, now or in the future.

In contrast, licensing allows designers to retain ownership of their creations, and thus to maintain control over their art — they have final approval over all uses of their designs, and can terminate the agreement at the end of the contract period if a manufacturer does not meet their expectations. They can choose which products to license and decide to whom they will license them. In addition, they will be earning a constant revenue stream that is tied to sales, rather than a one-time upfront fee that, for a successful product line, will generally be less than the royalty potential.

## BENEFITS TO LICENSEES

The major benefit to a manufacturer who ties in with a licensed property is the consumer awareness that the property brings to its product lines. A manufacturer without a well-known brand name can immediately become part of a brand through licensing. The "instant" brand can be a brand in the traditional sense (e.g. Betty Crocker or Dr. Scholl's). Or, it could be an entertainment, sports or other type of property, all of which boast consumer awareness and are, in a sense, brands in the same way that a corporate trademark is.

For example, Wal-Mart has created a successful hardware brand by licensing a magazine title (*Popular Mechanics*). The Disney name is viewed by most consumers as a brand, and Disney has launched several sub-brands as well, including Mickey & Co., Mickey Unlimited, the Princess Collection and so on, each appealing to a different target market. Sports properties can be considered brands, as well; consumers view all NFL Los Angeles Raiders merchandise as being under one brand umbrella, although it is manufactured by hundreds of different licensees. The major sports leagues have strengthened this perception, like Disney, by creating sub-brands. Major League Baseball, for example, instituted Rookie League as the brand umbrella for its licensed children's merchandise, Cooperstown Collection as its nostalgic brand, and so on.

By becoming part of an established brand through licensing, the manufacturer immediately benefits from the property's awareness, without the time and expense associated with building an in-house brand. Even if a high guarantee payment is required by the licensor, the guarantee is likely to be significantly less than the amount needed to build a brand over time.

A property's perceived brand benefits in the eyes of consumers could include: quality (such as Ralph Lauren), fun (Looney Tunes), educational benefits (Sesame Street), or an upscale image (Fabergé). Other brand attributes could include its appeal to a certain demographic group, a perception of value at a reasonable price, or other characteristics. Through licensing, the property's attributes become associated with the licensees' products.

A property also often brings a built-in market to the manufacturer's product line. If a domestics manufacturer licenses Elvis Presley for towels and sheets, it automatically gains a large potential market of Elvis Presley fans. If a stationery manufacturer licenses the Gitano apparel brand for school supplies, a large market of Gitano apparel buyers might have an affinity for Gitano notebooks and pens over other licensed products or generic merchandise.

Acquiring a license also provides additional marketing clout to the manufacturer. All of the licensed products associated with one property help sell the others. In addition, the core property helps sell the merchandise. *Playboy* magazine creates demand for *Playboy* men's underwear; the "Mighty Morphin Power Rangers" television series creates demand for Power Rangers action figures; Barbra Streisand concerts create demand for Streisand-licensed champagne glasses. This added awareness obviously benefits licensees; in fact, licensees of certain property types, especially entertainment and character properties, often have little or no need to additionally advertise their products, or at least are able to lessen their advertising expenditures. (This is not true for *all* property types; licensees of many corporate trademarks and sports properties are *required* to contribute to advertising in various ways.)

Licensing allows manufacturers that rely heavily on art and designs — domestics and home furnishings, giftware and tabletop, some apparel, stationery and paper goods companies, for example — to limit the size of their full-time in-house art staff and minimize development costs of art preparation. The time and monetary investment required to develop the designs rest with the artist; the manufacturer still may accrue significant development costs, but the portion of costs attributable to developing the design itself are not the licensee's responsibility. A well-chosen design license can help round out a licensee's selection, without internal development costs.

In some cases — although this situation is relatively rare — acquiring a license can also open up new distribution channels for a manufacturer. Usually, a licensee's existing distribution network is a major factor in a licensor's decision regarding which manufacturer to select, but in rare cases, other factors besides distribution (e.g. quality of products or willingness to pay a high advance) may be more important to the licensor's choice of licensee. If a licensee is trying to sell to a new retailer but is finding it difficult due to limited shelf space and the retailer's reliance on brands that it has purchased on a long-standing basis, a license may be what is needed to push the manufacturer into the store or chain. The fact that the retailer recognizes and values the license, or carries other products based on the same property, may lead it to consider buying from the new manufacturer. One example where this situation holds true is Fabergé, the upscale brand based on the works of Russian artist Carl Peter Fabergé. Fabergé chooses its licensees based primarily on the quality they can provide — distribution is secondary since the license itself can open doors for the right manufacturer.

All of these benefits, it should be noted, do not come just from so-called blockbuster properties. A marketer can gain the benefits of awareness and increased sales even if it is the only licensee of a particular property. For example, Weekend Exercise, a San Francisco-based apparel company, licenses Mikhail Baryshinikov's name for a line of bodywear, and does $35 million in sales annually; Pagoda, one of a handful of licensees for the foot-care brand Dr. Scholl's, has sold $100 million worth of Dr. Scholl's footwear thus far; Brut underwear licensee Nantucket reportedly sells $12 million worth of this line each year.

## RISKS TO LICENSORS

With all of these benefits come risks to both licensees and licensors. Licensors bear relatively little of the financial risk of licensing, of course. A portion of their revenues comes in the form of guarantees, which must be paid regardless of how the products sell. While the amounts of guarantees vary, it is unlikely that a licensor would lose much money from a licensing deal. Still, there are other risks.

One of the most significant is the possible loss of control over the property. If all products under a given brand are produced in-house or sub-contracted, the licensor has control over every detail — design specifications, quality, sales, distribution and marketing. With licensing, the manufacturer takes over many of these functions, leading the licensor to lose some control if it is not vigilant.

Of course, the licensor can, in various ways, maintain control over its licensing activities. Property owners have the ability to select appropriate licensees and distribution channels, to approve all products, to dictate terms in the licensing contract and to terminate the contract if the manufacturer does not meet expectations. The more seriously a licensor takes these responsibilities, particularly product approvals and selection of licensees, the more control it will have over the program. Still, the risk of a certain loss of control is inherent in the process of licensing.

Why is the potential loss of control such a significant risk? The licensor is in the business of owning a property. The value of that property forms the basis of the licensor's business and, therefore, maintaining the property's image is paramount. If a licensor loses control of its licensing effort, a number of factors could damage the licensor's property. Products that find their way into discount stores could harm the image of an upscale brand. Shoddy manufacturing will hurt a brand known for its "quality" (or any property, if the product is very poor). Frivolous merchandise could harm a children's property based on educational themes. An unhealthy item could hurt a property whose main reason for being is to promote good health (such as the American Heart Association or a health magazine, for example).

The existence of these potential disasters means that the licensor puts itself at great risk of diluting its brand image, unless it maintains control over its licensees and its licensing strategy. It is risky to license a property to a manufacturer and then let that company take it from there. It is also risky to license a property to an inappropriate manufacturer — a potential licensee that is known for making low-priced, low-quality items will not become a maker of quality, upscale items just because a licensor authorizes it.

The availability of too many products can also hurt a property's image and shorten its life. The market becomes saturated and a consumer backlash or a general cheapening of the image could occur. At minimum, consumers will eventually move on to the next "hot" thing. This phenomenon is most noticable in the entertainment area, but properties of any type are susceptible to this life-shortening phenomenon if the market is flooded with merchandise. In fact, product overproliferation is of more concern to licensors of corporate brands, for whom the core brand is the major business and licensing represents an ancillary business and revenue stream. In this case, the primary purposes of licensing are to support the brand image, protect the company's trademarks, extend to new product categories or increase awareness for the brand, as well as to generate revenue. It is more essential for corporate trademarks than for any other property type that the licensed products do not mar the integrity of the core brand.

A final risk occurs if the licensor does not live up to its end of the bargain in the licensing agreement. If that happens, the licensor will jeopardize its ability to license quality manufacturers in the future. Word gets around quickly in the relatively close-knit licensing community, and licensors that are perceived as unethical or who do not contribute their fair share to the relationship will have trouble finding quality manufacturers with which to work on the next property, or on the same property in the future. Of course, there will always be manufacturers lining up for a very "hot" property, no matter who the licensor is, but relatively few properties are truly must-haves. Licensors who lack good reputations, based on past experience, will have trouble marketing their properties, and will thus jeopardize their livelihood.

## RISKS TO LICENSEES

The major risk to licensees is a financial one. In addition to the required minimum guaranteed royalty, other non-recoupable investments include research and development, re-tooling and marketing expenditures (e.g. advertising and point of sale materials). And, besides these outlays, which become sunk costs if the license fails, there are the variable costs of manufacturing and shipping the licensed products. These will all be discussed in this section and in Chapter 6.

Even though a royalty is the main component of payment for a license — and is not really a big investment in itself since its payment is directly tied to sales — there is the question of the minimum guarantee against royalties. The guarantee, which is calculated based on expected sales, is payable no matter how many licensed products are sold. This requirement means that licensees must pay a sometimes-significant sum to the licensor; licensees will not recoup their investment if sales levels are not high enough to justify that expense.

Even for a property that looks like it will generate significant merchandise sales, the upfront portion of the guarantee (the advance) may be high enough to be a barrier to some potential manufacturers. Prohibitively high advances are particularly common in the entertainment area, where the laws of supply and demand dictate high advances for hot properties and where high advances are an important goal for the licensor, who often uses the money to finance production.

In addition to high guarantees and advances, as noted above, licensees often invest a lot in other costs, such as re-tooling, research and development, marketing and so on. If the licensed product line fails, these expenditures are irretrievable.

No matter what property a manufacturer chooses, there is no certainty that it will do well on that manufacturer's particular products. The property as a whole could flop. In the entertainment area, if no one goes to see a film or a television series gets cancelled after two episodes, there is not much chance of selling a lot of products. If a newly launched apparel brand fails, licensed accessories will fail too. More significant, however, is the fact that even if the property itself is a success, it is not a given that all licensed products will succeed. People may like the core property, be it film, television or some other type, but may not want to purchase merchandise based on it. Even billion-dollar properties do not drive success for every licensee — some products fly off store shelves, and some just sit there. (Conversely, a property that, overall, does not do well often has a couple of product lines associated with it that sell very well for one or more licensees.)

No single product line is guaranteed success, even for an established brand with a built-in market and a past record of solid licensed merchandise sales. This holds true of corporate trademarks such as General Motors' brands, a sports league such as the NFL or a non-profit group such as the Sierra Club. All of these properties are the focus of successful licensing programs, but each have been associated with certain products that did not sell. In some cases, there is a discernible reason: the target markets for the property and product did not adequately match, the price point of the product was too high or too low, the product category did not fit with the image of the property, and so on. In other cases, however, there seems to be no identifiable reason for the flop: the product fails, even though it seems to meet all criteria for success.

Another risk to licensees concerns inventory control. The popularity of a license — especially a faddish one — can increase to higher-than-expected levels very quickly. Then, with virtually no warning, demand can fall off suddenly. It is a challenge for licensees to, first, meet demand while it is at its peak; not being able to meet demand when it is high can cause bad feelings about the licensee's company on the part of both retailers and consumers. Second, it is important to ensure that inventory levels are not so high that excess inventory is left when demand falls off. Selling off excess inventory at close-out prices can wipe out the profits earned at the property's peak.

Finally, association with a property can become risky for a licensee if the property itself becomes the center of controversy — it may be deemed too violent, for example. Some products are relatively controversy-proof, such as t-shirts marketed to a college audience; others, especially family-oriented ones, could be damaged. Licensees who associate with living celebrities, including athletes or entertainers, are particularly vulnerable. Drugs, imprisonment or accusations, behavior unbecoming to a product spokesperson and so forth can make an attractive property very unattractive in an instant.

Even without the human element, entertainment properties can cause controversy. Each of the following properties, all of which have several licensees, have become controversial: "Beavis & Butt-head" (thought to encourage children to light fires), *Jurassic Park* and *Batman Returns* (both films considered more appropriate for adults, yet products appealed to younger children) and Mortal Kombat (accused by some of being too graphically violent). Even Barney the Dinosaur came under fire, being deemed by some observers to be more commercial than is appropriate for a PBS pre-school television series. Obviously, most of these properties drove a lot of licensed merchandise sales. All the same, there is still a risk that a licensed property could unexpectedly be considered controversial by a manufacturer's target market or by a vocal segment of the general populace, thus hurting sales of its products.

## RESPONSIBILITIES OF THE PLAYERS

Each participant in a licensing relationship has certain responsibilities to fulfill. Every licensing agreement is unique in its specifics, and therefore in the various roles required for each partner vary to some extent. Some guidelines can be outlined about how the responsibilities are normally divided, however.

The primary responsibility of the licensor is to legally protect its properties through trademark and copyright registration. Trademarks protect names and logos that distinguish the products of one company from those of others; copyrights protect creative elements of a property, such as graphic design, music and text.

Licensees desire to use the property because it is unique and allows them to differentiate their products from those of their competitors. If a property is not adequately protected, infringement is more likely to occur and less apt to be remedied. Therefore proper legal protection is a prerequisite of licensing, and the costs — with some exceptions discussed later — are borne by the licensor.

The graphic look of the property, whether it be a likeness, signature, logo or design, is created and its use monitored by the licensor. Licensors maintain the image of their properties by putting together a stylebook and other art reference materials for licensees to use as guidelines on the proper use of the allowable trademarks and copyrights. The stylebook illustrates the appropriate uses of logos, artwork, likenesses and other components of the property. It provides a range of artwork that can be used, including specifications such as exact colors. It often shows a variety of potential applications on goods in selected product categories.

The second major tool licensors use to monitor the image of their properties is the licensee selection process. As mentioned earlier, a licensee's track record speaks volumes about its ability to appropriately market and create products based on the licensor's property. The stylebook and other tools are not useful unless the licensee inherently has the capabilities required to do the job.

Once appropriate licensees have been selected, the licensor's next responsibility is a diligent product approval process. The licensor must approve samples of all products proposed by each licensee, usually at several key milestones during the manufacturing process, such as conceptual drawings or models, pre-production samples and production samples. Licensees then have a period of time during which to make the requisite changes. Some licensors take this responsibility very seriously and are notorious for their strict and lengthy approval processes. This diligence often pays dividends, though; these same licensors are generally those with the most sought-after brands. A diligent approval process benefits licensees too, of course, since the better the overall brand image, the better able the property will be to drive sales of the licensee's products. Licensors who are less strict about approvals open themselves up to potential problems later when a faulty or inappropriate product damages their brand, thus decreasing sales and making the property unattractive to potential licensees.

It is the licensor's responsibility to oversee anti-counterfeiting efforts. Counterfeiting, or the unauthorized use of a property, is a big problem in the licensing business. If poor quality, unauthorized goods find their way to the marketplace, the property will be hurt. In addition, sales of knock-offs cut into sales of legitimate products. The hotter the property, the more counterfeiting can be expected, so large licensors or those with hot properties tend to be the most active in their anti-infringement efforts. An effective anti-counterfeiting program is costly, and larger licensors have deeper pockets. Still, preventing infringement is an important concern for all licensors.

As for licensees, their responsibilities include the design and manufacture of the products, subject to approval by the licensor, as noted above. Licensees also handle sales and distribution of the licensed merchandise. They generally sell the licensed items to the same retail accounts that purchase their non-licensed products, although the property may allow them to achieve some extra distribution as well. (In some cases, where a licensor has a manufacturing business and is licensing as a means of brand extension, licensed products may be sold through its sales force as well. For example, a toy brand may be licensed for other non-toy-related children's merchandise. Some of these licensed items may be sold in toy departments, or at Toys R Us, or at other of the licensor's existing customers. Thus the licensor's sales force may handle this channel. Generally, however, sales and distribution are the licensee's jurisdiction.)

Responsibility for advertising and marketing support rests with both parties, depending on the situation. Licensors sometimes advertise to consumers in order to strengthen the brand. They also advertise to the trade to let retailers know where they can locate licensed products. For example, in *HFN*, a trade magazine for domestics, housewares, consumer electronics and other home furnishings, a licensor may run ads in the housewares section listing licensees of kitchen-related products. Manufacturers may also advertise their licensed products, either alone or with other product lines. In some cases this activity is a key part of the licensing effort. For example, the master toy licensee of a children's entertainment property advertises during Saturday morning cartoon shows; licensors and other licensees depend on this advertising to support the property.

For some licensors, such as corporate trademarks, fashion labels and some sports properties, licensees' products are viewed as a way to enhance the brand. In this case, licensees may be required to pay additional percentage points, on top of royalties, toward an advertising fund. Or, they may be able to deduct points off of the royalty if the money goes toward co-op advertising with retailers.

Licensors, especially of entertainment properties, are increasingly expected by licensees to play a role in pre-selling the property to retailers so store personnel understand and are aware of the concept before licensees approach them to make their puchase decisions. Licensors are expected to provide marketing support by encouraging retailers to merchandise licensed merchandise in concept shops, providing point-of-purchase materials and co-op marketing dollars, and creating retailer promotions.

## OTHER MAJOR PLAYERS IN LICENSING

Licensors often retain LICENSING AGENTS to manage their licensing programs. Agents bring experience and industry contacts to the table, which can be very valuable, particularly for a new licensor. In addition, agents can handle the approval process, oversee bookkeeping (including royalty compliance), and help with the contract negotiation and other duties. For their efforts, they receive a percentage of all royalty income. See Chapter 5 for more information on licensing agents.

Manufacturers also have help in the form of LICENSING CONSULTANTS or MANUFACTURERS' REPRESENTATIVES. These are companies retained by manufacturers to help them identify potential properties and aid them in acquiring appropriate licenses. Like agents, they have expertise and contacts, and specialize in licensing on a full-time basis. The manufacturer has other aspects of the business to attend to, and many find it valuable to retain an expert specializing in the license acquisition process, especially if the manufacturer does not have staff members dedicated solely to licensing.

ATTORNEYS specializing in licensing are another key component of the business. They have expertise in trademark and copyright law, in the particulars of licensing contracts and in the legal remedies available to counteract counterfeiting. Retaining an attorney for the legal aspects of licensing is essential, whether in conjunction with a licensing agent or a licensing consultant, or if the licensor or licensee is handling licensing duties alone. A number of these specialists are available to members of the licensing community.

# CHAPTER 2:
# SOURCES OF LICENSED PROPERTIES

As mentioned in Chapter 1, licensable properties come from a variety of sources. The largest, with $17.2 billion in retail sales in 1994 (or 25% of all sales of licensed merchandise), according to *The Licensing Letter*, is the entertainment/character segment, which includes television series, films, comic book characters and classics such as Looney Tunes and Peanuts.

The second largest property type is sports, comprised of sports leagues, colleges and other sporting events, which totaled more than $13.8 billion at retail in sales of licensed merchandise (20% of the market) in 1994. Corporate trademarks/brands, with $13.2 billion in retail sales (19%), and fashion properties with $12 billion (17%) round out the four largest sources of properties. *Figure 3 (page 22)* shows the relative shares of retail sales of licensed merchandise, by property type.

Categorizing property types is not a clear-cut enterprise. *The Licensing Letter* attempts to categorize properties by their origination — that is, a book title, such as *The Magic School Bus*, is classified under publishing even though its licensing program is, as of this writing, influenced more by the fact that it has developed into a television series on PBS. Similarly, the Nickelodeon licensing program, which we categorize under entertainment/character, is only partially dependent on character-specific licensing with its shows "Ren & Stimpy," "Rocko," "Rugrats," and so on. A significant part of its licensing effort focuses on Nickelodeon-branded merchandise, which theoretically could be classified under Trademarks and Brands as well.

As far as the creation of a licensing program goes, of course, it really does not matter what the source of a property is, as long as there is a market for it. In any case, *Figure 4 (page 22-26)* illustrates some of the properties that fall into each property type. This table is by no means comprehensive. Its purpose is to provide an overview of the types of licensed properties that spring from each source, and to provide an overview of the multiplicity of possible licensing programs.

While every licensing program is unique, certain trends and similarities exist within each property type. In this chapter, we look at the major sources of licensable properties and discuss some of their characteristics.

## ENTERTAINMENT AND CHARACTER LICENSING

The Entertainment and Character sector contains two groups of properties with very different characteristics — "hot" or short-term properties and "classic" or long-term ones. Short-term properties are expected, no matter how successful, to have a primary life span of about three to five years. Their sales curve spikes in the first year or two of this cycle — sometimes a very high spike indeed — but by the end of the three or so years, merchandise sales are very limited. When licensors determine that their property is short-

## Figure 3
## 1994 SHARES OF LICENSED PRODUCT RETAIL SALES, U.S. AND CANADA, BY PROPERTY TYPE
*Dollar Figures In Billions*

| PROPERTY TYPE | 1994 RETAIL SALES | PCT. ALL SALES |
|---|---|---|
| Art | $4.88 | 7% |
| Celebrities/Estates | $2.65 | 4% |
| Entertainment/Character | $17.22 | 25% |
| Fashion | $12.04 | 17% |
| Music | $1.05 | 1% |
| Non-Profit | $0.68 | 1% |
| Publishing | $1.56 | 2% |
| Sports | $13.80 | 20% |
| Trademarks/Brands | $13.15 | 19% |
| Toys/Games | $2.73 | 4% |
| Other | $0.26 | 0% |
| **TOTAL** | **$70.01** | **100%** |

*Source:* The Licensing Letter;
EPM Communications

## Figure 4
## SELECTED PROPERTIES BY PROPERTY TYPE

**ART**
American Greetings card art
Amy J. Wulfing
Boris Vallejo
Cat Clan
Cat Hall of Fame
Cheryl Ann Johnson
Colonial Williamsburg
Cynthia Hart
Donald Zolan
Edith Jackson
Frank Frazetta
Grant Wood
Gre Girardi
Greenwich Workshop
Greg Spiers
Gwen Connelly
Hallmark card designs
Helen Lea
Hillary Vermont
Hummel
Hunt Slonem
Ivory Cats
Jan Brett
Jared Lee

Joan Walsh Anglund
John Grossman
Judith Ann Griffith
Judith Kruger
Leslie McGuirk
Lisa Frank
Mabel Lucie Atwell
Mary Engelbreit
Maxfield Parrish
Norman Rockwell
Olivia
Paul Brent
Picasso
Ruth J. and Bill D. Morehead
Precious Moments
Stephen Lawrence
Sue Dreamer
Suzy's Zoo
Thomas Hart Benton
Vargas illustrations
Vicky Hart
Viv Eisner Hess
Winterthur Collection

*Continued Next Page*

*Figure 4 Continued*

## CELEBRITIES/ESTATES
Abbott & Costello
Albert Einstein
Mikhail Baryshnikov
Bette Davis
C.Z. Guest
Charlie Chaplin
Elizabeth Taylor
Elvis Presley
Emmett Kelly Jr.
Fabio
Humphrey Bogart
James Cagney
James Dean
Kathie Lee Gifford
Laurel & Hardy
Malcolm X
Marilyn Monroe
Martin Luther King
Roy Rogers
W.C. Fields

## ENTERTAINMENT/CHARACTER
ABC Daytime
Aladdin
Alvin & the Chipmunks
American Gladiators
Andy Griffith Show
Animaniacs
Archie & Friends
Barney
Batman
Beakman's World
Beavis & Butt-head
Beetle Bailey
Beverly Hills 90210
Blondie
Cabbage Patch Kids
Cartoon Network
Casablanca
Casper the Friendly Ghost
Coach
Dick Van Dyke Show
Felix the Cat
Fido Dido
Flintstones
Free Willy
Garfield
Godzilla
Gone with the Wind
Gumby

Hello Kitty
Home Improvement
Honeymooners
I Love Lucy
Indiana Jones
Inspector Gadget
It's A Wonderful Life
Jurassic Park
King Kong
Lamb Chop
Lassie
Looney Tunes
Marvel Comics (Spiderman, X-Men, etc.)
The Mask
Mickey Mouse
Mighty Morphin Power Rangers
Mr. Rogers Neighborhood
Mr. Wizard
MTV
Muppets
Nickelodeon
Nightmare Before Christmas
Nightmare on Elm Street
Northern Exposure
Peanuts
Popeye
Puzzle Place
Ren & Stimpy
Robotech
Rocky & Bullwinkle
Sailor Moon
Saturday Night Live
Sesame Street
Simpsons
Skeleton Warriors
Smurfs
Star Trek
Star Wars
Swan Princess
Tales from the Crypt
Teenage Mutant Ninja Turtles
Terminator 2
Thomas the Tank Engine
Tiny Toon Adventures
Tom & Jerry
Wizard of Oz
Woody Woodpecker
Ziggy
Zorro

*Continued Next Page*

*Figure 4 Continued*

## FASHION

Adrienne Vittadini
Alexander Julian
Anne Klein
Armani
Arnold Scaasi
Aspen
B.U.M. Equipment
Bebe Winkler
Bennetton
Bill Blass
Bob Mackie
Body Glove
Bonjour
BOSS
Brittania
Bugle Boy
Burberry
Calvin Klein
Capezio
Carolina Herrera
Carter's
Charlotte Moss
Cherokee
Chic
Christian Dior
Cotler
Cross Colours
Crunch Gear
Danskin
Debra Mallow
Diane Von Furstenburg
Donna Karan
Eagle's Eye
Easy Spirit
Faded Glory
French Toast
Gear
Generra
Gitano
Givenchy
Gloria Vanderbilt
Guess?
h.i.s.
Halston
Hang Ten
Health-Tex
J.G. Hook
Jacques Moret
Joe Boxer

Jones New York
Jordache
Jou Jou
Lightning Bolt
Lillian August
MacGregor
Marimekko
Members Only
Mighty Mac
Misty Harbour
Natori
Nautica
Nicole Miller
Ocean Pacific
Oleg Cassini
Oscar de la Renta
OshKosh B'Gosh
Perry Ellis
Pierre Cardin
Polo Ralph Lauren
Rampage
Sasson
Todd Oldham
Wrangler

## MUSIC

Barbra Streisand
Beatles
Billy Ray Cyrus
Clint Black
Country Music Association
Garth Brooks
Grand Ole Opry
Grateful Dead
Hank Williams Jr.
Janet Jackson
John Lennon
Madonna
New Kids On The Block
Prince, the musician formerly known as
Reba McEntire
Rolling Stones

## NON-PROFIT

American Heart Association
American Red Cross
ASPCA
CARE
National Audubon Society
National Park Foundation

*Continued Next Page*

*Figure 4 Continued*

National Parks & Conservation
  Association
National Troopers Coalition
National Wildlife Federation
Sierra Club
UNICEF
Wilderness Society
World Wildlife Fund
**PUBLISHING**
Babar
Baby-sitter's Club
Beatrix Potter
Berenstain Bears
Better Homes & Gardens
Budgie the Little Helicopter
Christy
Clifford the Big Red Dog
Cosmopolitan
Curious George
Eric Hill's Spot
Field & Stream
Good Dog, Carl
Good Housekeeping
Kipper
Little Engine That Could
Lyle, Lyle Crocodile
MAD Magazine
Magic School Bus
Old Farmer's Almanac
Pat the Bunny
Penthouse
Playboy
Popular Science
Rand McNally
Reader's Digest
Richard Scarry
Sports Illustrated for Kids
Very Hungry Caterpillar
Where's Waldo?
**SPORTS**
American Professional Soccer
  League
Arnold Palmer
Atlanta Centennial Olympics
Babe Ruth
Big Ten
Brickyard 400
Canadian Football League
Colleges
Goodwill Games

Indianapolis 500
IndyCar/Championship Auto Racing
  Teams (C.A.R.T.)
International Hockey League
Ironman Triathlon
Jack Nicklaus
Joe Montana
Johnny Tocco's Ringside Gym
Major Indoor LaCrosse League
Major League Baseball
Major League Baseball Alumni
Association
Major League Baseball Players
  Association
Major League Soccer
Michael Jordan
Minor League Baseball
Nancy Kerrigan
NASCAR
National Basketball Association
National Football League
National Football League Players
  Association
National Hockey League
National Hockey League Players
  Association
Negro Leagues Baseball Museum
Negro Leagues Baseball Players
  Association
New York City Marathon
Pele
PGA of America
PGA Tour
U.S. Hot Rod Association
U.S. Soccer
USA Basketball
Wayne Gretzky
Wimbledon
World Championship Wrestling
World Cup '94
World Wrestling Federation
**TRADEMARKS/BRANDS**
American Tourister
AMF
Anheuser-Busch, Budweiser
Apple
Betty Crocker
Big Boy
Borden

*Continued Next Page*

*Figure 4 Continued*

Brut
Buick
Burger King
Caboodles
Cadillac
Campbell Soup
Celestial Seasonings
Chevrolet
Chiquita
Coca-Cola
Coleman
Colt
Converse
Coors
Coppertone
Croscill
Crown Crafts
Dr. Scholl's
Dunlop
Everlast
Fabergé
Farberware
Fieldcrest
Ford
Formica
Frye
Harley-Davidson
Hawaiian Punch
Hawaiian Tropic
Hershey
Huffy
Jack Daniels
Jeep
Kawasaki
Keds
Kodak
Labatt's
Mack Trucks
McDonald's
Miller
Molsen
Pepsi
PEZ
Pillsbury
Rawlings
Reebok
Remington
Revlon
Riddell
Rollerblade

Samsonite
Sharper Image
Snap-On Tools
Spalding
Stanley
Sunkist
Voit
Western Union
Winchester
Zenith

**TOYS/GAMES**
Barbie
Bubsy Bobcat
Carmen Sandiego
Crayola
Creepy Crawlers
Dungeon & Dragons
Fisher-Price
Hot Wheels
LEGO
Magic Trolls
Mega Man
Monopoly
Mortal Kombat
Mr. Potato Head
My Little Pony
Nintendo/Super Mario
Norfin Trolls
Pac-Man
Play-Doh
Playskool
Polly Pocket
Sonic the Hedgehog
Street Fighter
Super Soaker
Treasure Trolls

*Note:* This list is not exhaustive, but should give a sense of the sorts of properties found in each property type.
*Source:* The Licensing Letter;
EPM Communications

term in nature, their optimum strategy is to maximize sales during the relatively short window of opportunity. This strategy is in stark contrast to the best strategy for a classic, outlined below. Of course, there is always the risk that this type of property will fail altogether, leading to a life span of zero years.

Long-term properties, on the other hand, are those that are seen as having a life span of decades. Mickey Mouse, created in 1928, is certainly among them, as are Peanuts (1950) and the "Sesame Street" characters (1969). When a licensor makes the decision to handle its property as a classic (or if it already is a classic in its original medium when licensing begins), its strategy will be quite different from that for a short-term property. Too high a level of merchandise sales in the early years could make the property fizzle out prematurely, and will leave little room for expansion of the program over the years. Licensors must also ensure that a classic property itself, as well as its associated merchandise, remains fresh (through new product designs, promotional activity, new media and entertainment vehicles) as its life span lengthens.

Because of the relatively conservative nature of classic-based licensing programs, annual sales levels for such properties are likely to be less in any one year than that season's crop of "hot" properties; the sales will, however, remain relatively constant for decades, rising and falling in cycles but hovering around a constant — and sometimes very significant — level.

An increasingly important trend in entertainment licensing is the tendency to look at most properties as having the potential to become classics. Manufacturers and retailers are risk-averse, and a property's potential longevity is an attractive selling point in their eyes. They examine a new property to see what media vehicles — films, TV, videogames, home videos and publishing — are planned, what promotional activities are being prepared at launch and in the future, and so on. As a result, even brand-new properties that would have automatically been considered short-term in the 1980s are now being pushed as being classics-in-the-making. Of course, not all will succeed. The main thing to remember is that there is a distinction between long- and short-term properties, and that each must be managed in an appropriate way. (See Chapter 5 for specific strategies applicable to each.)

There are exceptions to the rule, of course. Some initially hot properties, such as "The Simpsons" or the Teenage Mutant Ninja Turtles, begin to be managed as classics after their popularity as a "hot" property has peaked.

Children's entertainment properties make up the bulk of this segment of the business — as much as 70%, according to estimates by The Licensing Letter. But there are several licensed entertainment properties for adults, as well. They may not generate the record-breaking retail sales figures possible with a kids' property, but they can certainly be a solid niche business for licensors and licensees. Some of these properties include nostalgic television shows such as "I Love Lucy" and the "The Brady Bunch"; recent and current shows such as "The Critic" and "Saturday Night Live"; and films such as Forrest Gump. Properties also exist that appeal to both adults and children; the comic book/movie/TV show The Mask would be an example.

## SPORTS LICENSING

Sports licensing has been the fastest-growing segment in the business since the mid-1980s, with average annual gains of 27% from 1985 to 1993, according to TLL data. Now, however, the business is maturing. It is still growing, but not at the double-digit rates of recent years. Sports licensors are, as a result, changing the way they do business.

Future growth will be dependent on proactive marketing efforts, rather than on an inherent increase in demand and the subsequent signing of more and more licensees. This is particularly true for the four major leagues — Major League Baseball, National Football League, National Basketball Association and National Hockey League — and for colleges and universities, all of which together account for about 75% of all sports licensing, according to TLL.

The number of licensees for the leagues increased significantly in recent years, growing nearly sixfold for the NHL, tripling for MLB and doubling for the NFL from 1986 to 1993 (the NBA's licensee list has remained relatively constant at between 100 and 120 licensees over that period). Now, however, the leagues are actually cutting back their licensee rosters. This process enables them to maintain better control of their licensing programs, and to concentrate on the product lines that demonstrate the best sales potential.

It is more difficult, as a result of this process, for new manufacturers to become league licensees. A number of other sports properties exist, however, and their number is on the rise. These entities are increasing their licensing efforts for a variety of reasons. They have seen how lucrative sports licensing has been for the major leagues; in addition, they are now seeing demand from potential licensees. Some of the other major types of sports properties — outside of the major leagues and colleges — include auto racing, tennis and golf events, minor league sports, individual athletes and amateur and professional sports associations.

In addition, significant licensing campaigns are built around worldwide sports events such as the Olympics, the World Cup, the Special Olympics, the Paralympics and the Goodwill Games. While the four leagues and colleges dominate the field, each accounting for $1 billion to $3 billion in retail sales annually, other properties can rack up very respectable sales. NASCAR, for example, generates more than $500 million at retail, Wimbledon drives about $100 million annually and minor league baseball accounted for about $60 million in 1994 according to their licensors or agents.

Sports licensing attracts two types of custumers: the fan, whose purchases are primarily seasonal and local, and the fashion customer, who tends to purchase year-round with an eye toward likeable logos. The latter buys sports merchandise because he or she thinks it looks good, sometimes regardless of whether he or she is a fan of a particular team. Some wearers of San Jose Sharks' apparel may not even know what sport that team plays (hockey), and shoppers may buy one of the team's jerseys in Wisconsin (although the Sharks are Californian) in summer (while hockey is, of course, a winter sport).

## FASHION LICENSING

Fashion licensing consists of two major groups, apparel brands such as Gitano or B.U.M. Equipment and designer names (which can also develop into brands) such as Ralph Lauren or Josie Natori. In both cases, licensing primarily serves as a method of extending a fashion label into product categories where the designer or apparel company either does not have expertise (in manufacturing, marketing, design or distribution), or where licensing is more profitable than maintaining an in-house operation. Some labels, such as Donna Karan, license very few products, while other labels are full-time licensors, manufacturing nothing in-house. Sasson, Ocean Pacific, Perry Ellis and J.G. Hook are examples of the latter.

The decision of how extensive a licensing program should be is entirely individual, varying from label to label. For example, a company that manufactures certain core products (either in-house or sub-contracted out), including women's, juniors', missy and large-sized sportswear, blouses, suits and dresses, would, when it wants to extend its brand, examine whether it has the expertise to design, manufacture and market the new products, and whether it can do so profitably. The company would be likely to consider licensing certain apparel items for its primary target market (such as denim or outerwear); accessories (hosiery, headwear, handbags, footwear, belts, scarves and jewelry); fragrances; and products for new target markets (men's, children's and infants' products). Many fashion labels — Bill Blass and Laura Ashley, for example — also extend into home furnishings through licensing, as well as into international markets.

The fortunes of fashion licensing mirror those of the apparel industry as a whole, and have undergone some tough years of late. Some labels shy away from licensing in response to recessionary times and financial difficulties, preferring to maintain maximum control over what they produce. They may, in fact, cut back on their licensed, ancillary lines in order to concentrate on core products, as the footwear brand Sam & Libby has done, exiting the licensed apparel business. Conversely, some labels discover that it is more cost-efficient to increase their licensing activity in hard financial times, when licensing royalties can exceed profit margins on goods produced in-house.

Most consumers are not aware that some of the fashion merchandise they buy is licensed. To them, every Bonjour product is made by Bonjour; in fact, however, no merchandise is manufactured in-house by this full-time licensor. Therefore, it is essential that licensors maintain control over their licensing programs to ensure that no licensed products harm consumers' impression of the brand.

## CORPORATE TRADEMARK AND BRAND LICENSING

As mentioned in Chapter 1, there are a number of reasons that a corporate trademark owner would launch a licensing program: to create brand awareness, to protect the company's trademarks, to develop a new revenue stream, and as a relatively risk-free and cost-effective way to enter new product categories. Some corporate trademark licensors also use licensed merchandise for premiums to be used in promotions or provided to dealers. (As noted in Chapter 1, "trademarks" and "brands" refer here to the types of properties a corporation has available for licensing; it does not refer to trademarks in the legal sense or to brands in the sense of properties of any type with perceived brand identities.)

The main concern in corporate trademark licensing is not to hurt the company's core image, which is its reason for being. Revenues from corporate trademark licensing are usually miniscule when compared to sales of the company's major products. Wrong choices of distribution, lack of quality, incompatible price points, and other factors relating to a licensing program can all hurt the brand.

A large and growing number of trademarks are licensed, and their licensing programs vary extensively. They include:

- automotive (e.g., Harley-Davidson, Snap-On Tools, Chevrolet)
- food and beverages (Seven-Up, Betty Crocker, Hawaiian Punch, Hershey's, Chiquita, Celestial Seasonings)
- sporting goods (Spalding, Smith & Wesson, Everlast, Louisville Slugger)
- electronics/communications (Koss, Western Union)
- restaurants (Big Boy, Pizza Hut, Sardi's)
- housewares and home furnishings (Pfaltzgraff, Croscill, Farberware)
- cosmetics and fragrances (Brut and Revlon)

Each of these examples — which barely scratch the surface of potential branded licensing opportunities — all exhibit unique licensing strategies, and different reasons lie behind the launch of each program.

A great deal of brand-extension licensing is invisible to consumers. When they buy a Revlon hair dryer or a Betty Crocker kitchen utensil, they often believe the product is made by Revlon or General Mills. As with the fashion labels discussed earlier, this perception is a good reason for vigilant licensee selection and product approval processes.

## TOY LICENSING

Toy companies are often viewed mainly as licensees, but in reality several toy, game and videogame companies own properties that they license out as well. Some of these licensing programs are character-based, and thus are similar to the properties outlined in the section on Entertainment and Character licensing. Examples include trolls by several companies, which in the early 1990s were licensed out for all sorts of children's products; Mattel's Barbie, which has licensees for children's apparel, accessories and other merchandise; videogame characters such as Sega's Sonic the Hedgehog; and many others.

Toy companies are also active in brand extension licensing, with the same attributes as the programs discussed above in the section on Trademarks and Brands. These toy marketers are capitalizing on the equity they have built up over time, as they became known for quality toy products. Through licensing, they hope to extend their brand image further, becoming a children's products brand — extending to apparel, accessories, footwear, home furnishings, videogames, computer software and home video — rather than simply a toy brand. Some of the licensors that are using this strategy include Fisher-Price, Hasbro (Playskool) and LEGO.

## MUSIC LICENSING

Music licensing operates somewhat differently from other types of licensing. First of all, there are several types of licensing that are relevant to the music industry. Rights to perform music, rights to use music in conjuction with advertising or as a background in a product (e.g. a CD-ROM game), and rights for air play (e.g. in a restaurant) are all types of licensing that occur in the music business, in addition to authorizing merchandise incorporating the act's name, likeness or logo. The latter is the type of licensing germaine to this discussion.

In terms of product licensing, most musical acts are handled by one of a half-dozen major music merchandisers, which act as licensees for certain product categories, including most of the products sold at concert venues. The merchandisers also act as agents or sub-license other companies for product categories where they lack expertise either in manufacturing or distribution.

The field is very competitive. The number of merchandisers is on the rise, while at the same time the concert business is decreasing in the early 1990s. Fewer people attend concerts, and ticket prices are on the rise, leaving less discretionary income for ancillary products. The prices of merchandise sold onsite have also skyrocketed relative to goods sold elsewhere, since the venues take a cut of 40% of sales. As a result, the amount of merchandise sold at concerts has decreased, even as competition among merchandisers has risen.

Traditionally, most music merchandise has been sold by merchandisers on-site at concert venues, with very few groups making the cross-over into traditional retail channels. This situation is changing, however, as merchandisers try to find new channels of distribution to help them expand their businesses.

New product categories outside of the traditional t-shirts, tour jackets and collectibles are now being licensed, with particular emphasis on products that appeal to customers in traditional shopping environments. Examples include rock music comic books, toy trucks incorporating the likenesses and voices of country singers, and ties and apparel incorporating art by musicians including Jerry Garcia, Miles Davis and John Lennon.

In spite of this emphasis on traditional retail channels, music licensing is somewhat limited by the fact that most music groups have narrowly defined audiences, and that their fame tends to be transitory. There are exceptions, of course. The Grateful Dead have a robust merchandising program and recently retained a licensing agent to expand it further; Garth Brooks signed a deal with Wal-Mart for a wide variety of products in fourth quarter 1992; New Kids On The Block merchandise reached $800 million at retail in 1990; and significant licensing efforts revolve around nostalgic acts such as the Beatles and Elvis Presley.

## PUBLISHING PROPERTIES

Most properties with origins in publishing are either book characters (mainly for children), or magazine titles. (As mentioned, comic book properties are classified under the Entertainment and Character segment.)

Licensing programs based on children's book characters are, in general, handled like a classic character program. They often become the basis of various entertainment vehicles, particularly home video and television series (e.g. *The Magic School Bus* and *The Busy World of Richard Scarry*), but they also have a built-in audience due to the popularity of the books. For example, Beatrix Potter books have sold about 100 million copies, Paddington Bear 20 million copies and the Berenstain Bears over 180 million copies over their lifetimes through 1994. These properties have significant awareness with children. In addition, they often have the added benefit of being associated by consumers with quality and education, simply because they originate in books. Some children's publishing properties can generate very high retail sales figures — about $250 million worldwide annually for Beatrix Potter and $100 million for the Berenstain Bears — while others such as H.A. Rey's *Curious George*, Eric Carle's *Hungry Caterpillar* and Marc Brown's *Arthur* are associated with smaller efforts. More and more book properties are entering into merchandise licensing agreements.

Characters and content from adult books are also licensed, usually for use in other merchandise closely related to books and often sold in bookstores, such as desk calendars, computer software and CD-ROM reference works. Publishing-based brand names can be the focus of licensing efforts, as well. For example, the Berlitz name has been found on a number of CD-ROM applications and computer calendars, while Merriam-Webster and Random House are licensed for reference products.

Magazines ranging from *Sports Illustrated for Kids* to *Playboy* are also the basis for ancillary merchandise. *Popular Mechanics* and *Better Homes and Gardens* are licensed to Wal-Mart for hardware and gardening products, respectively. The *Cosmopolitan* name is authorized for videotapes and handbags and *Penthouse* has been licensed for fragrances and condoms.

Magazine-based licensing programs are limited by the fact that licensed products based on a magazine cannot compete with products marketed by that magazine's advertisers. After all, these advertisers provide the bulk of a magazine's revenues. Magazines logically want to avoid angering or alienating this important group.

## NON-PROFIT LICENSING

The most high-profile non-profit licensing programs are those launched by environmental groups such as the World Wildlife Fund (among the first to proactively pursue licensing in the late 1980s), the National Audubon Society, the Sierra Club and many others. More ecologically minded non-profit groups are entering licensing — or expanding licensing efforts. Licensed merchandise can generate income for an organization's cause, as well as create awareness of its mission and thus increase membership and charitable contributions.

Other non-profit groups outside of the environmental movement are also pursuing licensing more actively over the last several years. Some are relief agencies, such as CARE and Save the Children, some are crusaders for good health, such as the American Heart Association. Non-profit groups from the American Red Cross to the National Crime Prevention Council to the Humane Society of the U.S. are active in licensing.

Non-profit licensing programs can be limited in a number of ways. First, it is essential that none of their licensees' products detract from or contradict the mission of the group — or are perceived to do so. Secondly, most significant licensing programs must attract children to generate big numbers. While most non-profit groups look at children as a potentially important market, past experience does not provide evidence that non-profit products appeal to them. Children are not, as a rule, swayed by the fact that part of a product's purchase price goes toward a particular group's mission, even though they may be supportive of the cause itself. In addition, children's product manufacturers often do not want to pay for a non-profit license, since they do not perceive it as a competitive advantage in the children's market, where they are competing against character merchandise.

Most non-profit licensing programs are still in fairly early stages. As the groups become more attuned to the potential of licensing and better learn how to market their properties to manufacturers, retailers and consumers, this relatively untapped market should grow significantly.

## CELEBRITY LICENSING

Licensing of celebrities — both living and deceased — usually focuses primarily on promotional deals, such as the use of a famous person's name and likeness on packaging, premiums or advertising. A celebrity with a relatively high proportion of retail products, such as James Dean, still earns about 50% of licensing revenues from promotional deals. Others earn closer to 80%-90% of revenues to advertising and promotions, according to agents who specialize in this area. In some cases, licensed merchandise is manufactured as part of a broader promotional deal, especially for current celebrities. For example, signed memorabilia may be sold by a company for which the celebrity also serves as a spokesperson.

Some celebrities generate a great deal of merchandise sales, however. James Dean and Marilyn Monroe are prime examples. Other celebrities associated with products ranging from silk ties to plastic figurines include Babe Ruth, Albert Einstein, Laurel & Hardy, Charlie Chaplin, Bette Davis and many more. Most U.S. celebrity-based merchandise seems to strongly appeal to customers in international markets.

Celebrity licensing, when centered on living people, can be risky for licensees in some cases; there is no way to guarantee that celebrities exhibit good behavior — or that they stay popular. Estate licensing (licensing the names and likenesses of deceased celebrities whose estates are controlled by their heirs) is less risky. The way consumers perceive these former celebrities is not likely to change significantly, although their popularity may rise and fall. Deceased celebrities will not, however, be arrested or say anything controversial.

Most estate licensing is handled by licensing agents who represent the celebrities' heirs. Curtis Management Group and the Roger Richman Agency manage by far the bulk of all active programs, but other agents are involved as well. A few estates handle all product and promotional licensing themselves, with assistance from legal counsel.

Note: Some celebrities are included in other categories if they are associated exclusively with that area of the business. For example, athletes are included under sports, and some musicians such as Madonna are included under music.

## ART LICENSING

Art licensing comprises many different facets of the art world. They include museums, live and deceased fine artists, and designers who create their art with merchandise in mind.

Some museums are active in licensing. Many tend to run small, upscale programs, with most merchandise distributed in museum stores (their own and other museum shops). Occasionally, the name of the institution is used as a brand, such as Museum of Metropolitan Art silk scarves or Smithsonian science activity kits.

In addition, several institutions oversee active reproduction licensing programs, where items from their collections are reproduced on retail products such as greeting cards, gift items and home furnishings. Colonial Williamsburg manages an extensive licensing program with retail sales of $50 million per year, incorporating textiles, wall and floor coverings, furniture, pewter and brass objects, ceramics, house paint and moldings based on items in its collection. Art institutions sometimes shy away from licensing, preferring to maintain control of their merchandise programs through in-house manufacturing or sub-contracting.

Individual artists or their estates often oversee licensing programs, many of which are handled by agents specializing in this area. Reproductions of their works are licensed for various retail products, and occasionally their likenesses, names or signatures may be licensed as well.

Contemporary artists and designers often specialize in a certain genre, such as sports, fantasy, whimsical children's, realistic, illustrative, ethnic-themed or nature art. Some specialize in decorative patterns. In some cases, licensing efforts based on children's and illustrative art may be handled very much like a character program.

Currently active artists fall into one of two groups. The first is comprised of artists who create their art for art's sake, with licensing a secondary concern. In this case, licensing activity leans heavily toward publishing, gifts and stationery. The second group includes designers who create art with merchandise in mind. Their licensing activity is more wide-ranging, incorporating apparel, home furnishings and domestics, giftware, stationery, table-top items and housewares. Licensing enables them to develop coordinating ranges of merchandise in all product categories.

Consumers purchase art-licensed products simply because they like the way they look, unless the property is a recognized work of art or a famous artist, where name recognition also plays a role. Customers often do not know or even care who the artist is; they just know that they like the design of the product and want to own it. They may choose a certain pattern as the basis for a whole room's decor, but are not necessarily aware that the products are licensed and that each matching product is made by a different manufacturer.

Some designers eventually do become household names. The name becomes a brand, and shoppers go out looking for, say, Mary Engelbreit merchandise for their homes. They still do not necessarily realize that the products are licensed, but they do seek the Engelbreit brand name. When a designer achieves name recognition, he or she is more attractive to licensees. Not only do they gain a group of designs, without in-house development costs, which can be coordinated with products by other licensees, but more importantly, they also benefit from brand awareness. Thus they prominently display the artist's name as a selling point.

# CHAPTER 3:
# CHARACTERISTICS OF MAJOR PRODUCT CATEGORIES

Almost any product can be licensed, as long as the fit between property and that item is appropriate and there is a market for it. Fish bowls with major league team logos, condoms licensed by heavy metal musicians, salamis shaped like beer bottles sporting authentic beer logos, Grateful Dead skis, *Forrest Gump* frozen shrimp — the sky's the limit.

Most licensed merchandise, however, falls into one of 17 broad categories, as shown in *Figure 5 (pages 38-40)*. Some products are hard to precisely categorize; are lamps made out of NFL helmets home furnishings or novelties? Since they are probably sold in home furnishings departments and in specialty gift shops, they could legitimately be classified in either category. As a result of this difficulty, some of the broad categories in the table are admittedly catch-alls. Accessories, for example, comprises everything from jewelry to backpacks, while Gifts and Novelties ranges from signed memorabilia to novelty dog tags to animation cels and beyond. Still, these somewhat arbitrary categories lend structure to an overview of the business. Generally, the primary guideline is what department or type of store the merchandise would be sold in.

As *Figure 5* illustrates, apparel is the largest product category overall, accounting for 16% of all sales, according to *The Licensing Letter*. Toys and Games (11%), Accessories (10%) and Gifts and Novelties (9%) emerge as the second, third and fourth largest segments, respectively.

The relative importance of each product category for a specific licensing program varies enormously depending on the type of property being licensed. For an entertainment or character property with an audience primarily composed of children, Toys and Games can account for up to half or even two-thirds of total retail sales of licensed merchandise based on that property; for a teen entertainment property, videogames may account for a similarly high proportion. Sports properties, on the other hand, tend to be licensed heavily in apparel and accessories (up to 75% or even higher for some properties). Brand-extension licensing efforts vary hugely in terms of categories targeted, depending on where the core brand originates. A food brand may license heavily in food- and kitchen-related products; a sporting goods brand will target other sporting goods as well as apparel, accessories and footwear. Fashion brands tend to concentrate most of their activities in apparel, accessories, footwear, beauty products and home furnishings.

Thus, the overall product category breakdown of retail sales shown in *Figure 6 (page 41)* should not be taken as the norm for any individual property. Every property is unique, and targeted categories vary depending upon the characteristics of the property and its audience. With that caveat in mind, this chapter will briefly describe each of the major categories of licensed merchandise, including significant licensing-related trends in each.

*Figure 5*

# RETAIL PRODUCT CATEGORY BREAKDOWN FOR LICENSED GOODS

**ACCESSORIES**
backpacks
bandanas
belts
buckles
embroidered emblems and logos
eyeglass frames
hats and caps
jewelry
mittens and gloves
purses and handbags
scarves
shoelaces
small leather goods
socks and hosiery
sunglasses
ties
umbrellas
wallets
watches

**APPAREL**
boxer shorts
dresses
jackets
lingerie
nightshirts
pajamas
shorts
slacks
sportswear
sweaters
sweatshirts and sweatpants
t-shirts
underwear

**DOMESTICS**
bath mats
bedspreads
blankets
cloth placemats
curtains
fabric
laundry bags
pillowcases
pot holders
sewing patterns
sheets
towels

**ELECTRONICS**
cassette players
clock-radios
clocks
foot massagers
hair dryers
kitchen appliances
radios
tape players
telephones
walkie-talkies

**FOOD/BEVERAGES**
candy
cereal
cake & cake-decorating accessories
cookies
edible baking decorations
fresh foods
frosting
frozen meals
gum
health bars
juice
microwave meals
snack foods
soda
sports drinks

**FOOTWEAR**
athletic shoes
beach footwear
designer shoes
hiking boots
shoelaces
slippers
socks and hosiery

**FURNITURE/HOME FURNISHINGS**
appliances
beanbag chairs
beds
bookcases
ceiling fans
chairs
chests
clocks
desktop accessories
lamps
picture frames
tables
telephones
wall coverings and wallpaper

*Continued Next Page*

*Figure 5 Continued*

**GIFTS/NOVELTIES**
air fresheners
animated alarm clocks
animation cels
bow-biters
ceramic gift items
ceramic mugs
chess sets
Christmas decorations and ornaments
cloisonne pins
collectibles
commemorative coins
commemorative plates
erasers
gumball machines
key chains
lapel pins
lighters
magnets
milk caps
novelty watches
pencils
pencil toppers
pens
plush
pre-paid phone cards
PVC figurines
stickers
t-shirts
wind socks

**HEALTH/BEAUTY AIDS**
adhesive bandages
bubble bath
combs and brushes
cosmetics
dental floss
fragrances
hair accessories
lotions
shampoo
soap
tissues
toothpaste and toothbrushes
vitamins

**HOUSEWARES**
acrylic and melamine tableware
baking and cooking supplies
cups, plates, bowls
glassware
insulated beverageware

juice box holders
laminated placemats
lunch kits
mugs
silverware
tableware

**INFANT PRODUCTS**
baby bags
bibs
bumper guards
cribs
diapers
diaper bags
high chairs
infant clothing
infant furniture
infant housewares
infant toys
mobiles
playpens
rockers
strollers

**MUSIC/VIDEO**
audiocassettes
book and cassette packages
CDs
LPs
spoken-word audiocassettes
videocassettes, theatrical, music,
    direct-to-video

**PUBLISHING**
activity books
address books
bath books
book and cassette packages
calendars
cloth books
coloring books
comic books
diaries
how-to books
magazines
music and talking storybooks
novelizations
novels
one-shot publications
post cards
posters
stickers

*Continued Next Page*

*Figure 5 Continued*

## SPORTING GOODS
backpacks
bicycles
daypacks
fitness equipment
footballs, basketballs, baseballs
ice skates
inflatable water toys
ride-ons
rollerskates
skateboards
sleeping bags
slumber bags
sports equipment
sports jerseys
tents
uniforms
vinyl pool and water slides
wagons
water bottles

## STATIONERY/PAPER GOODS
bookmarks
candles, birthday
checks
erasers
gift bags
gift wrap
greeting cards, packaged and single
invitations
memo boards
mylar and latex balloons
note cards
notepads
paper party decorations
paper tableware
party goods
pens and pencils
postcards
rubber stamps and pads
school supplies
trading cards
Valentines

## TOYS/GAMES
activity kits
board games
craft and model kits
die-cast vehicles and models
dolls
dominoes
electronic toys

flying discs
Halloween costumes, makeup
  and masks
kites
learning toys
marbles
milk caps
playing cards
plush, stuffed toys
puppets
puzzles
rack toys
radio-controlled toys
ride-ons
science kits
trading cards
yo-yos

## VIDEOGAMES/SOFTWARE
arcade games
CD-ROM software
computer software, games and other
  electronic/LED games, handheld
  and tabletop
interactive games
pinball games
videogames for all platforms

## MISCELLANEOUS
automotive accessories
gardening supplies
hardware
luggage

**Note:** Several products are listed in more than one category, since they are often sold within more than one department or store type.
**Source:** The Licensing Letter;
EPM Communications

*Figure 6*

## 1994 SHARES OF LICENSED PRODUCT RETAIL SALES
## U.S. AND CANADA, BY PRODUCT CATEGORY

*Dollar Figure In Billions*

| PRODUCT CATEGORY | 1994 RETAIL SALES | PCT. ALL SALES |
|---|---|---|
| Accessories | $6.82 | 10% |
| Apparel | $11.37 | 16% |
| Domestics | $4.45 | 6% |
| Electronics | $1.11 | 2% |
| Food/Beverages | $5.45 | 8% |
| Footwear | $2.11 | 3% |
| Furniture/Home Furnishings | $0.78 | 1% |
| Gifts/Novelties | $6.54 | 9% |
| Health/Beauty | $3.92 | 6% |
| Housewares | $2.33 | 3% |
| Infant Products | $2.33 | 3% |
| Music/Video | $1.24 | 2% |
| Publishing | $4.53 | 6% |
| Sporting Goods | $2.39 | 3% |
| Stationery/Paper Goods | $3.26 | 5% |
| Toys/Games | $7.77 | 11% |
| Videogames/Software | $3.23 | 5% |
| Other | $0.39 | 1% |
| **TOTAL** | **$70.01** | **100%** |

*Source:* The Licensing Letter; EPM Communications

## ACCESSORIES

Accessories primarily include wearable items outside of apparel. Examples include costume and fine jewelry, hair accessories, hosiery, belts, scarves, hats and caps, handbags, backpacks and ties. Fashion properties, naturally, target this area particularly heavily, but virtually all other types of properties also do sigificant business in accessories.

In fact, non-fashion properties are increasing their activity in this category. So-called "conversational" accessories have become popular wearables in the 1990s; ties and socks adorned with Tabasco bottles, Star Trek characters or Marilyn Monroe can generate substantial retail sales. One major licensed tie manufacturer, Ralph Marlin, does $8 million annually in wholesale volume of licensed products, and its Three Stooges tie sold 40,000 units in the first half of 1993 alone. WEMCO, another marketer, makes *Wizard of Oz* ties, which sold about 100,000 units in their first four months on the market.

On the other hand, some accessories categories have been licensed heavily in recent years. A primary example is caps, particularly those licensed by the four major leagues and colleges. While sports-licensed caps (and caps embellished with other licensed properties) are still a strong-selling fashion item, the sheer number of cap licensees point to a shakeout. Some leagues have had as many of 30 cap licensees on board at one time. Walking through a sporting goods trade show's licensed products area in the early 1990s was a dizzying experience, with caps being exhibited as far as the eye could see. Now, the leagues are cutting back on the number of headwear licensees, allowing fewer companies to manufacture a wider variety of styles.

## APPAREL

Apparel is a major category throughout all property types. Products range from inexpensive t-shirts screen-printed with a corporate trademark and distributed through mass market outlets or as premiums, to leather jackets incorporating an NBA team logo and retailing for hundreds of dollars, to designer-licensed furs with price points in the thousands of dollars.

A recent trend in apparel licensing, especially for character merchandise, is the increasing importance of upscale products. This merchandise is characterized by high-quality manufacturing techniques, such as direct embroidery rather than appliques; by the use of costly materials such as leather or silk; by high prices and department or specialty store distribution; and by fashion-forward designs incorporating characters, usually of the classic variety, in unusual ways (such as large close-up designs wrapping around a garment rather than simply a character likeness on the front of a t-shirt). Screen-printed, mass market apparel is still a much more significant category of licensed merchandise, however.

## DOMESTICS

Domestics includes bedding — everything from sheets and pillows to quilts and bedspreads — as well as beach, bath and kitchen towels. The category also comprises placemats and tablecloths.

In children's domestics, especially sheets and beach towels, character and entertainment licensing — and to a smaller extent sports — play a significant role. In fact, licensed merchandise accounts for as much as 90% of the market for juvenile domestics, according to practitioners.

Designers are the main source of properties in the market for adult domestics. Both home furnishings designers such as Di Lewis and Mario Buatta and fashion designers from Laura Ashley to Bill Blass, who cross over into domestics and have successful signature programs, are active licensors. In addition, licensed designs from other home furnishings companies are proliferating. For example, dinnerware patterns might be licensed for tablecloths, or curtain designs for bedding.

Cross-merchandising of home-related products at retail is a major trend, and all the types of licensing outlined in the preceding paragraph lend themselves to cross-merchandising presentations. Coordinated programs highlighting products for every room are created through licensing and displayed together in retail concept shops.

Licensing also accounts for a large proportion of sales of beach towels, and properties from virtually every source can be found on towels appealing to both adults and children.

## ELECTRONICS

The electronics category incorporates telephones, cassette players, radios, walkie-talkies and the like. For example, novelty licensed telephones are a common category, ranging from phones that resemble Star Trek's U.S.S. *Enterprise* starship to those shaped like a pair of Jordache jeans to those that look like a Harley-Davidson.

Aside from novelty phones, most electronics products tend to be associated with properties that can be used as brands appealing to a certain target demographic group. For example, Barbie personal electronics, including telephones and radios, are targeted to young girls; MGM-licensed televisions and stereos are aimed at adults, for whom the MGM lion logo stands for entertainment; and Playskool electronics such as cassette players for young children are meant to appeal to parents of preschoolers.

Licensing is also a growing presence in personal-care appliances. The cosmetic organizer brand Caboodles, the cosmetics brand Revlon and the hair-care brand Vidal Sassoon all count licensed hair dryers among their product lines. And Dr. Scholl's, the foot-care brand, is licensed for electric foot-massage products.

## FOOD AND BEVERAGES

The majority of food and beverage licensing centers on brand extension licensing of food brands into other food categories. Sunkist soft drinks, Dole frozen fruit bars and Seagrams mixers are all examples of substantial revenue-generating licensed line extensions.

In general, other property types have less presence in the food and beverage category, although more licensors are targeting it. Most licensors have little experience with grocery store distribution and little knowledge of how food brands are developed. At the same time, most food manufacturers are not familiar with licensing and need to be sold on its value as a marketing tool. Since it takes a great deal of time and money to launch a food brand — and because the industry exhibits a high failure rate for new products — most food manufacturers are not interested in licensing what they perceive as short-term properties. They seek licensed properties that they feel have the legs necessary to make their substantial upfront investment in the brand worthwhile.

Despite these difficulties, there are a number of food and beverage products associated with non-food licensed properties. Colt 45 malt liquor, for example, is licensed from Colt, a gun and ammunition marketer. *The Old Farmer's Almanac*, a 200+-year-old publication, has licensed a number of grocery products, from dairy and fresh lettuce to hot cocoa mix and potato chips. Popeye canned and frozen spinach and Flintstones breakfast cereals are long-standing examples of licensed foods.

Some short-term licensing is done in this category as well, primarily for impulse products such as snacks (fruit candies, cupcakes and candy bars), frozen pizza and canned pasta. Some cereals (in addition to The Flintstones' Fruity Pebbles) and frozen entrees have also been marketed, but in the last two years many of the major players in these areas have left the business.

## FOOTWEAR

Several shoe manufacturers specialize in licensed children's footwear. Shoes, beach footwear, sandals and slippers are based on both short-term and long-term properties. Most licensed children's shoes are sold at mass market, and some observers estimate that as much as 90% of the children's mass-market footwear category is licensed.

A number of sports celebrities license their names for signature lines of athletic footwear. These products are usually part of a larger endorsement deal between the athlete and the shoe maker, where the celebrity participates in promotional events for the trade and consumers on behalf of the company and appears in corporate advertising.

Brand extensions are another significant aspect of footwear licensing, primarily affecting fashion labels and sporting goods brands. Most sporting goods companies (Spalding, Wilson, and so on) see athletic footwear as a natural extension of their sports equipment lines. Similarly, apparel brands and designer labels also consider footwear (dressy, casual or athletic, depending on the brand image) to be a key category. These labels often extend into footwear through licensing rather than setting up in-house operations; they do not usually have the expertise required to become footwear manufacturers.

## FURNITURE AND HOME FURNISHINGS

This category includes, among other products: furniture, lamps, wall coverings and floor coverings. As with the domestics category discussed earlier, the major licensors involved in home furnishings are designers and manufacturers that own brands and designs originating in other home-related categories.

Several museums have active licensed reproduction programs in home furnishings. For example, the Heart Castle licenses rugs, the Winterthur estate licenses wall coverings, among many other products, and many museums license works of art, such as sculptures, for decorative accessories.

A few character and sports properties have signed agreements for juvenile beds, while several children's licensors have signed manufacturers for wall borders and lamps. For the most part, however, home furnishings is a small category for these licensors. Most short-term properties are not appropriate, since home furnishings are a relatively large investment for the consumer and are expected to last for a long time.

## GIFTS AND NOVELTIES

Gifts and Novelties comprise one of the broadest categories in licensing, ranging from key chains and miniature plastic figurines that retail for a dollar or less, to animated cels and crystal figurines that cost thousands of dollars. It includes limited-edition products that are produced specifically as collectibles, items for gift-giving and low-priced novelties meant as impulse purchases.

With the exception of fashion labels, most types of properties are active licensors of gifts and novelties. Sports memorabilia, entertainment and character collectibles, gifts based on artists' designs and corporate-licensed merchandise based on nostalgic advertising art are all common.

Limited-edition collectibles are currently a growing area of the gift market, ranging from collectible plates featuring skater Kristi Yamaguchi's likeness and signature to framed photos signed by Mickey Mantle to animation cels signed by the creator to prepaid telephone calling cards based on Elvis Presley. Limited editions are often numbered, and come with some sort of verification of their authenticity. Of course, low-end novelty items, which are fun, impulse purchases for consumers, also are and will continue to be an important segment.

## HEALTH AND BEAUTY

Properties from the Ninja Turtles to Batman to Winnie the Pooh to Fisher-Price have all been found on children's cosmetics, colognes and bubble baths. *The Licensing Letter* estimates that about 19% of retail sales in the children's health and beauty market is attributable to licensed products.

As for personal care items for adults, licensing is less of a factor for most properties. Artists — especially those who specialize in Victorian or homey designs — have some presence in the personal-care area, especially with soaps and packaging for a wide variety of health and beauty products.

Licensing is a major factor in one product category within the health and beauty segment, however, and that is fragrances. Signature scents licensed by fashion designers — and a few other celebrities, such as Elizabeth Taylor — are a large influence in the marketplace. Calvin Klein fragrances, licensed to Unilever, reportedly generate $400 million in wholesale volume annually, while Ralph Lauren's Safari, one of several fragrances associated with the designer's name, does $30 million wholesale annually with licensee Sanofi. Most high-profile fashion designers have a signature fragrance associated with their names, and these lines — usually licensed — can be among their most lucrative.

## HOUSEWARES

Food brands that exploit their brand equity by expanding into kitchen-related non-food products are among the most visible licensors in housewares. Pillsbury, Betty Crocker and Campbell's Soup all oversee efforts in this area, with products ranging from kitchen appliances to bakeware to dishes.

Various home-related brands are also extended into housewares. Cookware maker Farberware, for example, licenses food storage containers and cutlery under its brand name. Makers of tablecloths license their patterns for coordinating dinnerware. Designers are also active licensors for dinnerware, glassware, cookie jars and mugs.

Primary product categories within the housewares segment for character, entertainment and sports licensing include thermal beverage containers and lunch kits, children's dinnerware and beverageware, ceramics from salt and pepper shakers to cookie jars, and baking supplies, such as cake pans and cookie cutters.

Housewares is still a relatively untapped category for licensing, with just 4.5% of sales attributable to licensing in 1992 according to TLL. It is, however, poised for growth. More licensors across several property types are examining the category as a potential area for expansion.

## INFANT PRODUCTS

This category contains a variety of products. Many could be categorized elsewhere (infant apparel under Apparel, layette under Domestics and infant toys under Toys and Games). They are classified together in a separate category, however, since they are often gathered into dedicated departments at retail, and one buyer is often resonsible for purchasing across categories.

Most property types are represented in this section. Several artists create designs that lend themselves to infant products because of their themes or color schemes. Fashion labels sometimes extend their brands into the infant category; the jeans brand Guess?, for example, licensed a company called Pour Le Bebe to manufacture its Baby Guess? infant line. The four major sports leagues and colleges license companies for bibs, diaper bags and infant-to-toddler apparel. Characters and entertainment properties, especially those that appeal to young children and also have nostalgic appeal for their parents, are also active in the area.

In fact, several licensors of classic characters have created sub-brands targeted specifically toward parents of new children. They are generally infant versions of classic characters, utilizing pastel color schemes and cuddly graphics. The purpose is to capitalize on the equity of the property — parents are familiar with the brand from when they were children and have a nostalgic affinity with the characters — and to build on this value by offering infant-themed merchandise that appeals to these brand-new parents. Some recent examples include the Looney Tunes Lovables and the Daisy Hill Puppy Farm (based on Snoopy of the Peanuts comic strip).

## MUSIC AND VIDEO

Video distributors or record companies are listed as licensees for home video or soundtracks, respectively, on most entertainment-based licensee lists. Most of these agreements are, however, essentially distribution contracts. They take existing intellectual property such as television episodes or theatrical films, and distribute them in the new form of home video or recorded soundtracks. While this type of licensing is a legitimate, necessary and significant part of marketing a property, this book does not deal with these sorts of agreements in-depth. (Distribution licenses are also not included in the numbers in *Figure* 6). This work focuses on the licensing of an existing trademark (and associated copyrights) for the purpose of creating a wholly new product based on it.

On the other hand, many licensors do license home video or record companies to create original programming, and these are what the numbers in *Figure* 6 represent. For example, the Simpsons were licensed to Geffen for a musical recording called "The Simpsons Sing The Blues," combining character voices and live musicians. The sports leagues have experimented with original videos; for example, the NBA has licensed CBS/Fox Video for a series of videocassettes that combine popular music with footage from NBA games.

Publishing is one property type that lends itself well to the creation of licensed audio and video. Several magazines, including *Cosmopolitan, Car & Driver, Esquire, Reader's Digest* and *Sports Afield,* license their names for special-interest videotapes, the content of which relates to the editorial focus of the magazines. Children's book properties also often lend themselves to original video or audio programming, incorporating original plots starring the characters in the book. Examples include *The Baby-sitter's Club* and *Where's Waldo?*.

Music and video — whether original productions or existing entertainment distributed in these forms — are key elements of children's entertainment property licensing programs. When young children own videos or musical recordings, they tend to play them repeatedly. Their frequent viewing or listening tends to strengthen their relationship with the characters, and ultimately to engender demand for other licensed products based on the same property. For this reason, and because video and music are often the products most closely related to the original entertainment vehicle, children's character licensors take this category very seriously.

## PUBLISHING

Publishing is a diverse product category. It includes books, comic books and magazines, and also comprises other published products, such as trading cards, milk caps (collectible items originating in Hawaii, which are increasingly popular across the country), posters and calendars.

Licensed books range from children's picture, bath and activity books to expensive coffee-table titles, from novelizations to original novels. New book releases can often drive sales of other licensed merchandise, much as new releases of other media or entertainment vehicles can. *Star Wars* is an example. Its first-ever original book series, starting in 1990, became a best-seller, and resulted in a rejuvenation of the property's licensing program.

Licensing is a significant factor in children's books as well. In *Publishers Weekly*'s best-seller charts each year, licensed books take up a significant proportion of the top 50 sellers.

Comic books are a major category for both children's and adult properties. Of the approximately $1 billion comics industry, *The Licensing Letter* estimates that about 9% of total sales are attributable to licensed titles. Nearly every entertainment and character property has a comic book version; sports properties are also experimenting with comics. The NFL, for example, has a joint venture with Marvel Comics for titles combining football and Marvel characters. Book properties for adults are also active licensors in comics publishing; many titles are translated into graphic novels, including books by Stephen King, Anne Rice, Clive Barker and others.

Comic books are sold primarily through comic book stores, which are known in the trade as the "direct market." (Young children's titles, which are distributed mainly through mass merchants, are an exception.) For comics retailers and manufacturers, licensing is a way to bring new readers into comic book stores. Although industry observers debate the effectiveness of licensed comics in attracting — and keeping — new customers, licensing is nonetheless a significant factor in the comics industry. Comic books are a staple on licensee lists for many property types.

Trading cards are another staple category. In 1991, trading cards hit their peak of popularity; since then, however, there has been a falloff in popularity due to oversaturation of product, especially in sports. While the trading card market increased by 20% from 1991 to 1992, according to TLL estimates, a drop of about 9% in sports cards alone was reported by Action-Packed research the next year.

In the mid-'90s, non-sports were growing as a property source for trading cards, although there is some disagreement about their long-term collectible value. Still, most entertainment properties do sign trading card licensees.

In fact, according to *Non-Sport Update* magazine, there were 64 non-sport trading card manufacturers producing 210 sets of cards in 1993, and TLL and *Non-Sports Update* both estimate that non-sports cards comprise about 10%-15% of the market. By far the majority of successful non-sport cards are comic book-related; some entertainment properties, notably "Star Trek" and Disney animated films, have also had success. Many trading card companies are beginning to specialize in niches, such as small runs of Harley-Davidson or Coca-Cola trading cards, where the market is relatively small, but definable, and where the consumer values the cards as collectibles and will continue to buy fresh designs as they are produced each season. Several contemporary and nostalgic artists, especially those specializing in fantasy art, have also signed lucrative trading card deals.

Licensed posters range from fine art reproductions to mass market one-sheets portraying musicians, celebrity heartthrobs and automobiles; calendars and desk calendars are based on properties from artists to entertainment to publishing and beyond. Art, entertainment and other properties are also found on book-related merchandise such as diaries and journals.

## SPORTING GOODS

Athlete-licensed merchandise is prevalent in the sporting goods area. It usually comprises a signature line of products such as sports balls, bats, hockey sticks and other equipment. Many of these products, like in the footwear category, are part of a larger endorsement deal, such as Spalding's Shaq Attack line of basketball equipment endorsed and licensed by NBA player Shaquille O'Neal of the Orlando Magic.

Line-extension licensing is also prevalent. Several sports-equipment manufacturers license another sporting goods company to manufacture items for which they do not have marketing or manufacturing expertise, but which they want under their brand umbrellas. For example, Spalding licenses Indian Industries for table tennis equipment and backboards.

Major league sports and colleges are also prevalent licensors in sporting goods, especially those related to their sport, of course. For example, the NFL licenses footballs, helmets and protective equipment; Major League Baseball authorizes bats, balls and gloves; the NBA grants rights to basketballs and hoops; and the NHL signs companies for skates, helmets, protective equipment, hockey pucks and in-line roller skates.

A number of sports products for children are also licensed, such as non-regulation balls, plastic bats and child-sized hockey sticks. Many of these products are made by toy companies who have set up sports divisions. Licensors include the sports leagues and colleges, sporting goods brands and also character and entertainment properties. In addition to the products mentioned above, other merchandise in the sporting goods category includes bicycles, sports toys and roller skates.

## STATIONERY AND PAPER GOODS

The Stationery and Paper Goods category incorporates a variety of products, from greeting cards and stationery to paper party goods, gift wrap, balloons, pens, pencils, erasers, pencil cases, folders, notebooks and a number of other school-related products.

Art and artists play a large role as licensors in this category; in fact, stationery and paper goods are among the largest categories not only for contemporary artists and designers, but also for fine artists' estates and museums. Their works are reproduced on greeting cards, gift wrap, gift boxes and other stationery.

In fact, almost all property types are sources for stationery and paper items. Children's entertainment and character properties play a role, especially in paper partyware (that is, paper plates, napkins, decorations and favors for birthday parties), balloons and back-to-school products. In fact, in these categories, licensed merchandise contributes a significant portion of total retail sales. *The Licensing Letter* estimates that 15%-25% of all paper school supplies sales are of licensed merchandise, while industry observers estimate that as much as 90% of all paper party goods are licensed. Sports properties and even some trademarks, such as Nike, also have a presence in licensed stationery and paper goods, particularly paper school supplies.

## TOYS AND GAMES

Between 40% and 50% of total retail sales of toys and games are attributable to licensed merchandise each year, according to *The Licensing Letter*. The figure is at the high end of the range in years where many of the best-selling toys are licensed — such as 1993, where Barney, "Star Trek," *Jurassic Park*, Disney and other licensed toys were among the top 20 sellers for the year — and at the lower end in years such as 1992, where the best-selling toys were mostly basics such as LEGO, Barbie, Hot Wheels and other non-licensed merchandise.

Within the toy industry, action figures are one category where licensing plays a major role, especially for film and television properties whose audience is composed of boys. Comic book and videogame characters, as well as sports celebrities, are also licensed for action figure lines. Other segments where licensing is a significant factor include:

- board games, licensed from comic book, book and entertainment properties;
- dolls, especially fashion dolls based on celebrities or characters or with clothes designed by fashion designers;
- plush, where book characters, such as Clifford the Big Red Dog, entertainment properties from Disney films to *Once Upon A Rainforest*, and classic characters including Looney Tunes and Betty Boop all play a role.

## VIDEOGAMES AND SOFTWARE

Videogames and software form what is probably the most dynamic and fastest-growing category in the licensing business today. As new technologies develop, opportunities will continue to become available for licensors. Licensors face the dilemma of how to get their feet wet at an early stage without knowing which of the current so-called "interactive multimedia" platforms (such as 3DO, various CD-ROM platforms, etc.), if any, will become the future standard. Many large entertainment licensors, in particular, want to be significant content providers in future interactive technologies; the question is whether to invest in technologies through joint ventures or subsidiaries, or whether to license at first to minimize risk but then face the possibility of not being positioned most profitably in the future.

No matter how confusing the multimedia area currently is, it is expected to be lucrative for licensors, given the track record of current interactive technologies such as videogames and computer software. Licensing plays a significant role here — *The Licensing Letter* estimates that over 60% of the total videogame market is attributable to licensed products.

Videogames can, in fact, drive some licensing programs, especially those for the often-elusive teen male market. In addition, videogames, like publishing and home video, are important to a property's success because they have become entertainment vehicles, with nearly as much power as filmed entertainment to drive sales.

Computer software is also a growing category. As the installed base of home computers has grown, licensed computer utilities and accessories have proven popular. Recent examples include screensavers starring dozens of properties from Disney's Goofy to the Sierra Club; computerized daily planners incorporating comic strips "The Far Side" and "Cathy"; sound effects utilizing voices from film and television; type fonts, such as "Bedrock," based on "The Flintstones"; and mouse pads, computer screen frames and keyboards.

CD-ROM software is a fast-growing area, and is expected by those in the licensing community to continue increasing at a fast pace. The installed base of CD-ROM hardware is still relatively small, however. In addition, technical glitches, software that does not hold purchasers' attention, and many users' lack of comfort with their own hardware all can cause customer service problems. Still, it is an area of great interest to licensors.

Even on-line services — such as America Online, Compuserve and Prodigy — are associated with licensed properties through chat lines, bulletin boards and realtime interviews, including the book series *The Baby-sitters Club* and the comic strip "Dilbert." And, as new technologies continue to develop and more people own the hardware needed to run them, new opportunities for licensed goods and services will continue to become available.

## OTHER LICENSING OPPORTUNITIES

In addition to retail products, licensors occasionally grant the rights to their properties for other purposes. For example, restaurants and bars are authorized by the licensors of Harley-Davidson, "Cheers," Popeye and others. Entertainment venues such as video arcades are also sometimes licensed, as are retail stores based on "Sesame Street" or Coca-Cola. Private label lines can be directly licensed to retailers, such as *Better Homes and Gardens* to Wal-Mart or Jaclyn Smith to Kmart. Direct-mail catalogs are sometimes licensed as well, such as one based on "The Andy Griffith Show." Advertising, theme park appearances or rides, ice shows, films and TV shows are all examples of instances outside of retail products where licensing can occur.

# CHAPTER 4:
# DISTRIBUTION OF LICENSED MERCHANDISE

Where licensed merchandise is sold depends on the characteristics of the property and its target market. Products associated with an upscale fashion brand sell primarily in department and specialty stores, while merchandise based on an adult-oriented entertainment property have very little presence in children's apparel or toy stores.

For corporate trademarks in particular, distribution of licensed merchandise is a crucial means of protecting a brand's image; the core business of an upscale brand, for example, can be hurt if licensed products find their way into discount chains. In addition, moving a property into inappropriate channels — that is, locations where target customers do not shop — will be a waste of resources. Expansion must occur within the constraints of brand image and target demographics.

Retailers are looking for ways to differentiate themselves from their competition. Licensed merchandise can be a factor in this effort; promotions based on licensed properties or exclusive merchandise deals can increase store traffic and sales, and make that store a preferred shopping destination. While distribution is primarily a licensee's responsibility, licensors can — and are increasingly expected to — make the sales job easier by coordinating promotions and concept shops directly with retailers.

## DISTRIBUTION CHANNELS

Licensed merchandise can be sold in virtually any distribution channel, and licensees and licensors are both increasingly interested in expanding to non-traditional outlets. *Figure 7 (page 54)* illustrates a wide variety of distribution tiers and a sample of stores that fall under each category.

### DEPARTMENT STORES

Department stores, along with specialty retailers, are considered upscale or "upstairs" distribution channels. Their prices are higher than at other types of retail outlets, and they buy products in relatively small quantities. Some department stores are national, while others are regional.

Fashion and designer labels often trace a large proportion of their sales to department stores. Other property types, such as entertainment, sports or corporate trademarks, are all present in this tier as well, but in general mass retailers (see below) rely more heavily on licensed merchandise than department stores do.

### National Chains

National department store chains include J.C. Penney, Sears and Montgomery Ward. These national retailers tend to buy in larger quantities than regional department stores, and their prices often tend to be somewhat lower. Some retailers who started out as regional department store chains, such as

## *Figure 7*
## SELECTED RETAIL STORES BY DISTRIBUTION CHANNEL

**UPSTAIRS** *(Higher-Priced, Lower-Volume\*)*

**Department Stores, National & Regional**
Abraham & Strauss
Bloomingdale's
Burdine's
Dayton's
Dillard's
Famous-Barr
Hecht's
Hudson's
J.C. Penney
Kohl's
Lazarus
Lord & Taylor
Macy's
May
Montgomery Ward
Nieman-Marcus
Nordstrom
Rich's
Sears
Woodward & Lothrup

**Specialty Stores**
Athlete's Foot
B. Dalton
Books-A-Million
Champs
Disney Store
FAO Schwartz
Kinney
Lechter's
Merle Harmon's Fan Fair
Merry-Go-Round
Moondog's
Nicole Miller
Sanrio Surprise
Sesame Street Retail Stores
Spencer Gifts
Warner Studio Stores

**DOWNSTAIRS** *(Higher-Volume, Lower-Priced)*

**Discount Department Stores, National and Regional**
Fred Meyer
Hills
Kmart
Meijer
Pamida
Rose's

ShopKo
Target
Venture
Wal-Mart

**Category Killers**
Barnes & Noble Superstores
Bed, Bath & Beyond
Kids R Us
Sports Authority
Staples
Toys R Us

**Drug, Convenience, Grocery and Variety Stores**
A&P
Ben Franklin
Circle-K
Dollar General
Family Dollar
Food Lion
Kroger
McCrory
Pay-Less
Rite-Aid
7-Eleven
Super Value
Thrifty
Walgreen
Woolworth

**OTHER**
Arcades
Concession Stands
Home Shopping
Mail-Order Catalogs, Property-Specific and Third-Party
Restaurants

*Note:* This list is not exhaustive. It provides an overview of the types of stores in each channel.

\* National department stores such as J.C. Penney, Sears, Montgomery Ward have fairly high volumes and lower prices than regional department stores, but are still classified as department stores.

*Source:* The Licensing Letter;
         EPM Communications

Macy's, Bloomingdale's and Saks Fifth Avenue, are currently expanding into new national markets (although consolidation and mergers within the industry may lead to fewer of these stores in any single market). Their prices remain higher than those at the national chains cited above.

### Regional Department Stores

Some department stores have just one or a few units, while others own many outlets in several states within a given geographic region. Most are shopping center anchors. They include Dayton's, Hudson's, Marshall Field's, Hecht's, Dillard's, Famous-Barr and Abraham & Strauss.

## MASS MERCHANDISERS

Mass merchandisers, or discounters, are characterized by low prices, low markups and limited customer service. Some are discount department stores, while others are discount specialty stores, usually of the warehouse type.

### Big 3 Discount Chains

The major national discount department stores are Kmart, Wal-Mart and Target. They sell a great deal of licensed merchandise across virtually all property types.

The Big 3 use licensing extensively to differentiate themselves from their competition. They not only participate in exclusive licensed promotions, but also license properties for private label lines. Kmart has licensed Jaclyn Smith's name for apparel, Martha Stewart's for domestics and Giggle Bunny, a property created by licensing company Those Characters From Cleveland (a subsidiary of American Greetings), for children's products. Wal-Mart has licensed *Popular Mechanics* from Hearst for hardware, *Better Homes and Gardens* from Meredith for gardening products and celebrity Kathie Lee Gifford for apparel. Target has associated itself with characters including Alvin and the Chipmunks, Lamb Chop, Casper the Friendly Ghost and the Velveteen Rabbit for short- and longer-term proprietary product lines and promotions.

### Regional Discounters

Aside from the Big 3, a number of other discount department stores operate on a regional basis. They include Venture, Pamida, ShopKo, Meijer, Rose's, Hill's and Fred Meyer. These chains have similar buying and merchandising structures to the Big 3 national discount chains, and often rely on licensed promotions to distinguish themselves from their regional competition.

### Category Killers

So-called "category killers" are huge superstores specializing in one product category. Those with substantial licensed merchandise offerings include Toys R Us (toys), Kids 'R Us (children's apparel), The Sports Authority (sporting goods and sports-licensed apparel), Bed, Bath & Beyond (products for the home), Barnes & Noble Superstores (books), to name just a few. Some category killers are regional while others are national.

The competitive advantage of these stores lies in their ability to charge lower prices and to carry a wide selection of merchandise within one category. They usually have several times the square footage of an average mall-based specialty store. For category killers, licensed merchandise is used more to enhance the variety of their merchandise mix rather than to help differentiate them from competitors.

## SPECIALTY STORES

Like department stores, specialty stores are considered upscale distribution channels. They offer a comparable level of merchandise in terms of price and quality. Unlike department stores, however, they specialize in one product category. They are usually small stores — ranging from chains to independent sole proprietorships — and compete not on price but on a shopper-friendly atmosphere and on the quality and uniqueness of the products they stock.

### Independent Toy Stores

Specialty toy stores face competition from Toys R Us, which they cannot beat in terms of price or selection. Many arrange promotions with licensed properties to distinguish themselves from the competition. For example, FAO Schwartz utilizes a number of in-store concept shops and promotions with properties such as Lamb Chop, Thomas the Tank Engine, Barney, "Bump In The Night," various Disney films and many others. FAO also has a free-standing year-round Barbie boutique.

### Gift Shops

Gift shops run the gamut from independent one-shop operations to national mall-based chains such as Spencer Gifts to airport gift shops. Some concentrate on upscale gifts and sell artist-licensed gift, tabletop and stationery creations. Others, such as Spencer, specialize in novelties, focusing on merchandise associated with entertainment properties and corporate trademarks such as beer brands. Gift chains often use licensed promotions to differentiate themselves from the competition as well as to enhance their reputation as a fun, unique shopping destination.

### Specialty Apparel Stores

Specialty apparel stores range from independent stores and regional chains to large, national chains such as the Gap and Merry-Go-Round. Apparel shops vary in how much they depend on licensed products: The Gap and The Limited, for example, stock primarily private label merchandise, whereas Merry-Go-Round carries licensed merchandise and occasionally participates in licensed promotions. Most specialty apparel stores also carry a good deal of licensed merchandise based on fashion labels; in fact, several stores exist that specialize in the apparel and accessories of one designer, much of which may be licensed.

### Housewares Stores

Licensed housewares products are sometimes sold in dedicated housewares shops, as are compatible products such as tabletop items, kitchen textiles and giftware. Any licensee of housewares or related products has an opportunity to sell to these shops. Licensing *per se* does not, however, play a large role in terms of licensed promotions or in-store concept shops, although larger chains such as Lechter's do occasionally set up concept shops for properties including Campbell Soup, among others.

## Sporting Goods Stores

Most sporting goods stores, including Herman's and Oshman's, carry sports and fitness equipment licensed from various athletes or the major sports leagues. They also carry a large quantity of licensed sports apparel. They often participate in regional promotions with the leagues and colleges, highlighting licensed merchandise of local teams and offering free or discounted tickets to games.

## Fan Shops

Fan shops are stores specializing in licensed sports apparel. They became an important channel in the 1980s, and were one of the primary reasons for the transformation in sports licensing during that time from a seasonal to a year-round business. They are often mall-based, regional chains, and face competition from category killers, sporting goods chains and every other outlet where licensed sports merchandise is sold. Some of the larger chains are Pro Image, Merle Harmon's Fan Fair, Champs and Going To The Game. Like sporting goods stores, fan shops often utilize promotions with local teams and with the major leagues to help differentiate themselves.

## Footwear Stores

Mall-based footwear stores sell licensed footwear, primarily associated with fashion designers or brands. Some also sell accessories and hosiery, which may be licensed. Athletic footwear stores such as Foot Locker and FootAction USA sell signature footwear lines based on athletes and footwear based on sporting goods brands. In addition, many do a brisk business in licensed sports apparel.

## Bookstores

While the majority of books are sold through national bookstore chains, there are also many independent bookstores. Some utilize licensed promotions with book-related properties to build visibility and store traffic, and to create excitement in their stores.

Many bookstores also sell licensed merchandise outside of books, called "sidelines" in the trade, including book marks, diaries, toys, videotapes, audiotapes, games and puzzles, calendars and CD-ROM software. Most are based on book-related properties, but merchandise associated with characters, trademarks, celebrities and other properties are sold as well. Books are sometimes co-packaged with licensed products such as plush figures or videotapes, bringing those products into bookstores.

## Entertainment "Fan Shops"

A number of specialty stores have arisen over the past few years that specialize mostly in licensed entertainment and character merchandise. These shops cater to baby boomers and others who seek products based on favorite current and past TV shows and films. The product offerings range from t-shirts and videotapes to collectibles and action figures. Virtually all of the merchandise carried in these stores is licensed, based on a variety of entertainment properties. The store atmosphere is pure fun, and these stores compete on the basis of their uniqueness, rather than on other factors such as price. Most are independent stores or small regional chains. Examples include Hall of Stars and Hollywood Legends, both at Mall of America.

## Property-Specific Stores

These chains have received a lot of visibility in the media over the past few years. They include The Disney Store, which started in 1987, Sesame Street Retail Stores (1990) and the high-profile Warner Bros. Studio Stores (1991). Coca-Cola also is associated with retail stores for gifts and other licensed merchandise. Several other studios and major licensors are considering or testing the market with their own property- or studio-specific stores.

These retailers market themselves not just as shopping destinations, but also as entertainment venues. Video walls, activities for children, costumed characters and galleries of animation art are among the draws, in addition to the merchandise. The products also sell, though; these retailers are reported to have well above the sales per square foot of an average mall-based store.

## Museum Shops

Museum shops are upscale gift retailers, usually located in a museum, selling merchandise based on their own logo and collections. In addition, most stores sell products based on other museums' collections, as well as other upscale gift items licensed from fine artists and designers. Much of the merchandise found in museum stores is sub-contracted out by the museum rather than licensed, but licensed merchandise is sold here as well.

In addition, the Museum Company, a mall-based chain selling museum-licensed merchandise and other gift items, many of which are licensed, has proven successful so far and is expanding rapidly.

## Comic Book and Trading Card Stores

Comic book stores — both chains and independents — sell a significant amount of comic book-related merchandise, especially in certain categories such as trading cards, action figures, role-playing games, toys and t-shirts. For example, the merchandise mix of one chain, Moondog's of Chicago, contains 10% apparel, 5% games and 20% videos, calendars and plush, according to an interview with the owner in *Comics Retailer*. Most of these products are licensed, primarily from comics licensors, but also from others such as fantasy art, sports and sci-fi entertainment. Trading card stores have shown a similar propensity and, in fact, the line between card stores and comic stores is blurring as both move into each other's territories.

## Video Stores

Video stores are seen as a good opportunity for licensed merchandise based on entertainment, because of a natural fit between licensed entertainment products and the core videocassette categories. Some national chains — in particular Suncoast Motion Picture Company, a division of The Musicland Group — sell a great deal of licensed products; Suncoast, in fact, stocks 10% of its merchandise mix in "trend merchandise." Suncoast is notable, however, in that it sells, rather than rents videos. Other national chains, as well as most mom-and-pop operations, focus on video rentals. It is more difficult to sell licensed merchandise in an atmosphere where customers go to rent products. Still, some products are sold in videostores, including videogames, figurines, candy and plush. It remains a small factor so far, however, with only 3.7% of the typical video store's sales attributable to "alternative merchandise" (not including videogames), according to the Video Software Dealers Association.

## Computer and Videogame Software Stores

Opportunities exist for licensed merchandise to be sold in software retailers, although it is somewhat rare at this point. Most of the licensed merchandise sold here is the software itself (computer software and videogames based on various types of properties), computer accessories, such as mousepads, and videogame accessories, such as joysticks or gloves. Licensed books with tips on how to play various games are also sold in software stores.

## GROCERY STORES

Many people do not realize it, but grocery stores are a large outlet for licensed merchandise, mainly because so many food lines are licensed. Food-related brand extension programs record virtually all of their sales in grocery stores, as do other licensed food items such as snacks based on characters. Packaged food companies also participate in short-term promotions with entertainment properties, where grocery stores are the major focus. Other types of licensed merchandise are not prevalent in grocery stores, although an increasing number sell licensed kitchen-related items, books, school supplies, toys and other products.

## DEALER NETWORKS

Dealer networks are retail or wholesale outlets where a brand's core products are sold. Licensed merchandise based on the company's brands are sometimes sold in these venues as well. For example, caps based on Snap-On Tools may be sold through hardware stores, Corvette auto vacuums may be sold in Corvette showrooms and Budweiser can coolers may be sold to convenience stores though Bud distributors. Dealer networks also provide opportunities for licensors and licensees of corporate trademarks to sell licensed merchandise to dealers as premiums for consumers or the trade.

## DRUG STORES, VARIETY STORES AND CONVENIENCE STORES

All of these retail channels can be significant purchasers of certain types of licensed merchandise. Stationery and back-to-school products, insulated beverageware, health and beauty items, lunch kits and paper partyware are often sold through drug stores such as Pay-Less and variety stores such as Woolworth's. Convenience stores such as 7-Eleven sell licensed food products, beer-licensed novelties and other low-priced licensed items.

## CONCESSION STANDS

Concession stands are significant distribution channels for certain types of merchandise. For example, music-licensed products are sold on-site at concert venue concession stands. Sports merchandise is sold at arena concessions. And entertainment merchandise is sold at theme parks. Not all the merchandise seen at these venues is licensed, however; much of it is purchased from a sub-contractor specifically for that purpose by the licensor. The merchandise is often theme park- or arena-specific so as not to compete with merchandise sold through traditional retailers.

## RESTAURANTS AND ARCADES

Some merchandise is sold at property-specific restaurants such as Cheers bars at airports, Popeye's Fried Chicken restaurants and the Harley-Davidson Cafe, which are themselves licensed, as mentioned in Chapter 3. Videogame and pinball arcades provide an opportunity to sell licensed merchandise based on characters from the games. As in the situation with concessions stands, this merchandise is usually specific to the arcade or restaurant, so as not to compete with traditional retailers and the licensees who sell to them.

## MAIL ORDER

Mail order is an increasingly important category for sales of licensed merchandise. Third-party catalogs such as Signals, Sharper Image, Wireless, Athletic Supply, Sound Exchange, The Mind's Eye and many others all sell licensed merchandise ranging from mugs to ties to apparel to novelties. Sometimes the products are unique to that catalog, while at other times the same items can be purchased at retail. Property types of all sorts are represented — sports, entertainment, publishing, art, corporate trademarks, music and so on.

In addition, the number of property-specific catalogs selling merchandise based on a single property or family of properties is growing. Properties such as NASCAR, Coca-Cola, Doonesbury, Elvis Presley, "The Andy Griffith Show," Hershey's, "thirtysomething," Disney, Warner Brothers and Budweiser have all experimented with selling merchandise via dedicated mail order catalogs.

## TELE-SHOPPING

Home shopping is increasingly being tested by licensors across all property types. Fashion designers and celebrities were among the first to try it, and their success led licensors of other types of properties, including entertainment, sports and corporate trademarks, to successfully test home shopping as well. An estimated $1 million in merchandise based on the film *A League of Their Own* and $260,000 worth of soap opera "All My Children" products were sold on QVC in 1993, while Woodstock merchandise rang up nearly $1 million in sales in 1994 on MTV.

The majority of home shopping sales currently occur on one of the two major networks, Home Shopping Network and QVC, which together accounted for $2 billion in sales in 1993. A number of other outlets are also available for home shopping, including smaller networks and various transactional television programs found on ESPN2, MTV, in syndication and so on. (See *Figure 8 [page 62]* for a selection of home-shopping activity involving licensed properties.)

## OTHER

This wrap-up is intended to demonstrate the wide variety of retail outlets that are possible distribution channels for licensed merchandise. Licensed products can in fact be found almost anywhere and are not limited to these channels. For example, pet supply stores would sell licensed pet products such as leashes and other pet accessories, as well as bird seed and aquariums, all of which come in licensed varieties. Some licensors and licensees have experimented with licensed movie merchandise sales in movie theaters with mixed success. On-line services have tested selling merchandise as well; CBS is selling David Letterman "Late Show" merchandise (although non-licensed) online via Prodigy, for example. And more non-traditional retail channels should continue to be tested as licensors and licensees look to expand distribution and increase sales.

## RETAIL BUYING

Retailers buy merchandise on a department-by-department basis. Individual buyers have responsibility for one or more departments, or sometimes for several products sold within one department. The smaller the retail operation, the more departments one buyer may be responsible for; mom-and-pop operations may have one buyer for the whole store, while buyers for large chains may be responsible for just one or a few categories. (Small independent stores may utilize a purchasing company to serve as a middleman between itself and manufacturers.)

The buying structure for a given store or chain varies depending on that store's needs. Normally, buyers of soft goods (apparel and domestics) do not purchase hard goods (toys, hardware, furniture and so on), but buying responsibilities vary. A buyer for one chain may purchase toys, gardening supplies and outdoor furniture; at another chain a buyer may handle toys, lunch kits, paper partyware and greeting cards.

A divisional merchandise manager (DMM) usually oversees several buyers, and a VP or higher level employee normally oversees several DMMs. *Figure 9 A & B (see included sheets)* shows two typical large-retailer organizational charts.

## ORGANIZING CONCEPT SHOPS AND PROMOTIONS

The fact that purchasing decisions are decentralized means that a manufacturer deals with a certain buyer or buyers at each store who is in charge of

*Figure 8*

## SUMMARY OF SELECTED DIRECT-RESPONSE TELEVISION VEHICLES FOR LICENSED PRODUCTS

| PROPERTY | NETWORK/FORMAT | DESCRIPTION |
|---|---|---|
| All My Children | QVC | $260,000 worth of merchandise reportedly sold; exclusive products made by licensees of ABC Daytime. |
| Batman: Mask of the Phantasm | Two QVC programs, one hour each. | Sold out of everything (9 items) including 2 signed lithos for $110, a Bob Kane one-sheet for $150, t-shirts, etc. Set decorated like a rooftop scene from the movie. |
| Elvis Presley | Three shows on QVC within last 12 months. | Products include CD boxed sets ($75), Hasbro dolls ($49), collectibles, apparel, jewelry, framed items, steins, trading cards, etc. Hasbro dolls sold out in 2-3 minutes. Tied to stamp issuance, birth and death dates. |
| Free Willy | 9 hour-long programs on QVC. | Sold 9-12 items per show, including crew merchandise, signed prints, t-shirts, etc. Three licensees involved. Movie's producers were guests. |
| Maverick | 20-minute vignette within another QVC segment. | Products included signed lithographs, t-shirts, caps, framed one-sheets. |
| NASCAR | NASCAR Shop Talk on ESPN. Generally airs after races. 11 original airings in 1994, plus repeats (1/2 hour). | At most, 6 products are featured per half-hour show. Include jackets, t-shirts, caps, lithos, collectible die-cast items, etc. Sell in the hundreds of thousands of dollars per show. Merchandise ties in with the guest (e.g. signed memorabilia is featured). |
| Northern Exposure, Coach | Short-form commercial, on CBS and ABC respectively. | Aired immediately after shows. Both were 20- to 30-second spots featuring sweatshirts. Northern Exposure was followed up with merchandise catalog containing other merchandise. |
| Peanuts | 2-hour QVC segment. | $500,000 worth of merchandise sold, including 2,580 units of a Charles Schultz book in 4 minutes; 1,885 units of a Logotel sweatshirt in 3.5 minutes and 1,440 of a Logotel t-shirt in 6 minutes. Other sell-outs included watch and Bibb throw. |
| Warner Studio Stores | Monthly two-hour show on QVC during consistent time period. | Sales average $300,000-$450,000 retail per show. Sell Looney Tunes and other store merchandise. None of the products are licensed; all are contracted by Studio Stores. |
| Woodstock | 3 half-hour segments on Friday and 6 on Saturday during MTV's coverage of Woodstock 94. | Reportedly around $1 million worth of merchandise sold in total. Products included an event package (program, hat and t-shirt) for $50, a $75 raincoat, $40 sweatshirt and $75 collectible (framed coin and ticket). Merchandise supplied by licensor Polygram's wholesale division rather than by licensees (except for the coin). |

*Note:* This table is by no means complete. It is intended to provide a snapshot of patterns in licensed product-related home shopping. Many other licensors and individual licensees have also tested home shopping and direct-response commercials.
*Source:* The Licensing Letter, December 1994; EPM Communications

purchasing that licensee's products. From a licensor's point of view, this buying structure can make the creation of concept shops or promotions rather challenging. The licensor needs to find the person at each retailer who is the major organizer of such promotions or boutiques, and who can coordinate all the various buyers who would be involved in purchase decisions for the products included in the concept shop.

This job is becoming easier than it was a few years ago, because retailers are aware that concept shops are the most effective way to sell licensed merchandise, and therefore often have a structure in place to oversee their creation. When concept shops were first being tested, the challenge was greater, because there often was no one person at a given retailer that was willing and able to coordinate all the various buyers. Now, however, a senior DMM or someone in the marketing department is usually the point person for such promotions.

## TRENDS IN DISTRIBUTION

The increase in the use of concept shops in virtually all channels of distribution is one major trend in licensed merchandise retailing. Another is the fact that licensees are increasingly looking for opportunities to cross-promote and cross-package different licensed products based on the same property. One licensed product, such as a comic book, trading card or plush, is packaged together with another compatible licensed product, such as a video- or audiocassette, videogame or book. Not only does this cross-packaging add value in the eyes of consumers — they receive a free trading card with a comic book or a free poster with a videogame — but it can also open up distribution channels that would not normally be considered. For example, a book and video package can be sold in bookstores and in video stores (as well as mass market or department stores), while a toy and comic book package can be sold in comic book stores and toy stores (as well as other channels). Since video stores are not traditional channels for books, this activity is a good way to expand distribution for each manufacturer, and to increase the average price per transaction for the retailer. In fact, retailers may embrace a non-traditional product that is cross-packaged with a traditional one much more quickly than they would accept it alone, so this technique is a good way for a manufacturer to gain entry to a new channel.

Licensors and licensees are continually looking for creative new ways to increase sales of licensed merchandise as the market matures — leading to slower growth — in the U.S. and Canada. While the licensing community continues to rely heavily on mass merchants and, to a lesser degree, department and specialty stores, many licensors and licensees are experimenting with new channels of distribution such as independent video stores, online services and teleshopping channels.

The major perceived danger of expanding into new distribution channels is the fear of cannibalization. Many existing retailers and licensees feel that sales in the new distribution channel may adversely affect their sales.

When Major League Baseball products are sold on a home shopping channel, for example, owners of fan shops may fear that they will lose sales, although an argument can be made that TV shopping efforts can actually drive sales at retail. Or, a licensee distributing Disney t-shirts through specialty stores for $15 may fear that similar products sold in Kmart at $10 may take sales away from them.

## AVOIDING CANNIBALIZATION

In order to alleviate retailers' fears, licensors often approve different products for different channels of distribution. For example, direct-embroidered apparel, a relatively costly manufacturing technique, can be licensed for distribution in department and specialty stores, while apparel sporting embroidered appliques can be authorized for mass merchant sales. Similarly, plastic toys can be licensed exclusively for mass market, while wooden toys may be approved for department and specialty distribution. In any product category, different designs can be authorized for each outlet, so that that particular design may only be found in one type of store. For example, the NBA allows apparel with the authentic NBA logo on the sleeve to be distributed only through upscale channels; mass market apparel may exhibit team logos, but not the official NBA league emblem.

Another technique increasingly used by licensors to differentiate among channels is to create sub-brands, each applicable to a different distribution tier or demographic group. The Walt Disney Company is a good example of how sub-brands can be used to segment merchandise by distribution channel and by demographics. Some of their sub-brands include:

- Minnie & Me: girls' products
- M. Mouse: Women's bridge sportswear
- Perils of Mickey: Children's products based on nostalgic comics from the 1930s
- Mickey & Co.: Women's and children's department store merchandise
- Mickey & Co. Sport Club: Sports-themed merchandise
- Disney Babies: mass market infant products
- Mickey's Stuff for Kids: mass market products for age 2-10
- Princess Collection: girls' merchandise based on various film characters

The major sports leagues have also experimented with sub-branding, creating logos for children's products, nostalgic marks, authentic reproductions and so on. For example, the NFL has launched the following sub-brands:

- NFL Pro-Line: authentic on-the field apparel for sale in fan shops and sporting goods stores.
- NFL Pro Shop: golf apparel and accessories sold through sports-related specialty stores.

- NFL Throwbacks: merchandise based on nostalgic marks sold at a mid-to-high price in upper-end retailers including department stores and fan shops.
- NFL Spirit: women's merchandise for the upstairs market.
- NFL Kids: mass market children's merchandise.
- QB Club: mass market merchandise endorsed by NFL quarterbacks.

Licensors also offer exclusives to certain stores as a differentiation technique. Individual retailers or mail-order catalogs then have a product or product line that can be purchased only at that outlet, at least within the store's geographic area. Exclusivity can be for a short time period, or can sometimes be a long-term arrangement.

While the above methods help to alleviate retailers' fears, the main method of lessening licensees' fears, of course, is to grant rights to all distribution channels to one licensee. This tactic is not always practical, however. Licensees may not be capable of handling all channels adequately, or a licensor may opt for several licensees if maximizing upfront money is its primary goal. Yet, true exclusives are an effective way to eliminate the threat of cannibalization.

No matter what differentiation techniques are used, it is worthwhile to note that the average consumer may not be able to perceive the sometimes-subtle differences that distinguish products in one channel from another. To them, a $10 Pepsi t-shirt in Kmart may be basically the same as a $20 t-shirt with a slightly different design spotted in a specialty store. These methods usually add to the comfort level of existing retailers, however, and demonstrate to licensees that licensors are keeping their interests in mind.

## BARRIERS TO EXPANDING DISTRIBUTION

In spite of the trend among licensors to expand distribution to new, untapped channels, certain barriers to expansion exist. The challenges are not insurmountable, but can cause problems initially.

First, in distribution channels where licensed merchandise is a relatively new category — particularly in those where independent stores dominate — demand from retailers will be small at first. This situation may lead licensors and their licensees to ignore a distribution tier in favor of larger markets. Any independent store can still purchase licensed products, of course, but licensors and licensees may not feel it is cost-effective to aggressively target that segment until evidence develops of a greater demand. Independent retailers may also resent the lack of attention paid to them, and sometimes complain that they face resistance when trying to order small quantities.

Secondly, distribution methods in various retail industries affect how easy it is to sell licensed products to those retailers. In several industries — including video rental, comic book and book stores — a network of distributors sell the core products to retailers. Retailers, especially small ones, are used to buying all their products from their distributor. They are not accustomed to going directly to manufacturers, which is where they would need to go for most licensed merchandise; their core-product distributors are unlikely to carry it at present. Some distributors are beginning to look into carrying licensed products, however, and some licensees actively target independent retailers as customers.

Another challenge is the fact that many independent retailers do not have experience in merchandising licensed products so as to achieve maximum sales. They assume that the products will sell themselves. For example, video stores may put licensed products in an out-of-the-way place or beind glass to prevent pilferage, thus eliminating impulse sales. Similarly, movie theaters selling merchandise for the first time may put very little of it out on the floor where filmgoers will see it, thus reducing potential sales. Some distribution channels — especially independent specialty stores — need to be educated in selling licensed merchandise before they can become viable.

Finally, the purchasing habits of consumers in various distribution channels must be considered. For example, if consumers are used to renting in a certain retail outlet, such as a video store, will they be willing to change their behavior to accommodate the availability of licensed products? They may be in the habit of only bringing to the store the two dollars they need to rent a video, thus eliminating the possibility of purchasing additional items. Similarly, if the retailer sells low-priced items, such as trading cards or movie tickets, will customers purchase a much more expensive item on impulse? Consumers will need to become used to the fact that these venues are destinations for licensed merchandise before they will change their purchasing patterns.

# PART 2:
# LICENSING STRATEGIES

CHAPTER 5:
# STRATEGIES FOR LICENSORS

Every licensing program is unique, and there is no "correct," step-by-step method of creating one. This chapter provides a framework within which licensors can make decisions about their properties, and outlines some of the issues that arise when launching and maintaining a licensing program.

Property owners should remember that licensing is a business technique, not an end in itself. A licensing plan should be created within the context of the licensor's marketing plan, taking into consideration the advertising and promotional strategies for the company as a whole.

Licensors should also outline their goals for the licensing effort, before any other decisions are made. Objectives vary depending on the property and the licensor; they may include earning upfront dollars, extending into new product categories, protecting trademarks or any of the other possible goals outlined in Chapter 1.

## DEFINING THE PROPERTY

No property can be successfully licensed until its characteristics are defined. Manufacturers, retailers and, especially, consumers must be able to understand what the property stands for. Some of the attributes to be considered include:

- The property's brand image; that is, whether it is primarily upscale, "fun," educational, health-related, adult entertainment and so on.
- The size and demographic characteristics of the target audience. Demographics include age, sex and economic level. Psychographic or behavioral information can also be helpful, such as where the target audience likes to shop, what they do in their free time and what sorts of products appeal to them.
- Specific property characteristics, such as what the logo and other graphic representations should look like, what color schemes should be used, how many logos and graphic variations should be trademarked, personality traits (for characters) and sample plot lines (for entertainment).
- Competitive properties. Other properties available that target the same demographic audience and have similar characteristics will affect the strategy for any property. A thorough investigation of competitive properties — whether corporate brands, characters or whatnot — will be beneficial.

Licensors should also be aware from the outset of whether their property is essentially long-term or short-term. Most corporate trademarks and fashion labels are long-term; it is not worth the investment to launch such a line unless it is expected to last for years or even decades. Most book properties and artists' works also have the potential to endure over the long term. On the other hand, many films and television shows are inherently short-term, at least as a stand-alone property. They tend to have consumer appeal for one to five years, and then fade out. The New Kids On The Block, for example, was certainly lucrative, with retail sales of $800 million, but the group lasted just about a year as a licensed property.

As mentioned earlier, some short-term properties can be managed so they will not disappear after they become outmoded as a fad. They can even become classics — the *Batman* licensing program based on the first live-action movie, for example, started as an essentially faddish licensing program in 1989, when the Bat-logo was ubiquitous and Bat-merchandise racked up $1.5 billion in sales worldwide. But, through promotions and constant new media reincarnations, the property has become a long-term classic.

Whether the property promises to be short- or long-term affects the licensing strategy. With a short-term property, a licensor wants to maximize revenues during the property's life span without worrying about its performance after that time. Consequently, every appropriate product category will be licensed from the beginning, and all possible distribution channels will be utilized right away. Every effort will be made to meet demand while it exists.

On the other hand, with a long-term property, the goal is to have demand increase steadily over time until it reaches a strong, consistent level year after year. Product categories will often be limited initially to allow for later expansion, and distribution may be narrowly focused at first. In addition, steps will be taken to keep the property fresh over the long term, such as media, updated designs, promotions and so on.

## CREATING A LICENSING STRATEGY

Before the selection of licensees begins, property owners should develop a licensing strategy. Strategic elements include distribution, product categories, timing, and media and promotional support.

## DISTRIBUTION

Licensed products may be sold through any of the distribution tiers discussed in Chapter 4. The primary retail channel to target is determined by the property itself. An upscale property lends itself to department and specialty stores, while a short-term entertainment property may be primarily directed at mass merchants. Niche programs may be aimed exclusively at gift shops, direct mail or home shopping channels. Some licensors initiate multi-tiered programs, allowing certain products to be sold in the mass market while other more upscale merchandise is distributed through department and specialty stores.

Geographic distribution is also an important consideration. Some corporate trademarks are already known internationally. Similarly, many musicians have worldwide followings. Both of these properties would probably be appropriate for a worldwide licensing program from the start. On the other hand, a television property's licensing efforts will be dependent on the broadcast schedule and its rollout internationally. Some properties even have narrow distribution within one region of the U.S., such as a minor league sports team or a college without significant national appeal.

## PRODUCT CATEGORIES

The products that are appropriate for a particular property are determined, of course, by the property's characteristics and target audience. If the average target customer has a relatively low income, screenprinted t-shirts would be more appropriate than direct-embroidered denim jackets. Children's educational properties may lend themselves to activity kits or science sets, but perhaps not to more frivolous products. For a property that skews toward adults, plush or action figures would probably not be appropriate, whereas a board game might be. A designer property with an upscale image may lend itself to decorative tabletop accessories, but not keychains or plastic figurines. An environmental non-profit organization would not license environmentally unsound products.

Licensors should also consider the number of products to license. For a short-term, faddish type property, a wide range of products may be authorized from the start; on the other hand, a licensor of a children's book property may want to preserve its longevity and image of quality by limiting the number of products.

How many individual licensees should be selected? This decision has nothing to do with the expected sales or even with the number of products planned. Rather, it is a strategic decision. Some licensors prefer to authorize a relatively small number of licensees, each having broad, exclusive product lines and selling in a number of distribution channels and geographic areas. Others opt for many licensees, each with very narrow or no exclusivity and manufacturing a small range of products. The former method allows more control over the property's image, as long as demand can be met by one or a few licensees; the latter allows the licensor to earn more upfront money in terms of advances.

The property type is irrelevant in this discussion — Pierre Cardin has 840 licensees worldwide, while Bill Blass has 70 in the U.S. and 70 internationally; both have similar licensed merchandise sales of between $325 million and $350 million wholesale annually.

## TIMING

A number of timing issues arise when planning a property's licensing effort. First, when is the appropriate time to launch the property? For a fashion brand, launching at the beginning of a major selling season — rather than at a time when retailers and customers are not buying much merchandise — makes sense. For a film, a licensor might wish to make film-goers aware of its release and to increase the opening-day box-office take, in which case products would appear in stores all at once, a couple of weeks — or in the case of some very high-profile releases, several months — prior to the film's premiere. For a classic comic book property, a few products might be tested initially, perhaps in conjunction with a promotion, and more products rolled out slowly. A TV show licensor would want to wait until the series becomes established before products reach retail; if merchandise gets to market too early and does not sell, retailers will turn from the property, leaving little chance of recovery later, even after the series catches on. In general, launching all products together makes the biggest statement at retail, whereas staggering product introductions may help maintain the property's longevity.

Another timing issue has to do with the roles of certain licensees. A few key categories drive some types of licensing programs. For a children's entertainment property, the master toy licensee usually devotes funds to advertising, thereby encouraging sales of other products. Therefore, the master toy licensee is usually signed and sometimes even launched at retail before other licensees come on board. Similarly, for a new fashion label, core apparel categories will often be launched prior to secondary categories such as accessories or footwear.

Selling seasons also play a role in when products should be launched. For example, a large majority of all toy sales for a year are sold in the fourth quarter. Thus, introducing a toy line in January may not be optimal. Similarly, apparel is sold in two major seasons, Spring and Fall, with smaller in-between seasons known as Resort and Holiday. Products are sold to retailers at trade shows about six months prior to the start of the consumer selling season. Introducing new apparel lines outside of this accepted schedule would hurt sales.

Finally, lead times — the time required for products to get to market — also play a role in the timing of a property's launch and roll-out. Length of contract negotiations vary (although a rule-of-thumb average is six to eight weeks). Licensees must have products or prototypes ready to show to retailers at industry trade shows such as Toy Fair in February or MAGIC, for apparel, in February and September. And, while the average lead time from contract signing to retail is one to one and a half years, different products require different lead times, depending on product development and manufacturing needs.

Thus, the length of time between contract signing and the product's appearance at retail dictates when licensees should be sought. Videogames, computer software, footwear and toys need a long time to complete product development and manufacturing, and therefore need to be signed earlier than other categories. Apparel, on the other hand, can, in a pinch, get to retailers as little as three months after contract signing. In general, imported goods require longer lead times than goods produced in this country.

A timing issue of importance to film licensors is the scheduling of the home video release date. Videos can drive further sales of licensed merchandise, especially for children's films that are purchased rather than rented — children watch the tape over and over, which drives demand for other merchandise — but retailers may not keep merchandise on shelves until the video is released. Film merchandise has a short window of opportunity, and if sales are slow early, retailers will most likely bail out before the video has the opportunity to jump-start product sales.

## MEDIA AND PROMOTIONAL SUPPORT

If a property is intended to be around for a long time, licensors need to plan how to keep it fresh and maintain its awareness in customers' minds.

There are several methods of keeping a property fresh. For entertainment properties, one method is to create new entertainment and media vehicles, including book publishing, comic strips and comic books, films and sequels, home video releases, television series and videogames. Not only do they help retain the interest of the property's customers, they also add new fans.

Promotions also serve to maintain the longevity of all types of properties. Entertainment promotions often occur in conjunction with the new media releases described above, but there are all sorts of other opportunities simply because there is a fit between the property and a promotional partner:

- Homer Simpson of "The Simpsons" serves as spokescharacter for Winchell's donuts, since the character loves donuts;
- Pigpen from the Peanuts comic strip acts as spokescharacter for Regina carpet cleaners, since his main personality trait is that he spreads dirt wherever he goes;
- Garfield the Cat is a spokescharacter for Golden Cat's Kitty Litter MAXX.

Sports properties may be involved in promotions in conjunction with championships or All-Star games; fashion labels may enter into promotions at the start of a new season. Promotional activities are discussed further in Chapter 12.

No matter how many media events or high-profile promotions surround a property, products will not continue to sell over time if they remain the same year after year. Adding new product categories to the merchandise mix keeps a property alive. Many fashion labels, for example, start off with apparel and accessories, and then expand into home furnishings or personal care products. A children's book character may be focused initially on videos, CD-ROM, music, plush and publishing, and then slowly expand into other categories such as board games, apparel and accessories. A corporate trademark licensing program may focus on collectibles based on its nostalgic advertising, and then expand to apparel; an artist may start out in stationery and gifts and expand to tabletop items or domestics. All of these product additions give repeat customers new items to purchase, as well as providing new opportunities for advertising and promotions.

Even within existing product categories, fresh designs each season are essential to maintain demand over the long term. Designs on apparel, accessories and footwear need to be updated each season to reflect fashion trends;

new toy lines must be introduced each year, so children can add to their collections. Every product category can become stale over time without being enhanced by new designs and new product incarnations.

Another method of extending a property's life is to introduce it to new audiences. Cross-licensing — combining two properties on one product — is one way to achieve this. For example, a t-shirt showing the Looney Tunes' Tasmanian Devil in an NFL Los Angeles Raiders uniform helps keep both properties fresh by introducing a new, fun product; it also expands both properties' audiences by encouraging fans of the NFL to buy Looney Tunes merchandise, and vice versa. And, while sports-character cross-licensing is the most common type, infinite possibilities exist: the Teenage Mutant Ninja Turtles toys masquerade as Universal Studios Monsters, Mickey Mouse rides in a Cadillac (on a t-shirt) and the above-mentioned Taz rides a Harley, as portrayed on a leather jacket.

A property's demographic appeal can also be expanded through the use of sub-brands appealing to different demographic groups. For example, Major League Baseball launched its Rookie League brand to increase its sales of children's products; many classic characters have spun off infant sub-brands; and fashion label Guess? introduced Baby Guess for the same reason.

## SELECTING LICENSEES

After setting its overall licensing strategy, licensors must select their licensees. Either the licensee or the licensor can initiate the relationship. Potential licensees are screened by filling out a licensee evaluation form that covers many of the points discussed below; the information provided creates a basis on which the licensor may make its decision. While evaluation forms vary in terms of length and amount of detail, *Figure 10 (pages 75-76)* outlines the basic contents of a typical licensee application.

### CRITERIA FOR SELECTION

Licensors evaluate potential licensees against several criteria before ultimately deciding which manufacturers are most appropriate.

#### The Product Line

What products does the potential licensee propose to make under the licensing agreement? Licensors should ensure that those products fit with the strategy for the property and that they are compatible with its characteristics. The design, the materials used, the product's quality and the way the property is incorporated into the product are all important considerations. Samples of similar items to those proposed should be analyzed.

#### The Potential Licensee's Track Record

Does the licensee have experience manufacturing and selling products similar to those it is proposing? The quality of these lines, and of other products manufactured in the past, should be acceptable. If the licensee has experience marketing licensed products, how successful were results? Were the design and product quality up to the licensor's standards?

*Figure 10*

# TYPICAL CONTENTS OF A LICENSEE EVALUATION FORM

## GENERAL COMPANY INFORMATION
Company name
Primary contact person
Name of person who provided information on the form
Address and phone numbers of headquarters and other locations
Number of years in business
Previous names of company, if any
Other companies operated by the principles of this company
    within the last five years
Corporate officers, owners and partners
Number of employees
Parent company, if any
Other names under which business is done
- subsidiaries
- labels
- brands

Top competitors

## RECENT BUSINESS HISTORY
Annual gross sales volume for last three to five years
- in dollars
- in units
- by SKU
- by distribution channel

Annual net profits for last three to five years
Amount spent on advertising over the last three to five years
Description and history of manufacturing facilities, distribution facilities, sales
    force/organization, showrooms
Major competitors

## COLLATERAL MATERIALS
Name of advertising, public relations, promotional agencies
Copies of price lists, brochures, promotional materials depicting the company's
    products
Audited financial results such as annual reports

## RETAIL CUSTOMER INFORMATION
Three to five largest retail customers, sometimes by brand
- type of retail account
- address
- phone number
- name of buyer

Last year's wholesale volume with each top retail account
Summary of current distribution by % of sales volume in each channel, with
    largest customers in each

## FINANCIAL AND CREDIT INFORMATION
Insurance
- type
- amount of insurance
- names of insurance companies
- policy numbers

Type of business (corporation, sole proprietorship, etc.)
Credit rating or other credit references

*Continued Next Page*

*Figure 10 Continued*

Bank references
- name
- address
- phone number
- contact person

Federal tax I.D. number
Litigation currently involved with, if any

## OTHER BUSINESS INFORMATION
Description of quality control procedures
Description of in-house design and artwork capability

## LICENSING HISTORY
List of current licenses held with the prospective property holder
List of current licenses held with other property holders
- contact information
- number of years held

Annual wholesale dollar volume of similar licensed products, if any
Reason for interest in prospective property

## PLAN FOR THE PROPOSED LICENSED PRODUCT LINE
Trademarks to be used
Products to be made
Territory to be covered
Estimated wholesale selling price per unit
Product samples of similar products to those proposed
Retail accounts where licensed products will be sold
Timing of sample completion, production, product launch, shipping and other
    marketing dates
Collateral materials and promotional plans
- trade and consumer advertising
- in-store materials
- co-op advertising funds
- sales incentives

Trade shows where product line will be exhibited
Amount of advertising, promotion and merchandising funds
Materials (or drafts) showing products incorporating the property
- catalogs
- brochures
- advertisements
- price lists

Names and addresses of sub-contractors or manufacturing plants where each
    product will be made
Financial forecasts of gross sales and units for each line for two to three years (or
    the number of years proposed for the license)

## OTHER
Any other information that will help demonstrate the licensee's ability to success-
    fully market the product
Other trade contacts, in addition to retail, bank and licensor references

*Note:* Few licensee evaluation forms contain every element listed here, but all elements are contained in some forms. Exact contents of the evaluation form depends on the licensor's objectives.

*Source:* The Licensing Letter; EPM Communications

## Manufacturing

Licensors should find out if manufacturing will be done in-house, through a sub-contractor or sub-licensee, or if the products will be imported. If in-house, it is worth paying a visit to the facilities. If manufacturing will be done by a third party, the licensor should get as much information about that company as possible. The licensor should also ascertain that the licensee or its sub-licensee is capable of adequate production levels to meet demand expected for the line.

## Distribution

Is the licensee's sales force adequate to achieve the sales levels desired? In most cases, the licensee should already have relationships in place with key retailers where it proposes to sell the product. In addition, if past experience shows that a potential licensee may approach unauthorized distribution channels (e.g. selling to Kmart for an upscale brand or exporting when it has domestic rights only), it should not be signed. Distribution is, with very few exceptions, an extremely important criterion for licensee selection.

## Sales Forecasts

The sales forecasts for the proposed products should be in line with the licensor's expectations. They should also be realistic given the track record and the manufacturing and marketing capabilities of the licensees.

## Long-Term Capabilities

The licensee should be capable of producing a new product line each season. It also may be beneficial if the licensee can expand into other, related products if initial merchandise sells well.

## How Many Other Licenses Does The Manufacturer Hold?

Does the licensee intend to treat the property as one of its primary brands or does it maintain a stable of licenses? The first option may be important for a fashion brand looking for a significant advertising and promotional commitment from its licensees. On the other hand, an entertainment licensor to whom advances are a primary goal and awareness secondary may value a licensee who will pay the required advance, even if it stockpiles the license and does not produce merchandise.

## Marketing Plans for the Property

Some licensors, especially fashion and corporate property owners, desire licensees who plan to actively promote the brand. To a licensor of a short-term entertainment property, this consideration may be less important, although in many cases the advertising done by certain manufacturers (in particular the master toy licensee) is critical to the program and is a prerequisite before other licensees even consider the property.

## Financial Strength of the Potential Licensee

Is the company financially stable? Specifically, does it have the financial ability to achieve all that it proposes to achieve in the marketing and manufacturing of licensed merchandise? Licensors ask for bank references and credit references to help them evaluate a manufacturer's financial status.

## Reputation as a Vendor

Licensors ask for retailer references from potential licensees, in order to ascertain if the company's retail customers value it as a vendor. Important factors include whether the licensee delivers products on time, has a reputation for quality, maintains good, long-term relationships with retailers and provides good customer service.

## What Is the Potential Licensee Willing To Pay?

The ability and willingness to pay desired royalties, advances and guarantees is certainly not the sole, or even the most important, criterion in the selection process. In cases where all else is equal between two licensees, however, the willingness to agree to a better monetary deal for the licensor may be the deciding factor. For short-term entertainment properties, where there is a surplus of demand from manufacturers and where licensing fees are a primary goal of the licensor, price may be an important consideration.

## Personnel

The relationship between the licensee's and the licensor's personnel is a very important factor in how well the arrangement works. The licensor should feel comfortable that the licensee will communicate any problems that arise, and should trust the manufacturer's staff to treat their assets with care. Licensors should have a gut feeling that they can work well with the licensee's staff.

## LICENSEE PRESENTATIONS

When presenting a property to potential licensees, all of the elements in the licensing strategy should be outlined clearly. This includes giving a brief synopsis of the property, its target audience and its attributes, as well as demonstrating its look. A style book or other art reference materials will help with the latter by showing various logos and/or characters available and by presenting some sample products incorporating the property. If the property has a track record in terms of sales of a core product, sales of products by other licensees, TV ratings, sales of videos or theatrical box-office figures, these results should be outlined. Any known interest from retailers, promotional plans and proposed media vehicles, if applicable, are all strong selling points. The more professional and well thought-out a licensor's presentation to potential licensees, the more chance of generating interest in the property.

## RETAILER PRESENTATIONS

Although licensees are primarily responsible for selling the licensed products to stores, licensors often — and increasingly — make presentations to retailers as well, to set up promotions or in-store concept shops. Licensors may make presentations to retailers alone, or may bring a group of licensees along. Initial retailer meetings usually occur about nine months before the introduction of the licensed merchandise. It is important to have the appropriate personnel attend the meeting; also, since each department has a separate buyer, it may be necessary to present the property to several buyers as well as a manager or someone from the marketing department. It is also important that licensors and licensees — whether meeting with retailers together or separately — deliver a consistent message about the property.

Because the retailer is such an important part of the licensing equation, many licensors and licensing agents hire a staffer dedicated to servicing retailers on a full-time basis. This person should have retail experience and know what the retailers' needs are, so the licensor, and its licensees, can better address them.

The provision of promotional materials to support the property is also an incentive for the retailer to get behind that license. Promotional support can include pre-fabricated boutique displays, point-of-purchase materials and the provision of co-op marketing dollars.

## ADMINISTERING THE LICENSING PROGRAM

Once strategies are developed and contracts are signed, the licensing program still requires day-to-day administration. Most observers suggest that this be the job of at least one full-time person if the licensing program is being administered in-house.

Day-to-day adminstrative duties include approving products at various stages of the design and manufacturing process, not just for the first line of products but for all merchandise developed under the licensing agreement; collecting royalties and monitoring royalty accounting statements, usually on a quarterly basis; and communicating on an ongoing basis with licensees and retailers. It is essential that licensors communicate any changes in the property or its strategy — changes in promotional time frames, movie release dates and concert tour schedules, injuries to athletes who are celebrity endorsers and the like — to licensees and retailers, whose businesses may be greatly affected by these developments. The more time they have to react, the more likely any problems that arise will be resolved.

Finally, licensors must oversee an ongoing anti-infringement program. Anti-counterfeiting techniques will be discussed in depth in Chapter 10, but they include policing retailers and flea markets for counterfeit merchandise, overseeing investigators in the U.S. and abroad, maintaining adequate legal protection and seeking remedies where counterfeiting does occur.

## FINANCIAL FORECASTING

Determining the financial gain likely to accrue from a licensing program is not easy, given the vast number of variables with which to contend. While royalties and other money matters are the subject of Chapter 7, this section examines some of the considerations involved in financial forecasting.

Financial forecasts follow directly from the strategic decisions outlined so far. The number of products available, when those products are introduced, how fast the program rolls out and the property's total expected life span all play a role in determining the property's financial value over time. The assumptions behind the financial forecast should be in line with the property's planned strategy.

One reasonable way to examine potential revenues is to start by looking at retail sales levels generated by licensing programs based on comparable properties. For example, a mass-market fashion brand might be compared to sales of Sasson or Bonjour, or a children's book property to the Berenstain Bears or Clifford the Big Red Dog.

It is not easy to find retail sales figures on most properties, especially if they are not "home-runs." Most are not readily available. Licensors can start, however, by researching retail sales of as many comparable properties as possible. Trade magazines usually print such information now and then — *Women's Wear Daily* for women's apparel, *Playthings*, *Toy & Hobby World* or *The Toy Book* for toys, and so on. Some licensing publications, including *The Licensing Letter*, also include such information.

The licensor can then compare the potential of its property with the sales generated by other, fairly similar properties, trying to be as realistic as possible. (Most new properties are not "the next Mickey Mouse" or "the next Ninja Turtles" or "the next Coca-Cola.")

To estimate annual royalties, the licensor divides retail sales figures in half to estimate wholesale sales, which are, in general, about half the retail level. Multiplying wholesale sales by the average royalty rate (see Chapter 7) gives the licensor an estimate of royalty income. For example, if a property is forecast to reach $50 million in annual sales, wholesale sales would be about $25 million. Assuming a royalty of 7%, annual revenues to the licensor — before agency commissions — would be $1.75 million. Revenues for the first year of a property are not indicative of eventual sales; advances will be tallied, but royalties will not begin to appear until at least year two.

Estimating a property's economic potential is not science. The point of coming up with a reasonable forecast is to help the licensor determine if launching the program is worth it. It may also highlight areas in the original strategy that need rethinking. Forecasting best-case, worst-case and realistic scenarios is often a good idea, in order to get an overview of the implications of each.

*Figure 11 (page 81)* illustrates a sample format for forecasting sales; the product categories and number of years included will vary depending on the property, of course.

## USING A LICENSING AGENT

For new licensors, agents offer instant expertise: They know how to negotiate contracts, what going royalty rates are, how to identify the best licensees and how to target appropriate product categories. They can also help a licensor develop a strategy based on their experience of what works and what does not. Agents make sure licensors get paid, ascertain that product approv-

## Figure 11
### SAMPLE GRID FOR FINANCIAL FORECASTING
### PRE-SCHOOL ENTERTAINMENT PROPERTY

| PRODUCT CATEGORY | YEAR 1 | YEAR 2 | YEAR 3 | YEAR 4 | YEAR 5 |
|---|---|---|---|---|---|
| Accessories | $0,000.00 | $0,000.00 | $0,000.00 | $0,000.00 | $0,000.00 |
| Apparel | $0,000.00 | $0,000.00 | $0,000.00 | $0,000.00 | $0,000.00 |
| Domestics | $0,000.00 | $0,000.00 | $0,000.00 | $0,000.00 | $0,000.00 |
| Housewares | $0,000.00 | $0,000.00 | $0,000.00 | $0,000.00 | $0,000.00 |
| Infant Products | $0,000.00 | $0,000.00 | $0,000.00 | $0,000.00 | $0,000.00 |
| Music/Video | $0,000.00 | $0,000.00 | $0,000.00 | $0,000.00 | $0,000.00 |
| Publishing | $0,000.00 | $0,000.00 | $0,000.00 | $0,000.00 | $0,000.00 |
| Stationery/Paper | $0,000.00 | $0,000.00 | $0,000.00 | $0,000.00 | $0,000.00 |
| Toys/Games | $0,000.00 | $0,000.00 | $0,000.00 | $0,000.00 | $0,000.00 |
| Videogames/Software | $0,000.00 | $0,000.00 | $0,000.00 | $0,000.00 | $0,000.00 |
| Other | $0,000.00 | $0,000.00 | $0,000.00 | $0,000.00 | $0,000.00 |
| **TOTAL** | **$0,000.00** | **$0,000.00** | **$0,000.00** | **$0,000.00** | **$0,000.00** |

STEP 1: Find historical sales figures for comparable properties. Make sure you know if the figure is for retail or wholesale and for what time period.

STEP 2: Estimate the life span of your property, and determine what sales levels it will be able to generate once the program gets under way, in comparison to the historical examples.

STEP 3: Based on step 2 and your anticipated growth rate, fill in total expected retail sales for each of years 2 through 5 in the bottom line of the spreadsheet.

STEP 4: Estimate what percentage of total retail sales is likely to be attributable to each product category targeted. Apply these percentages to the total retail sales for each year to fill in the blanks for likely retail sales for each product category.

STEP 5: Figure out wholesale sales by applying average retail markups for each product category using the formula:
### WHOLESALE = RETAIL X (1 - MARKUP)
If markup is unknown, use 50% (e.g. wholesale is approximately half of retail), a good rule of thumb.

STEP 6: Apply average royalty rates for each product category to the wholesale sales in each category to determine royalty income. Use average royalty rates in Chapter 7 if exact rates are unknown. Add up royalty income for all product categories to determine total royalty income for each of years 2 through 5.

STEP 7: For year one, estimate total advances likely for each category, given the number of licensees and products planned. Year 1 income is from advances only.

**Note**: This procedure offers one method of estimating approximate royalty revenues for a given property. Actual revenues may vary significantly as variables change.

*Source:* The Licensing Letter; EPM Communications

als are achieved in a timely manner, help create designs and style books, and assist with most of the other duties the licensor would otherwise have to do in-house, freeing up time for property owners who are not full-time licensors. Agents also bring their contacts within the industry to the new licensors; licensing is a business of relationships, which take time to develop.

Most licensing agents receive approximately 25% to 35% — although some rates are as low as 15% (or even lower for some well-established programs) and as high as 55% — of all royalty income, including advances and guarantees. An upfront fee is occasionally required, especially for licensors of corporate trademarks, to demonstrate good faith. These costs are balanced, however, by the fact that the licensor will not need a full-time in-house licensing staff. A good agent may very likely bring in incremental revenue that an in-house licensor, especially one new to the business, would not be able to achieve. For that reason, new licensors often use an agent to get the program up and running and then take it in-house after it is established.

Financial considerations play a role in whether or not to use an agent. For example, if setting up an in-house licensing operation overseen by at least one full-time manager costs $250,000 for the first year, and an agent charges a commission of 25% for its services, royalties of at least $1 million (about $10 million in wholesale sales of licensed merchandise at a 10% royalty) would have to be earned for the amount paid to an agent to exceed the amount required for the in-house division:

$$25\% \times \$1 \text{ million} = \$250,000$$

Thus, in this situation, it is more cost-effective to retain a licensing agent until royalties exceed $1 million.

Contracts with agents usually are 2-3 years in duration, often with an option to renew if certain performance criteria are met.

## SELECTING A LICENSING AGENT

A number of directories, including the *EPM Licensing Letter Sourcebook*, list licensing agents and a sampling of the properties they handle. Licensors use a number of criteria to select one that is right for them.

It is helpful to examine what types of clients potential agents specialize in. For licensors of corporate trademarks, an agent focusing on sports or entertainment may not be the right fit. While the mechanics of licensing are the same among property types, strategies and contacts usually vary somewhat, so specific expertise can be beneficial.

A licensing agent's track record is also a good indicator. Licensors should feel free to talk to the agent's present and past clients about their working relationship, and about what strategy the agent recommended. If the agent manages primarily short-term properties, but a licensor envisions slow, steady growth for its property, perhaps this isn't a good match.

Personal relationships are as important with the agent as they are with the licensee. Does the agent forthrightly answer the licensor's questions? Offer adequate support services? Communicate openly? Does the agent's way of doing business fit with the licensor's?

The number of properties the agent represents may also be a deciding factor. Some agents represent a whole stable of properties, have a relatively large staff and a lot of experience with different types of clients; they most likely have also built a variety of relationships throughout the business. On the other hand, some agencies handle one or just a few properties, and may have a small staff or even be a single person. Because these agents represent few properties, they devote a large percentage of their time to servicing those properties — and their income depends on their performance. There is no right or wrong choice; the selection depends on the licensor's objectives.

## CHAPTER 6:
# STRATEGIES FOR LICENSEES

Manufacturers who are thinking of entering the licensing business should remember that licensing is just one facet of their company's overall marketing efforts, one business technique that can increase company sales. Licensing should fit logically and comfortably into a company's total business plan. Licensees' participation in the business ranges from acquiring a large stable of properties in the hope that a few will be home runs, to associating with one or a few strong brands that the company depends on for a significant portion of revenues over the long term.

## SETTING OBJECTIVES

Many potential licensees are aware that licensing is an effective marketing tool, and go out to seek properties based on that knowledge alone. Licensing can provide a number of very different benefits to a manufacturer, however, depending on which, and how many, properties are selected. If a licensee wants a ready-made customer base, then perhaps it would opt for a property that has an ongoing, definable fan contingent, such as Elvis Presley. If it wants to associate with an established brand that is known to and valued by the company's target customers, then it may choose a corporate trademark, a fashion brand, a classic character or an established publishing-based property.

A company that seeks to make its products perceived as "fun," in order to increase impulse purchases, may select a Saturday morning cartoon character for children's items or a classic comedy television series for adults. Does the manufacturer want a line that has a good chance of increasing sales drastically, bringing in a lot of money in a short time? In that case, perhaps a potential blockbuster such as *Jurassic Park* or a short-term, hot property such as New Kids On The Block would be appropriate.

The point is for the manufacturer to know what its goals are before it selects a license, and then to match potential properties with those objectives.

## WHAT LICENSORS WANT FROM THEIR LICENSEES

Many licensors desire distribution, first and foremost. They want products based on their property to be found in as many appropriate distribution channels as possible, and they depend on their licensees to get them there. Distribution is becoming increasingly important for many licensors; most expect licensees to have existing relationships with major retailers *before* they acquire the license. While some manufacturers hope to use a license as a point of entry into new distribution channels — and this is still possible in some cases — it is more common for property owners to consider a licensee's existing retail customer base as a significant factor in their selection process.

Licensors are also looking for monetary compensation from the licensing arrangement, from royalties, minimum guarantees and/or upfront advances. While money is rarely the exclusive reason for selecting one licensee over another, it certainly can be one aspect of the decision.

The manufacturers' products — both those proposed under the agreement and those that the licensee has marketed in the past — are also important. Licensors seek products that fit with their property's image in terms of price, quality and design. They look for unique, fashion-forward products that take advantage of trends in consumer tastes. They may also desire licensees with the manufacturing capability to expand into other product lines if initial merchandise is successful.

Many licensors are concerned with the potential licensee's willingness and ability to commit to the brand through advertising, promotion and sales activities. They want to know how important the licensed line will be compared to the company's other lines. They want some assurances that the licensed line will be emphasized on sales calls to retailers and not become lost among a variety of competing lines.

This commitment can be costly to the licensee — for a large line of home furnishings based on a designer name, for example, where the licensee is building a new brand in its category, marketing dollars spent by the manufacturer can reach seven figures, while the cost of getting the product to market can require hundreds of thousands of additional dollars.

The relative importance of the criteria outlined above varies depending on the licensor's objectives. An entertainment licensor with a brand-new animated series or film may depend on upfront money; in the eyes of this property owner, the licensee's willingness to pay high advances will be a point in its favor. An established fashion brand, on the other hand, may count on advertising and promotional contributions by licensees to help market the brand and create awareness. This licensor may want the licensed line to be the manufacturer's only brand, or one of only a few, so that it will get adequate support. The size of the guarantee would be secondary.

For an artist, the licensee's existing distribution network may be the overriding factor, since a small design house has virtually no ability to market products to major retailers and would depend on the licensee to do so. One of the main concerns of a corporate trademark licensor is the integrity of its brand; it may value the licensee's ability to make quality products as its most important attribute. For a sports league, which already has hundreds of licensees in every distribution channel, the major factor for selecting a new licensee may be the uniqueness of the proposed product; with so much sports merchandise on the market, a fresh idea may be more attractive than a huge distribution network or deep pockets for an advance.

So, if licensors want significant promotional dollars, large advances and guarantees, and huge existing distribution networks, can a small company with limited resources become involved in licensing? In some cases, yes. A new licensee may be willing to commit to producing a large number of SKUs (stock-keeping units, the identifying numbers assigned to all retail products) within its category, in lieu of a high advance or guarantee. If a property owner is looking primarily for presence at retail rather than for huge fees, a small manufacturer willing to make this commitment may have an edge over a large licensee who will pay the money but cannot guarantee that products will get to market.

Similarly, small licensees without a large distribution network may have a superior ability to distribute in a particular retail niche. They may offer a unique product or design that fits exceptionally well with a given property. Or, they may be willing to get on board early with an unproven property. While the latter can be risky — there is no guarantee the property will be successful — the licensee's payments to the licensor will be lower than for an established property. The licensor, whose goal is to get licensed products based on an unknown property into the marketplace, will meet its objectives as well.

## LOCATING POTENTIAL PROPERTIES

One way to find out what properties are licensed and what products in a particular category are associated with certain products is to attend various trade shows. An annual exposition sponsored by the Licensing Industry Merchandisers Association (LIMA), held in June in New York City, is a show-case for licensors of many property types. It is especially helpful for locating entertainment and character licenses, but many corporate trademarks, artists, celebrities and a few sports properties can be found there as well. Browsing this show will give licensees a good overview of what's available for licensing, and will also enable them to discover who handles various properties. The show also provides opportunities to make initial contact with licensors and to pick up descriptive materials, including licensee lists. Another smaller trade show, the Worldwide Licensing Exposition, held in April in London, provides many of the same opportunities for international properties.

Other trade shows are intended for manufacturers to sell their wares to retailers, but are also useful for licensees trying to learn more about licensing. A licensee may not be able to ascertain immediately who handles a certain property, but it will get a sense of which properties are being licensed for certain categories. For example, if a licensee is interested in fashion trademarks, a staff member could attend one of several apparel-related trade shows held throughout the year, such as the International Fashion Boutique Show, Men's Apparel Guild in California (MAGIC) or National Association of Men's Sportswear Buyers Show (NAMSB). Trade shows exist for every industry; most trade publications list upcoming exhibitions. Many of these shows highlight licensed products; in 1995 alone there are at least 100 exhibitions of interest to those in the licensing community. A list of significant trade shows is included in the Appendixes.

Trade journals are also good places to find out about various properties. The licensing publications are the primary sources of this type of information but all consumer product-oriented trade magazines cover recent licensing agreements in their fields, and many also run ads from licensors and licensees. For example, in a publication for the sporting goods industry, editorial coverage and advertisements contain licensing-related information on apparel, sporting equipment, sports accessories, caps and footwear based on sports leagues, colleges, sports events, sporting goods brands, fashion labels, corporate trademarks such as gun brands and even character or entertainment products on occasion. See the Appendixes for a list of licensing publications and journals covering consumer products categories where licensing is a factor.

The easiest way to find out who handles specific properties is to purchase one of the licensing industry directories published by various companies, including EPM Communications (see the Appendixes). These books list agents, licensors and licensees, as well as the properties with which they are associated, and are updated annually.

## EVALUATING PROPERTIES

A licensee needs to consider several interrelated criteria when evaluating a potential property. It should also find out everything possible about a property, including:

- the past sales history, if any, for other licensed products based on a given property. Methods of determining such figures, in addition to information from the licensor, include TRSTS reports (a toy sales ranking researched by the NPD Group) and similar research for other categories.
- the popularity of the property. Several measurements exist, such as Nielsen ratings for TV shows, box-office receipts for films and sales figures for videocassettes.
- consumer awareness of the property, gauged by survey data such as Cartoon Q (research conducted by Marketing Evaluations) or other similar research.
- the specifics about the property itself. Reading scripts, finding out who the stars are in entertainment productions, reading books or magazines if the properties are based on them, and examining advertising for fashions or corporate brands can all be enlightening.

## DEMOGRAPHICS

The demographic, psychographic and behavioral characteristics of the property's target audience — age, sex, income level, shopping habits — should match those of the licensee's customers.

## FIT BETWEEN PROPERTY AND PRODUCT

The combination of the property and the product should make sense. To take an obvious example, foot massagers and shoes both make sense for the Dr. Scholl's brand, but hair accessories probably do not. Cosmetic accessories and hair-care products make sense for the Revlon brand, furniture does not. School supplies and apparel make sense for "Beverly Hills 90210," diamond jewelry probably does not. These examples seem to be common sense, but many licensed product lines have failed because a good fit did not exist. In addition, the designs, logos and colors authorized by the licensor should be able to be logically incorporated into the licensee's products in a way that will appeal to its target audience.

## AUDIENCE AWARENESS

One of the benefits of a license is the instant awareness it can bring to a manufacturer's product line. The licensee should evaluate each property in terms of whether its target market, specifically, is aware of the property. If a trademark or fashion label is being considered, the licensee's customers should know the label exists and value its attributes. A brand-new entertainment property may not fit the bill; on the other hand, an extensively hyped property may bring with it significant consumer awareness.

## PROMOTIONAL SUPPORT

The promotional support planned by the licensor to back the property — whether packaged goods or retail promotions, fast food tie-ins, advertising or entertainment vehicles — can be an important decision factor for a licensee. Some properties have built-in awareness, as discussed above, but others need periodic boosts.

## IMAGE

Potential licensees need to be sure that the brand image of a property — the way customers perceive it — is one with which they want their products and company associated. Sometimes these images are not constant; an agreement with a well-known celebrity could seem very beneficial one day, and controversial the next. An upscale brand may change its strategy and start distributing low-priced products, thus diluting the brand in the eyes of the licensee. It pays to carefully consider a property's image, and to be aware of how it may change over time.

## VISUAL APPEAL

No matter what the licensee's goals, the property should look good on its products. On any type of merchandise, whether apparel, a plate, a gift box or a chair, the property's graphic look should appeal to the licensee's customers.

## LIFE SPAN

The property's likely life span is an important consideration. Both short- and long-term properties can be beneficial, depending on the licensee's objectives, of course. The licensee treads a fine line between meeting demand while it is strong, and not possessing excess inventory when that demand falls off. Thus, the property's anticipated life span and growth (and decline) rate affect inventory and production decisions. Furthermore, short-term properties may not be appropriate for products that require major retooling, capital-intensive products or those with significant product development costs.

## TIMING

The launch of a new licensing program and its expansion should coincide with the licensee's goals. Negotiations with the licensor should begin soon enough so that contract negotiation and product development can be completed prior to the licensee's selling season to retailers. In addition, enough leeway must exist for manufacturing, so that products arrive on retail shelves in time.

## RIGHTS

The licensee should be aware of exactly what rights the licensor owns and is authorized to grant. In some cases, such as auto racing, the rights the licensee wants may be owned by a number of different licensors. Similarly, in entertainment, being granted the rights to a film does not automatically guarantee the right to use the actors' likenesses. (See Chapter 8.)

## LEGAL PROTECTION

The licensee is paying for the right to utilize a legally protected — trademarked and/or copyrighted — property on its products. Legal protection means that other companies cannot make merchandise that is confusingly similar to the manufacturer's licensed line. If a property is not adequately protected by trademark or copyright in all countries where the products are expected to be sold, the licensee may lose sales to infringers. Therefore, manufacturers should make sure that trademarks and copyrights are in place — or in progress — before signing a licensing agreement.

## EXCLUSIVITY

Some licensors grant exclusive rights, while others grant non-exclusives or very narrow exclusivity. For example, a licensee could be granted the exclusive right to manufacture all headwear worldwide, or the right to make baseball-style caps, in cotton, adjustable, with a button on top, in two colors, with one basic design, for U.S. only, to be sold in department stores only. The latter may be fine if the licensee feels the property is valuable enough to justify such a narrow grant of rights. Other licensees may prefer much broader exclusivity in order for the property to be attractive. (Business-wide, non-exclusives are becoming more frequent.)

## PREMIUM RIGHTS

Acquiring the rights to distribute products as premiums is a way for licensees to gain additional sales. A retail licensee may therefore want to acquire the rights to manufacture premiums as well as retail products in its category. In addition to incremental sales, being granted the rights for both premiums and retail products allows a manufacturer's retail sales to be undamaged by the distribution of low-priced or give-away premiums as part of a promotion; these items compete with the licensee's retail products if similar. Some retail licensees, such as major players in the toy industry, will not sign a licensing agreement unless they have the rights to both premiums and retail products, thus eliminating the possibility that their retail line will be cannibalized by a promotion utilizing similar products as premiums.

## LICENSOR'S BUSINESS PLANS

Many licensees want to be sure that a licensor is not overextended, handling too many properties or being involved with more promotions than they can manage. Licensees should be confident that the licensor can deliver on its promises; an analysis of the licensor's total business can be instructive.

## ROYALTIES

The royalty, guarantee and advance should all be acceptable to the licensee given the benefits it feels it is receiving by its association with the property. Furthermore, if a licensee is undecided between two properties with similar benefits, which equally meet its objectives, then a comparison of royalty/guarantee/advance packages will be an important tie-breaker.

## MINIMIZING RISKS

Any licensing arrangement can be risky. Some properties lead to success for licensees in virtually every category, while others fizzle out across the board. Even the most successful programs have a few licensees who find that the property does not drive sales in their category; conversely, properties considered to be a licensing failure overall can have a few licensees who do very well.

One method of minimizing risk is to ensure that the fit between the property and the product is appropriate, as mentioned earlier. If a property is popular, but does not fit with a certain product in terms of demographics, brand image or product design, the property probably will not help drive sales of that product. Conversely, if a property is not popular among the general populace but has a small, loyal fan base that is compatible with the licensee's customers, it can drive sales of certain niche products.

The fit between property and product should be more than just a good theoretical match. The execution — the way the property is integrated into the product — must be appropriate. The combination of product and property has to offer a competitive advantage over similar merchandise in the same category. Simply tacking on a logo or character isn't enough in itself; the property must have some reason for being incorporated — a unique design on a scarf or a plate or an additional element of play value in a videogame, for example.

The product itself has to be something consumers want. A licensed property cannot drive sales of merchandise that has no appealing attributes aside from the fact that it is associated with that property; on the other hand, a license can add incremental sales to a product that stands alone as a good product. No matter how popular a property is, it will not in itself cause people to buy a toy that isn't fun to play with. The play value of the toy comes first, then the property, if appropriate, enhances that play value or creates more play value. The property may get kids to look at the toy in the first place if they like the TV series or film on which it is based, but if the toy isn't fun to play with, that demand won't last long. A good licensed product, on the other hand, can still sell, even after a property's popularity fades.

Finally, marketing efforts by the licensee also minimize risk and enhance the success of a licensed product line. Most successful manufacturers emphasize the licensed line in sales calls, advertise it to the trade and consumers, and encourage their entire sales force to get behind it. Properties do not necessarily sell themselves; licensed lines need the same amount of attention that a manufacturer's own brands get.

## FINANCIAL IMPACT OF LICENSING

It is difficult to forecast the economic impact to a manufacturer of acquiring a license. Manufacturers should consider the following points when trying to determine the financial impact of a licensing agreement:

### ADVANCES

Since advances are paid upon contract signing, rather than as sales accrue, and are non-refundable, a licensee may feel that a given property is not worth it if the upfront payment is prohibitively high in its eyes. Royalties are paid as sales mount, and thus are less of a burden to cash flow. While guarantees can be a burden if sales do not accrue, they are due at the end of the contract period, and royalties on sales that do occur go toward meeting the guarantee, thus decreasing its financial impact (see Chapter 7). Advances, on the other hand, require cash upfront as the relationship begins.

### INVESTMENTS

Since most guarantees are required minimum payments (although in certain cases involving non-exclusive guarantees may simply be performance benchmarks rather than required minimums), they are a significant financial burden to licensees, *if* sales do not reach expected levels. In addition to guarantees, however, licensing agreements require other investments — retooling, product development, and marketing costs associated with the license — which also become sunk costs if the line fails. A licensee should examine whether it can afford these expenditures if a worst-case scenario occurs. (Manufacturing and shipping costs accrue as the products are produced and delivered and, while significant, are not upfront fixed costs but rather variable costs that are dependent on the number of units made and shipped.)

In addition, manufacturers should consider not just whether they are likely to recoup these investments, but also how long this is likely to take. Guarantees can be negotiated so as to be reasonable–or rejected if too high–but manufacturers should consider what will happen if sales are slower than expected, and how this will affect their businesses.

### MARGINS AND PRICING

Royalties affect a manufacturer's gross margins. The effect can be either positive or negative, depending on the industry; if a license can command a premium price, margins are likely to increase, whereas if licensed products are sold at equivalent prices to generic or in-house designed merchandise, margins will be squeezed (see Chapter 7). If margins narrow, can the licensee still compete with other companies in its industry? If a royalty requires the manufacturer to charge higher wholesale prices to the retailer, will this adversely affect sales?

## VOLUME

In some cases, manufacturers may feel that narrower margins may be worth it if a license generates increased volume, compensating for the lower per-unit profits. The licensee should also consider, however, whether similar sales gains can be achieved some other way without a negative impact on margins. If so, a license may not be the best choice.

## INVENTORY CONTROL

Another financial consideration is the question of inventory. Hot licenses can cause demand to ramp up extremely quickly, causing inventory shortages. While short-term sales in this case will be strong, licensees should keep in mind that an indirect long-term effect of this situation could be damage to its retailer relationships, and possibly bad feelings on the part of its customers. Lags in filling orders could cause problems down the road.

A more important inventory concern related to licensing, however, is the excess remaining if demand falls precipitously. In fact, a huge inventory surplus due to an unexpected drop in demand could lead to major losses for the licensee, which will have to dispose of the inventory at greatly reduced prices or even at a loss, and which also has to absorb the cost of shipping products back — if returnable. These costs can be considerable. This situation could wipe out profits generated during the peak of demand. Licensees should consider whether their business can withstand such a situation before taking on a license whose life span seems as if it could be a short one.

## LICENSING CONSULTANTS

Many companies, especially those who maintain a stable of licenses and who do not have a full-time person on staff to seek and evaluate properties, retain a manufacturer's representative or licensing consultant serving manufacturers. These licensing specialists represent manufacturers in their licensing activities — evaluating properties, staying on top of what properties are available, helping negotiate agreements and assisting the licensee in developing a strategy. They provide value by offering years of experience in licensing and a multitude of business contacts. In addition, they serve as the client's full-time eyes and ears in the business. More than a dozen licensing consultants who specialize in serving manufacturers' needs are in business; in fact, it is a growing field, with more than half of them having launched their consultancies within the last two years of this writing.

Licensing consultants vary in terms of how they are paid. Some require a flat retainer fee, some receive an advance fee against a commission (averaging 1%-2% of net sales of the licensed lines) and some demand a retainer plus a percentage of net sales. Still, they may be more cost-effective than a full-time in-house employee or staff with licensing responsibility, depending on the licensee's business and objectives.

# PART 3:
# THE DETAILS

# CHAPTER 7:

# MONEY MATTERS

Compensation for most licensing deals centers on a royalty per unit of merchandise sold. Details about royalties, along with other facets of payment, are explained in this chapter.

## THE BASICS

The basic unit of payment in licensing is the royalty, around which advances and guarantees are structured. Royalties, advances and guarantees vary widely depending on a number of factors.

## ROYALTIES

The royalty percentage is most commonly between 5% and 12%, but can be as low as 1% or as high as 20% and beyond. Royalties are usually applied to the wholesale price of each item sold. If a licensee sells 1,000,000 t-shirts at a wholesale price of $5.00, paying a royalty of 5%, the payment would total:

$$\$250,000 = (1,000,000 \text{ units} \times \$5.00 \times 5\%)$$

## GUARANTEES

The minimum guaranteed royalty, or "guarantee," is the minimum amount that the licensee agrees to pay the licensor each contract period. In other words, if royalty payments over the period *exceed* the guarantee amount, no further payments are required because the guarantee has been met. If, however, total royalty payments over the contract period are *less* than the guarantee amount, the licensee owes the licensor the difference between the guarantee and actual royalties at the end of the period.

Guarantee amounts vary depending on the licensor's objectives for the program, but they are often based on a percentage (often about 50% but varying widely) of expected sales over the contract period. For instance, continuing with the previous example, suppose the licensee estimates it can sell somewhere between 250,000 and 300,000 units. After a negotiation, the licensee and licensor agree to base the guarantee on half of a figure in the middle of the expected sales level:

$$1/2 \times 275,000 = 137,500 \text{ t-shirts}$$

Therefore, applying the 5% royalty rate to the sales units at $5 wholesale, the guarantee amount for the contract period would just exceed $34,000:

$$\$34,375 = (137,500 \text{ units} \times \$5.00 \times 5\%)$$

If the licensee sells only 125,000 shirts, it still owes the licensor $2,750, the difference between actual royalties and the guarantee (rounded to $34,000:

$$\$34,000 - (125,000 \text{ units sold} \times \$5.00 \times 5\%) = \$2,750$$

If, however, the licensee records sales high enough so that royalties exceed the guarantee amount — more than 137,000 — the guarantee has been met, and no further money is owed. If the t-shirt licensee sells 300,000 units, for example, it has exceeded its guarantee by $41,000:

$$\$41,000 = (300,000 \text{ units sold} \times \$5.00 \times 5\%) - \$34,000$$

This hypothetical example illustrates the concept of the guarantee and how royalties are applied against it. Actual guarantee amounts can vary widely depending on licensees' and licensors' objectives, and are subject to negotiation. While licensees and licensors report that many deals fall into the $10,000 to $50,000 range, guarantees can be as low as about $350 (for some artist-licensed items) and as high as $2 million (for a long-term videogame deal) or higher.

The main purpose of the guarantee is to ensure that the licensee makes its best effort to sell the licensed merchandise or, if not, that the licensor is compensated anyway. During the contract period, the licensee ties up a certain category. No other licensees can be signed for those products (unless the agreement is non-exclusive), regardless of whether the licensee does anything with the property. The broader the exclusivity the licensee is granted, the more important this consideration is for the licensor.

On the other hand, however, the licensee is required to pay the guarantee even if it made its best effort, but the merchandise underperformed anyway. Perhaps the property itself did not catch on with consumers; perhaps it suffered from a lack of awareness. It could be argued that the licensor bears responsibility for the failure, but the guarantee — with few exceptions — must be paid in any case.

Licensees are usually required to pay an advance, as well. It is often calculated as a percentage — such as 25% — of the first year's portion of the guarantee, and is payable upon signing the contract. Advances are not always calculated based on this formula, however. A low guarantee may be paid in full as an advance, while at other times the advance is a token amount of a few hundred dollars. In some cases, there may be no advance at all. If very large, the advance can be remitted half upon contract signing and then completed in a series of payments every six months, rather than as a single lump sum upfront.

## FACTORS AFFECTING ROYALTY RATES AND GUARANTEES

Royalty rates vary widely, as *Figure 12* *(page 99)* shows. A number of factors contribute to this variation. First, rates are affected by the laws of supply and demand. A property that many licensees desire, such as *Batman Returns* or *Jurassic Park,* can command royalties of up to 10%-14%, or even higher. On the other hand, properties that are not in great demand, such as a new syndicated television show with low national household coverage, command lower rates because the licensor has more to gain by signing on licensees (to generate awareness for the show) than the licensee benefits from signing on. The same phenomenon occurs for all property types — the major sports leagues and the Olympics command a higher royalty than other less-

## Figure 12
### AVERAGE ROYALTY AND RANGE OF ROYALTIES
### BY PRODUCT CATEGORY
### 1994

| PRODUCT CATEGORY | AVERAGE ROYALTY | RANGE |
|---|---|---|
| Accessories | 7.3% | 4%-12% |
| Apparel | 7.6% | 4%-15% |
| Domestics | 6.7% | 4%-8% |
| Electronics | 8.0% | 4%-12% |
| Food/Beverages | 5.8% | 3%-8% |
| Footwear | 6.4% | 4%-10% |
| Furniture/Home Furnishings | 5.9% | 5%-15% |
| Gifts/Novelties | 8.6% | 3%-10% |
| Health/Beauty | 6.0% | 5%-12% |
| Housewares | 8.5% | 5%-12% |
| Infant Products | 6.7% | 3%-10% |
| Music/Video | 8.9% | 6%-15% |
| Publishing | 8.0% | 5%-10% |
| Sporting Goods | 8.0% | 4%-15% |
| Stationery/Paper Goods | 8.5% | 5%-15% |
| Toys/Games | 7.8% | 4%-12% |
| Videogames/Software | 7.6% | 5%-40% |
| **TOTAL** | **7.4%** | **3%-40%** |

*Note:* Ranges are typical reported ranges. Royalties can fall below or above these ranges within a given category.
*Source:* The Licensing Letter; EPM Communications

in-demand sports properties, while a long-popular fashion brand commands a higher price than a newly launched, little-known brand.

In very competitive arenas, such as children's apparel brands or contemporary artists — in the latter, there are hundreds if not thousands of properties vying for licenses — royalty rates tend to be lower, and vary less than the entertainment examples cited above. Within any field, however, some properties are more in demand and thus attract higher royalties than other, similar properties.

Distribution tiers also play a role in determining royalty rates. Royalties tend to be lower for manufacturers who sell to mass merchants, yet enormous sales levels compensate for this fact. For example, products sold through Kmart or Wal-Mart or grocery stores achieve much greater sales (albeit at lower prices) than those sold through department or specialty stores or niche distribution.

Average gross margins within the licensee's industry also influence royalty rates. The margin, usually referred to in the form of a percentage, is the gross profit divided by the wholesale sales price. Gross profit is the wholesale sales price minus the cost of goods sold (the unit cost of each item sold).

Companies that operate in industries with low margins, such as food manufacturers, would not be able to cost-effectively acquire a license if the royalty rate were too high, because margins would be squeezed even lower, which would be a competitive disadvantage for the manufacturer (see Chapter 6.). This situation is particularly true for industries where licensed products are sold at the same price as generics or products sporting in-house graphics. In the case of children's domestics or paper school supplies, for example, wholesale prices are nearly equivalent for licensed merchandise and products designed in-house. Thus, manufacturers that have to pay a royalty have higher costs — and consequently lower margins — than their competitors:

*Example 1:* If margins in a certain licensee's industry average 50%, and licensed merchandise cannot command a premium price at retail, a 10% royalty would lower margins from 50% to 40%, producing 20% less profit. For example, if the wholesale price of a nonlicensed item is $10, and the cost of goods sold (the variable unit cost of each item sold) is $5, the margin would be 50% (the gross profit is half of the wholesale price). If the same item is licensed, and still commands a $10 wholesale price, a 10% royalty ($1 per item) is added to the cost of goods sold, increasing it to $6 and reducing margins to 40%. This example, as well as the others in this chapter, assumes that the cost of goods sold for generic and licensed items are approximately the same (which may not always be the case).

*Example 2:* Similarly, if margins in the industry are 20%, the same situation would cause margins to decrease to 10%, a 50% drop in gross profit. For example, at a wholesale price of $10 and a cost of goods sold of $8, the gross margin is $2 or 20%. But with a 10% royalty ($1 per unit), the cost of goods sold rises to $9 per unit, cutting margins in half to $1 per unit.

◆

On the other hand, in some markets, such as alarm clocks or hair-care appliances, a license is viewed as a competitive advantage and a licensed product can command a higher price. Customers are willing to pay more for a licensed item, so wholesale prices can in turn be higher without complaints from retailers. In this case, manufacturers' margins can be maintained, or even improved, by association with a license. The licensee can in essence transfer the entire royalty to retailers, who pass it along in turn to their customers:

*Example:* If a manufacturer receives a $10 wholesale price for a generic (non-licensed) item, the customer would pay $20 at retail, assuming a 50% markup. (The retail markup is the difference between the retail and wholesale price, divided by the retail price.) However, if the item is licensed, the manufacturer must pay a 10% royalty on the wholesale price of each item. By increasing the wholesale price to the retailer to $11.11, the manufacturer can still net $10 per item after the royalty is paid:

$$\$10 \text{ net} = \$11.11 \text{ wholesale} - (10\% \text{ of } \$11.11)$$

And, if the wholesale price increases to $11.11, the customer's retail price rises to $22.22 at the same 50% markup. This is the ideal situation in a licensing deal, but it can only be accomplished in industries where consumers are willing to pay an extra $2.22 for a licensed product versus a generic item.

Note that, in order for net receipts to remain the same, the increase in wholesale price must not necessarily equal the royalty amount.

◆

Licensees' and licensors' objectives also affect royalty rates, guarantees and advances. Some licensors look for high advances to help pay for an entertainment production, but may offer a lower royalty rate in return for more upfront funds. To attract a licensee's commitment to a longer contract, a licensor may offer a lower royalty rate. A licensor seeking broad exclusivity may be required to pay a higher royalty rate or guarantee in return. Licensees may be able to lower their guarantee by offering a greater commitment in terms of the number of SKUs they present to retailers or by other increased marketing support. Since this commitment ensures that products get to market rather than properties being stockpiled, licensors may agree to this sort of arrangement in lieu of high guarantees.

Since every licensing agreement is unique, any number of royalty-guarantee-advance combinations may ultimately be agreed upon. Negotiations between licensee and licensor determine the ultimate outcome. Some property types are, however, more negotiable than others — entertainment and artists' contracts vary significantly, while major league sports properties tend to fall along similar lines.

The following examples illustrate the wide variety of possible royalties, guarantees and advances:

- A multiyear contract for apparel based on a non-major league sports entity commands a $50,000 advance for apparel and $15,000 for novelties.
- A guarantee for a long publishing contract based on a group of very well-known classic characters is $13 million, whereas for many publishing deals, a $20,000 - $30,000 advance would be considered quite high.
- A designer with good name recognition commands a $35,000 guarantee and a 5% royalty with a 2% override for co-op advertising expenditures.
- Some properties receive royalties of just 1% for products such as domestics, while the Atlanta Olympic Games commands royalties of up to 20%.

In some cases, separate royalties, guarantees and advances are tied to different products or different geographic areas within an agreement, in order to ensure that the licensee puts equal effort into each product or territory, rather than being able to earn out the entire guarantee with one product or area, ignoring the others.

## FREE GOODS

Some merchandise within the context of a licensing agreement can be exempt from royalties. Examples might include samples for use in the selling process; merchandise for in-house use by the licensor or licensee; and products sold to the licensor for re-sale (such as in the case of on-campus college bookstores that sell collegiate licensed merchandise; the college is the licensor and the retailer). In other cases, licensed products may be sold at a discount to companies affiliated with the licensor or licensee.

In all of these cases, the royalty may diverge from the rate charged for normal sales to retailers. There may be no royalty required (although there might be a cap on the amount of free goods that can be given away without a royalty requirement). On the other end of the scale, licensees may be required to pay a full royalty (as if for a full-priced product) even if goods are discounted, such as those sold to a sister company.

## ALLOWABLE DEDUCTIONS

Royalties are normally based on the "Net Sales Price," which means the wholesale price less allowable deductions. Very few deductions are authorized, but some include:

- Cash or volume discounts to retailers
- Returns (in product categories such as publishing where items are sold on a returnable basis); a reserve for returns of about 10% - 20% is often created
- Freight

Total deductions are limited by the licensor to a cap of about 2%-5% of the first billing amount. In addition, as noted, there are certain items, such as samples, for which royalties may not be required.

## CO-OP ADVERTISING ADJUSTMENTS

Entertainment licensees are not, as a rule, willing to agree to any extra payments or requirements for advertising, because their reason for choosing the license in the first place is that consumers are already aware of it.

On the other hand, for fashion labels, corporate brand-extension programs and some sports properties, the situation is different. In these cases, one of the licensor's main goals is for the licensees to strengthen and support the brand. A strong ongoing advertising and promotional campaign is essential to this effort, and licensees are expected to contribute; this support benefits the licensees as well as the licensor. Licensees' contributions may come in several forms:

- Licensors may require licensees to pay an additional one-half to two percentage points on top of the royalty rate. This money is earmarked for advertising by the licensor to strengthen the brand. The NBA, for example, has a "2% clause," meaning that 2% on top of the royalty is required of licensees. The 2% goes toward TV campaigns, retail promotions and co-op advertising with retailers, all coordinated by the licensor.
- Licensors may allow a licensee to deduct a point or two off its royalty payments if it spends the equivalent on co-op advertising with retailers. The Aspen apparel brand asks its licensees to pay a total 4% royalty. Up to 1% of that royalty, however, can be deducted if the licensee spends the equivalent on co-op advertising with its retail customers, subject to approval by the licensor.
- Licensors may require licensees to devote a certain percentage of total licensed volume to advertising the brand. For example, Pierre Cardin, according to reports in *Women's Wear Daily*, requires its approximately 840 licensees to devote 1% of total volume to advertising the brand, which translates to about $3.5 million in advertising expenditures worldwide.

## ROYALTIES APPLIED TO THE RETAIL PRICE

As noted, royalties are usually based on the wholesale, or net sales, price of the licensed merchandise. There are times, however, when the royalty is based on the retail price. Book publishing is one example. Royalties are based on the book's suggested retail price, thanks to publishing industry conventions. Publishers traditionally pay authors their royalties based on the retail price, mainly because it is easier for authors to calculate — the suggested retail price stays relatively constant whereas wholesale prices vary drastically based on type of distribution channel and volume purchases. Royalties are also based on the retail price in cases when there is no wholesale price, such as when a retailer or mail order catalog or other direct-response marketer is the licensee and sources the licensed products itself, rather than buying merchandise from third-party licensees.

Royalty percentages are normally lower in such cases, making royalty rates roughly comparable to what would be expected if the rate was based on the wholesale price. Or, a flat fee per unit may be agreed upon, or a royalty against the cost, rather than the price, of each item.

## FLAT FEES

Occasionally a flat fee per unit will be paid by the licensee in lieu of a royalty percentage. For example, a licensor may receive $.75 to $1.75 per unit for a videogame license. The main benefit of this arrangement is ease of accounting, but the situation is rare.

Multimedia software licensees, who utilize a number of different properties within one product, may pay flat fees for some content. For example, they may pay a publisher a few hundred dollars per year for the use of a book in a software product. Trademark licensors on whose trademarks the game is based, however, usually receive a royalty.

Licensors who associate their properties with online services for bulletin boards or other services often receive a flat fee per customer use, while payment for the use of a licensed property in a 900-number game usually comes in the form of a flat fee, such as $.25 or $.50, per call.

## MULTIPLE ROYALTIES

There are many cases where royalties must be paid by the licensee to more than one licensor. For example, a character and sports league may be cross-licensed, or paintings from several artists may be incorporated into one deck of cards or board game. Normally each licensor takes somewhat less than what it is used to, if it wants to be involved with the product; if the licensee's price is prohibitively high, the product will not happen. Still, the licensee ends up paying a higher total royalty for multiple properties than it would for one alone.

## DEVELOPERS, INVENTORS AND AUTHORS

In the videogame industry, the manufacturer must deal with several parties: the licensor for the right to use a licensed trademark (such as a celebrity, a film or a sports property); Nintendo or Sega or another videogame company for the rights to make a game for a certain platform (e.g. SuperNintendo or SegaCD); and often also to a third-party game developer who creates the game architecture. Each of these entities demand a royalty.

Other examples of dual royalties include toy manufacturers who may be required to pay a royalty of about 5% to a toy inventor as well as a royalty to the licensor of the trademark on which the game is based, and a publisher who must pay an additional royalty to an author of a novelization or other book being created, as well as to the licensed trademark. Multimedia is another area where many parties may receive royalties or fees, such as developers, licensed property owners and various content providers including publishers, owners of film clips, authors, photographers and so on.

## CROSS-LICENSING

Cross-licensing occurs when a manufacturer acquires the rights to use more than one licensed property on one product, such as portraying Fred Flintstone in an NFL uniform on a sweatshirt. If each property normally commands 9% in the relevant category, the licensee might pay a total of 12% for the cross-licensing agreement, with 6% going to each of the licensors.

Dual licenses often occur in sports licensing, as well, when a product portrays the likeness of an athlete in uniform. Royalties must be paid to the athlete through his agent or a league's players association, and also to the league for the rights to use the logos of the league itself and its teams. If the athlete is a member of the players association, both licensors lower their typical royalty rates somewhat when working together, so the licensee might end up paying 8% to the league and 4%-5% to the association. In the case of a dual license with a league and an athlete or athlete's estate handled by an agent rather than by the players association, however, the licensee might be required to pay the full combined amount (perhaps 10% to each licensor, for a total of 20%).

Sometimes cross- or multiple licensing agreements can get quite complicated. For example, a manufacturer who wants to produce auto-racing merchandise may need to pay royalties to the governing body (e.g. NASCAR or IndyCar), a racetrack, a driver, the driver's corporate sponsors and the manufacturer of the driver's car. Similarly, licensee Cameo Guild put together a "Golden Era of Baseball" chess set that involved the Major League Baseball logo, *The Sporting News*, seven players handled by the same agent, two athletes each with their own agents, and five players represented by Major League Baseball. A total of 10 separate licensing agreements were signed, and Cameo Guild paid a total royalty (some portions in the form of flat fees per unit) of nearly 20%.

## ADJUSTMENTS WHEN MILESTONES ARE REACHED

Sometimes — quite rarely — royalties are adjusted when various milestones are reached throughout the life of the property. These hurdles are written into the contract and are intended to protect the licensee if the licensor's promises do not come true, much as guarantees protect licensors. For example, the licensor of a brand-new animated television series being launched in syndication may believe that it will achieve 90% coverage of the country by the time the show airs. At the time it is negotiating with licensees, however, the show has only been purchased by enough stations to achieve 65% coverage.

The licensee is interested in the show, but feels that it is a risky property at current coverage levels. As an incentive for the licensee to sign, the licensor may arrange a lower royalty rate or guarantee in the initial stages of the merchandise campaign, with the promise that, as syndication levels reach certain milestones, the royalty rises. When the show achieves the predicted 90% coverage, the royalty reaches the level that the licensor wanted in the first place, which the licensee is now willing to pay. Similarly, Nielsen ratings or other measurable milestones (e.g. sales of a toy line) can be used for other categories. As noted, these types of arrangements are very rare, but can be negotiated.

Conversely, negative milestones may affect the royalty rate. For example, if a licensee misses a certain crucial deadline, such as a product introduction or delivery date, it may be required to pay a penalty. This situation might occur, for instance, in a case where a selling season is short and a missed deadline would have a critical effect on sales.

## PAYMENT FOR NON-RETAIL LICENSING AGREEMENTS

Non-retail licensing agreements vary in how payment is structured. For example:

- For use of a licensed property in advertising, the licensor might receive a flat fee or a percentage of the total media buy.
- For premiums as part of a promotion, licensees might pay a flat fee per unit, or a percentage of the cost of the premium; alternatively, the cost could be part of the overall fee for the promotion, with no separate payment.
- Promotional licensees may pay a single flat fee, a separate fee for various promotional elements, a combination of flat fees and premium royalties, or no fee at all. In the last case, payment may take the form of providing something of value — such as advertising or point-of-purchase signage — other than cash.
- Owners of restaurants or arcades that are licensed may pay for the use of the property through a percentage of total sales of food and/or merchandise.

Promotions will be discussed further in Chapter 12.

# CHAPTER 8:

# PROTECTING YOUR RIGHTS

Licensing agreements require that a legally protected property exists to lease. It is the licensor's responsibility to register its property as a trademark before attempting to license it out. First, legal protection is what gives a property its intrinsic value. A licensor has legal remedies with which to battle infringers — companies that utilize its trademarks illegally — if the property is adequately protected in the countries where it will be marketed. Legal protection also makes a property marketable, since it does not provide a competitive advantage in the marketplace if it can be knocked off.

Nothing in this chapter or book should be construed as legal advice. Licensors should consult with counsel — preferably with expertise in licensing — when examining any legal aspect of their properties.

## TRADEMARKS AND COPYRIGHTS

The primary tool for protecting properties is the trademark. Most property owners also supplement their trademarks, however, by registering copyrights for graphics, text and other creative aspects of their properties.

### TRADEMARKS

Words, phrases, symbols, designs — or any combination of these — that identify and distinguish the goods of one company from those of another can be trademarked. As far as licensing is concerned, this means that titles, character names, brand names, depictions of characters and logos can be protected through trademark registration. There are some exceptions; for example, place names cannot be trademarked unless combined with other words (Minnesota Golden Gophers) or logos (the word Minnesota graphically depicted in conjunction with a portrayal of the Gopher mascot).

The primary criteria for a property to be considered a trademark is that it is used in commerce. In other words, the act of utilizing a property on merchandise signifies that it is a trademark within the classification(s) of goods where it is being exploited, and therefore should not be infringed upon. For full legal protection, however, "marks" should be registered with the Patent & Trademark Office under their appropriate classifications. (A total of 34 classes exist for goods, with an additional eight for services.)

Registration also signifies "intent to use," thus offering trademark protection even in cases where merchandise is not yet on the market. Trademark registrations can be renewed in perpetuity, as long as they are exploited in each classification where they are registered. Marks can also be registered in additional classifications, if their use is expanded or planned for expansion into new categories.

All products, printed matter and so on that show the trademark should be marked as follows:

- The ™ symbol can be used by anyone. It demonstrates that the property owner considers the brand or depiction to be a trademark not to be infringed upon; it does *not* signify that the trademark has been registered with the Patent and Trademark Office.
- The ® symbol can be used only with names, depictions and so on that are registered as trademarks with the PTO.

The licensor's style book should outline the correct methods of marking each element of the property.

Trademarks must be registered in each country separately, under the laws of each of those countries; it is usually recommended that the registration procedure begin approximately a year and a half before the launch of a licensing program in each region. In several countries, whoever is first to register a trademark owns it; licensors benefit by a proactive approach to international trademark protection in order to prevent unauthorized parties from legitimately usurping their marks.

## Cost Versus Protection

Fees are required for each trademark registration. The more registrations, the better protection, but costs can mount quickly. For example:

- various depictions, names, slogans and logos associated with one property may all be registered separately;
- marks may be registered under various classifications. There are about a dozen major classes covering the typical products in a children's licensing program, for example, including class 25 (clothing, footwear, headgear), class 28 (games, playthings, sporting articles, Christmas decorations) and class 16 (paper, cardboard and goods made from these materials, including printed matter, stationery and playing cards);
- trademarks may be registered internationally, typically at least in Canada, Europe and Japan, where most international sales will occur, as well as various countries where piracy is likely. This basic roster totals about 25 major countries.

It should be noted that trademark protection and enforcement differs from country to country. Some regions have strong laws, but do not enforce them, some have weak or no laws covering trademarks, and some have strong laws and strong enforcement (and the registration procedure tends to be lengthy). Licensors should be aware of the particulars of each country's legal protection of trademarks before entering the market.

The costs of several depictions in several classifications in several countries can add up fast. Thus, licensors need to weigh, with their legal counsel, the need for adequate protection versus budgetary constraints. Some registrations may need to be delayed, for example. Or, perhaps certain elements can be combined under one registration. It is worth noting, as well, that registering and exploiting too many marks could dilute the value of the most important ones.

## Registration Procedure

Trademarks for the U.S. are registered with the Patent and Trademark Office (PTO) of the U.S. Department of Commerce (703-308-HELP).

Within about three months after filing an application, a PTO attorney reviews it. If the application is refused, the licensor receives a letter explaining why. One common reason is that the proposed trademark is confusingly similar to an already-registered mark. The licensor has six months to respond with arguments as to why these objections should be overcome.

If the application is approved (or the initial refusal is overcome), the proposed mark is published in a weekly PTO publication, *The Official Gazette*. Anyone who believes that the proposed trademark damages one of their own marks has 30 days to respond. If there is opposition to the mark, a hearing before the PTO's Trademark Trial and Appeal Board occurs to resolve the conflict.

If there is no opposition, a Notice of Allowance is sent to the licensor about 12 weeks after publication of the mark in *The Official Gazette*. The licensor then has six months in which to either exploit the mark in interstate commerce or to file an extension. If the mark is exploited and a Statement of Use is filed and approved, the PTO issues a Certificate of Registration. Barring any difficulties, the whole procedure takes about six months.

## COPYRIGHTS

Unlike with trademarks, copyright is valid upon a work's creation. The work does not technically have to be exploited, but to receive full copyright protection, a work should be registered with the Copyright Office of the U.S. Library of Congress (202-707-3000).

Copyright applies to original works of authorship, such as graphics, music, written works and so on. Names, titles, short phrases and slogans, ideas or anything in the public domain cannot be copyrighted; a logo and lettering style associated with a name can be, however. Copyright registrations made in the U.S. are valid in all countries that are parties to various international copyright conventions, or parties to separate agreements with the U.S., and so do not need to be registered separately in those countries.

There are about a half dozen copyright conventions, the major ones being the Berne Convention and the Universal Copyright Conventions of Geneva and Paris. Virtually all major markets for licensed merchandise are parties to one of the conventions or bilateral copyright agreements with the U.S.

The use of a copyright symbol (©) or other copyright notice (Copyright © 1994 by EPM Communications, Inc.) is optional, but is strongly recommended.

Unlike trademark registration, copyright protection expires after a time, no matter if the copyrighted property is exploited or not. For copyrights registered as of January 1, 1978, the term is the author's life plus 50 years, or, in the case of a work-for-hire (registered by the company that commissioned it rather than by the author), 75 years after publication or 100 years after creation, whichever comes first. It should be noted, however, that new copyrights can be registered for similar but different depictions of the expiring properties. For example, new representations of Bugs Bunny or Mickey Mouse would be copyrighted periodically so that there is no danger of the character falling into the public domain. Copyrighted graphic depictions can also be trademarked, which provides better and non-expiring protection (if exploited).

## PUBLIC DOMAIN WORKS

Once copyrights expire, they enter the public domain. Anyone can then exploit the property without charge or permission. Essentially, the work is owned by the public, rather than by any one entity. Trademarks can also revert into the public domain (e.g. yo-yo), but only through a lack of exploitation and/or enforcement by their owners.

As noted above, trademarks can protect properties even after copyrights have run out, if appropriately registered and diligently exploited and enforced. For example, the characters of Beatrix Potter are protected by trademarks, so even though many of the copyrights are running out in the mid-1990s, meaning that her books are entering the public domain, graphic representations and names of Peter Rabbit and other Potter characters are still legally protected from use by unauthorized parties. If a book is in the public domain, a publisher can produce a new version of the story, but cannot use any trademarked depictions of characters or logos associated with the original. (Text/content cannot be trademarked.)

## FEES AND PERMISSIONS

Incorporating public domain works into products occasionally requires fees and permissions. These fees are due to the fact that access to some public-domain works is limited, not because anyone owns the rights. For example, a work of art painted two centuries ago is definitely in the public domain, meaning that a person could take a photograph of the work and use it on merchandise. If the work is in a museum, however, which restricts photo-taking, and there are no other known or accessible photos of the work, the only way to acquire reproducible art would be to get permission from the museum and to pay a fee.

## LICENSING PUBLIC DOMAIN EVENTS

Properties based on public domain events can also be licensed. Licensors — often governmental bodies or associations — create a logo and slogan related to the event, which will be used to identify "officially" licensed merchandise. While the event itself cannot be trademarked, being in the public domain, a unique logo that suggests the event can be protected. Of course, anyone can establish a trademark on a public-domain event, and sometimes several licensors create different logos based on the same event, each managing a separate licensing program with a separate identifying logo. For example, the 500th anniversary in 1992 of Christopher Columbus's discovery of America in 1992 had at least four licensing efforts associated with it. Some confusion in the marketplace may occur in a case like this (and in fact it did), but from a legal perspective it is perfectly acceptable. Other public domain events that spawned licensing programs include the 100th anniversary of the Statue of Liberty and the 50th anniversary of World War II.

## RIGHT OF PUBLICITY

Legal protection of celebrity likenesses, signatures and names — on behalf of the celebrities themselves or of their estates if they are deceased — can be complicated. Laws governing the protection of celebrities (collectively known as the right of publicity, or the right to control the use of one's own name and likeness in commercial endeavors) vary on a state-by-state basis. Most states, in fact, do not explicitly offer such protection to celebrities, although some (e.g. California and Indiana) have quite strong protection.

Much of the so-called right of publicity relies not on statutory (written) law, but on common law, which is based on legal precedent. Trademarks can be established for celebrities' names and likenesses, of course, which allows for more clear-cut legal protection than the somewhat fuzzy area of right of publicity.

## MULTI-LICENSOR PROPERTIES

Division of ownership of properties can become complex when several rights holders are involved in the development of a property. Each owner may have a hand in managing the licensing program, particularly with regard to product approvals, and each may receive some portion of royalties from merchandising.

This situation holds especially true for entertainment properties. A television show, for example, may be based on a book or comic book. New made-for-TV elements may be copyrighted or trademarked by the producer, however, depending on the agreement it has with the original licensor. Either the publisher or creator is the owner of the original trademarks or copyrights, and a television producer licenses the rights from the original rights holder. Either the publisher or the original creator or the TV producer may handle the licensing effort for the show, and all three will in most cases receive merchandising revenues. Other entities, such as syndicators or licensing agents, may be involved as well.

Luckily for licensees, one of the rights holders normally takes the lead in the licensing program, becoming the main contact with manufacturers. No matter how rights, responsibilities and rewards are divided up behind the scenes, the licensee primarily works in partnership with just one party on a day-to-day basis.

Just a few of the many examples of such multi-licensor properties include:

- *The Flintstones* movie. Turner Home Entertainment and its sister company Hanna Barbera (owner of the cartoon on which the film was based), producer Steven Spielberg's Amblin Entertainment and movie studio MCA/Universal all were partners in the licensing effort, with MCA/Universal being the primary contact for licensees on film-related merchandising. (A separate classic character program exists, as well, handled by Turner.)
- *The Mask,* distributed in theaters by New Line Cinema and based on a Dark Horse comic book. New Line handles licensing for both the film and TV versions.
- "Babar," a Nelvana animated television series based on the French book series, the rights of which are owned by Clifford Ross. Licensing is handled jointly by the two companies.

## NEW PROPERTIES DEVELOPED BY LICENSEES

Within the context of a licensing agreement, a manufacturer may create a new property, which may in turn be licensable. For example, a t-shirt maker may create a new design, a book publisher may create new characters based on an existing property or a videogame publisher may create a new "look and feel" in a game based on an existing trademark. The new property incorporates the original property, and either the original licensor or the licensee may be able to trademark or copyright the new entity (and both may share in merchandising revenues). As noted in Chapter 9, details about ownership of newly created entities within the context of the licensing relationship should be ironed out in the contract, prior to the development of such properties.

## LIKENESSES

Licensing agreements involving entertainment properties that include live performers often bring up the question of likeness rights and approvals. Licensees often desire the rights to a film or television show only if they know that they can count on the use of the major stars' likenesses in conjunction with their product lines.

Many observers point to the fact that the talent's likenesses were not available as one (but certainly not the only) reason for the poor performance of certain properties, such as *Robin Hood: Prince of Thieves*, starring Kevin Costner, and *Hook*, starring Robin Williams and Dustin Hoffman. These actors did not allow their likenesses to be utilized on products, thus limiting many manufacturers to items sporting logos or other graphics. These designs may have been less appealing to consumers than likenesses of the actors would have been, particularly for certain product categories. Even when actors allow their likenesses to be associated with products, they may be very picky about *how* they are used, making it virtually impossible to survive the product approval process.

There are cases when actors give up the rights to approve their likenesses for products that show them in character, but in most cases major stars will have some say over how their names and likenesses are used, if at all. Thus, it is important for licensees to ascertain up front if actors' likenesses are available and for licensors to be honest about any approval problems that might arise. Some manufacturers and promotional partners even recommend that prospective licensees have their lawyers look over relevant portions of the film contract between the studio or producer and the talent. Contracts can be interpreted in various ways, and some licensees feel more comfortable getting their own counsel's opinion on what the contract implies for the licensing relationship.

Also, while a contract between an actor and a studio may explicitly grant the use of his or her likeness, if the actor has some celebrity and decides he or she does not want his or her likeness exploited, the studio may back off just to keep the talent happy, with an eye toward an ongoing relationship and/or the actor's good will for media tours and the like.

## PRODUCTS CONTAINING SEVERAL PROPERTIES

Some products incorporate several properties, as was touched upon in the discussion on royalties in Chapter 7. Auto racing merchandise and a sports chess set were two examples outlined there. Similarly, a pack of playing cards might have a different celebrity or the work of a different artist on each of the 52 cards, requiring rights to be obtained separately for each entity. A line of collegiate merchandise may require going to several individual universities. Or, a multimedia product may require rights from publishers, writers, photographers, musicians, music publishers, celebrity likenesses, actors and writers unions, copyright and trademark holders and so on. For example, a *New York Times* article noted that a person pursuing permissions for a five-second clip of *Star Wars* to be used in a CD-ROM product had to go to nine sources: the rights holders for the movie (Lucasfilm), actors, the Screen Actors Guild, stunt performers and coordinators, the director, scriptwriters, the musician's union and a music publisher.

Licensees can sometimes make their job easier by selecting a group of celebrities handled by one agent or a group of public domain paintings whose reproduction rights can be acquired from one museum. Still, the perfect complement of properties for a particular product line may require a significant investment of time in order to research and negotiate all the various rights needed.

CHAPTER 9:

# CONTRACTS

The licensing contract ensures that both parties — the licensor and the licensee — know what their roles and responsibilities are. Many licensors have developed a standard boilerplate (a contract containing the standard clauses that the licensor wishes to include), although the specific points in a deal are virtually always negotiable. The licensor is normally the party who offers a contract to the licensee, but this can vary; in the case of book publishing, for example, it usually works the other way around.

Both licensors and licensees should consult an attorney who specializes in licensing before entering into an agreement. We cannot stress often enough that the information in this book should not be construed as legal advice, but rather as a guideline and overview.

## MAJOR POINTS IN A LICENSING CONTRACT

The items outlined here are not necessarily in the order that they would be found in a licensing contract, and they are certainly not in the language suggested for a legally binding agreement. They are simply intended as a plain-English description of the major elements.

## DESCRIPTION OF THE PROPERTY

The contract should clearly specify exactly which property is to be included under the agreement, including which trademarked names, graphics and logos are allowed. For example, is a license granted for the Disney family of classic characters, or is it for Goofy alone? Does the contract cover Teenage Mutant Ninja Turtles merchandise utilizing film-based Turtles, live-action Turtles, or animated TV-style Turtles? Are the Coca-Cola and Diet Coke logos both included under the terms of the agreement? An explicit description of the property or elements of the property is designed to prevent confusion later.

## GRANT OF RIGHTS

The grant of rights is the section of the contract that outlines the products, territories, distribution channels and price points for which the licensee is authorized to market products.

### Products Manufactured

The contract should explicitly describe the products covered by the agreement. It should specify designs, materials and sizes allowed, in order to distinguish these products from any others being manufactured under license.

In addition to the product descriptions, the licensing contract also outlines whether the licensee has the right to *sell* the licensed products or the right to *manufacture* them (or a combination). There is a distinction between the two. The right to sell implies the possibility of importing products from overseas or selling products made domestically by sub-contractors. The right to manufacture means that the licensee will make the products without sub-licensing (where a licensee grants the rights to another company for certain items within the context of its agreement with the licensor, in return for a royalty) or sub-contracting (sourcing from third parties).

Licensors retain the right to approve any sub-licensees or sub-contractors. The sub-contracting companies or sub-licensees are indirectly associated with the licensor and its assets; thus, in order to maintain maximum control over the property, the licensor wants to know who those companies will be, and desires the right to reject them if they are not appropriate for the job.

## Distribution

The contract should outline the distribution channels to be utilized by the licensee, to ensure that two licensees' distribution rights do not overlap, and also that upscale brands do not find their way into mass market outlets. Is the agreement for department and specialty stores? Mass market? Direct mail only? In a single direct-mail catalog? Distribution by one licensee can cover all channels, too, of course. The possible combinations are many, depending on the capabilities of the licensee and the strategy of the licensor.

If a product line is expected to be sold through a network of distributors, as opposed to directly by the licensee, many licensors reserve the right to approve distributors. For example, a sports league-licensed sweatshirt could have a hangtag or sewn-in label that identifies the name of the distributor rather than the licensee. Thus the distributor is associated with the league, whether or not the league has authorized it or has had any contact with it. If that distributor acts in such a way as to anger retailers or customers, it reflects poorly on the league. Therefore licensors want to okay distributors, or sometimes even to disallow the use of distributors at all (as the NBA has done).

The agreement should also specify whether the licensee is able to distribute its products as premiums, through retail outlets or both. Retail licensees are often granted the rights to distribute premiums in their categories, because free or inexpensive premiums can cannibalize sales of similar retail products.

As in the case of distributors, licensors often retain the right to reject purchasers of premiums. The reason for this is that a purchaser of premiums, who plans to use them in a promotion, is indirectly associating itself with the licensor's property in the eyes of consumers, even if it is not directly connected with the property owner as a licensee. Thus, many licensors want to be able to reject premium end-users, to prevent an incident in which their assets are damaged through their use in a promotion.

## Geographic Territory

The contract should also specify geographic areas where sales are allowed. The agreement could cover the U.S. and Canada, or it could apply to a small region of the country. For example, a t-shirt licensee of one minor league sports team or one university may cover only the metropolitan area in which the team plays. On the opposite end of the spectrum, the contract could authorize worldwide distribution. The agreement often explicitly states that licensees cannot knowingly sell to retailers that they have reason to believe will distribute outside of the approved territory.

In certain cases, licensors are legally prohibited from explicitly restricting licensees geographically — namely, within the European Community, where licensees cannot be stopped from exporting into other European countries outside of the territories granted. Of course, licensees who do so will be unlikely to work with the same licensor in the future.

## Exclusivity

Exclusivity can range from a wide definition (such as all apparel in all territories for all distribution channels) to a narrow one (caps made of cotton, in a particular range of graphics, with an image on the front of the cap only and a button on the top, with adjustable sizing). The grant of exclusivity can be limited to certain designs, specific distribution channels, a few geographic areas, certain sizes, specific manufacturing materials, or any number of other criteria. No matter how narrowly exclusivity is defined, however, the contract should note that the products covered by it are exclusive. Conversely, if the agreement is non-exclusive, the contract should state this fact as well.

## Rights to Newly Created Properties

The ownership of rights to new properties that may be created by the licensee within the context of the licensing agreement, using the core property as a basis — new logos, new characters or new designs, for example — should be specified in the contract up front, before these entities are created.

## Advertising and Promotional Materials

The licensee is normally granted the right to use the property in advertising and promotional materials supporting the licensed product line, subject to approval by the licensor.

## PAYMENT AND AUDITING PROCEDURES

The contract should fully outline and explain all matters relating to payment.

## Compensation

The major elements of compensation to be included in the agreement are:

- The royalty rate, including any boosts in that rate tied to various milestones.
- The minimum guarantee, including the fact that royalty payments will count toward the guarantee amount, and that the guarantee is a required payment (the most common situation, especially for exclusives). Alternatively, the guarantee may simply be a performance benchmark upon which renewal depends (for

some non-exclusives). If so, the contract should state that fact.

- The amount of the advance, and when it is to be paid (usually in full upon contract signing).

The agreement should also include the payment schedule for all of the above. Royalty statements are normally required on a quarterly basis, with payment usually following within 30 days. The portion of the guarantee remaining, if any, after all royalties have accrued is due at the end of the contract period. The agreement should outline the method of royalty reporting, including if reports should be broken down by SKU, by geographic area, by retail account and so on. Units sold, invoice amounts, allowable deductions taken and returns are usually all reported. These breakdowns help licensors keep track of sales along important variables, which helps fine-tune the program over time.

Other payment-related issues that may be contained in the contract, depending on the situation, include:

- The licensor's cut of the licensee's revenues from sub-licensing agreements.
- What royalties, if any, should be paid on samples or other free goods, as well as a limit on the amount of royalty-free goods allowed. In addition, discounted goods sold within the company or to users associated with the company may require a special royalty situation.
- The fact that all outstanding royalties and any still-owed portions of the guarantee must be paid upon termination of the contract.
- What penalties will be charged for late royalty payments (such as 1% to 2% per month overdue).
- What items, such as freight, returns and cash discounts, are allowed to be deducted from royalties, and what maximum amount of such deductions is authorized. (Other selling, manufacturing and distribution costs are rarely deductible.)
- How exactly the royalty is to be calculated.

## Definitions

All terms that might be unclear should be specified, particularly when they relate to royalty payments. One common example is the term "net sales." Most royalties are payable on net sales, but, since the term can be ambiguous, its definition should be clearly set out in the contract. For example, net sales may be defined as the invoice amount to retailers, less certain allowable deductions as outlined above. What constitutes "samples" or other "free goods" or "discount goods" should also be clarified.

## Auditing Procedures

Licensors retain the right to audit the licensee's books. The contract should state this right, as well as specifics about its being carried out. For example:

- what prior notice should be given to the licensee?
- how often can audits be done?
- how long after termination of the contract can audits be requested?
- how long must a licensee keep its books relating to the agreement?

The licensee is required to pay royalties owed to the licensor as a result of any discrepancies (with a penalty for each month overdue, and with interest). Licensees must usually also pay for the cost of the audit if discrepancies surpass a certain level. For example, if an audit uncovers the fact that a licensee owes 5% or more royalties than it has paid, it would be required to bear the costs of the audit, as well as paying the overdue royalties.

## PRODUCT APPROVALS

The contract should specify the method and time frame for product approvals. For example, it should outline the number of samples to be sent to the licensor for approval, the time within which the licensor must approve or disapprove (e.g. within 10 days of the receipt of samples) and the different stages in the manufacturing process where approvals are necessary (e.g. conceptual models, pre-production samples and/or production samples). Licensors should also approve promotional and advertising materials and packaging utilizing the property.

The agreement should also clearly state whether the failure of the licensor to approve within the given time frame signifies approval or non-approval. Most licensors will want the lack of approval to constitute a non-approval, since products will not slip through and be approved accidently. Licensees, on the other hand, often want a lack of response by the licensor within the given time period to be interpreted as approval, so there are no unnecessary delays. A strong approval process benefits both parties, however.

If a product is not approved, licensees are given a certain amount of time (such as 30 days) to remedy any problems. If they do not respond adequately within the given time, grounds for termination may exist. Licensees may also want licensors to provide a reason for any non-approval of a product.

Licensors often request the right to inspect the licensee's production facilities as part of their quality control procedure.

## TERM OF THE CONTRACT

The contract should state the time period during which the contract will be valid. Two to three years is the average duration, but this may vary depending on a number of factors, including how long the licensee and licensor have had a mutually acceptable relationship with one another, what type of property is involved and the licensee's history. Terms can range from as little as six months to a decade or more, depending on the circumstances. The effective date of the agreement (the date the relationship officially begins) should be specified as well.

---

## Termination

All contracts will end eventually, whether through an amicable parting when sales run their course, through a disagreement or some violation of the contract terms, or because one of the parties did not meet specified performance criteria. The agreement should outline what consititutes a breach, or contract-terminating behavior. Failure to meet crucial production schedules, failure to meet a product introduction date or a first sales date, failure to continuously sell the merchandise, failure to earn out the guarantee, failure to pay royalties and bankruptcy are among the possible reasons for termination. A licensor may reserve the right to terminate one aspect of the agreement (such as one geographic area). All rights revert back to the licensor after termination.

In addition, what happens *after* termination should be clarified, including the fact that outstanding royalties must be paid, what happens to remaining inventory, and so on. For example, a licensee may be granted 60 to 90 days to dispose of inventory after termination; royalties must be paid on these items (which may be disposed of at a greatly reduced price). After the disposal period, which is usually non-exclusive so the licensor can seek a new licensee for the same products, the manufacturer is barred from allowing any of the licensed merchandise to enter the market.

## Options

Some licensing agreements contain an option to renew. The possibilities range from an automatic renewal if certain performance criteria are met, to no contractual option. Similarly, the licensee may be granted a first look at or rights of first refusal for the licensor's next property. Even if the contract contains an option to renew, royalties and guarantees, as well as other terms of the agreement, are usually renegotiated.

## INDEMNIFICATIONS AND INSURANCE

The licensor indemnifies (protects) the licensee against third parties who dispute the licensor's ownership of the property.

The licensee indemnifies the licensor in the case of injury or death due to the licensed product. While the licensee is technically responsible for any suits brought against it of this type, the licensor — often having deeper pockets — may be held responsible as well.

For that reason, the indemnification is usually backed up by insurance. For example, a licensor may require a minimum $1 million each in personal injury and product liability insurance; those sums may be higher in categories where lawsuits often occur, such as food or toys.

Most companies already carry insurance like this, or maintain a risk-management policy in industries where insurance is prohibitively expensive or difficult to acquire. In a licensing agreement, however, the licensor will want to be named as a co-insured on the licensee's policy. In addition, the licensor will want to be informed of any changes to the licensee's insurance or risk-management policy during the term of the agreement.

## OTHER PROVISIONS

Other contractual terms may be incorporated into the agreement, to protect both parties. Some are contained in virtually all deals, while others are optional. They include, in no particular order:

- Warranties on the part of the the licensor that it owns the property and has not granted the same rights to other licensees, and that the trademarks covered in the agreement do not infringe on other trademarks. Also, the contract should state that the agreement does not imply ownership by the licensee.

- Warranties on the part of the licensee that it will make its "best effort" to market and distribute the products under a schedule specified in the agreement.

- Warranties that both parties have the authority to enter into the agreement and to live up to all the responsibilities contained in it.

- Provisions that licensees must mark products and collateral materials with appropriate trademark and copyright indicators. Licensees are often also required to use specific labeling to ensure consistency among all licensed products.

- Statements regarding which party has the right to take legal action against an infringer, if counterfeiting occurs, as well who must pay for such an action and which party gets the rewards, if any. (Normally the licensor takes all responsibility for combatting knock-offs and also reaps the rewards, if any, but there are occasions when the licensee may want some participation in anti-infringement, such as when a licensor decides not to pursue a counterfeiter.)

- Provisions allowing the licensor to approve any changes in ownership of the licensee, including large financial investments or an outright sale. Such changes of ownership, if not satisfactory to the licensor, may be grounds for termination of the agreement.

- A schedule dictating product introduction and first product shipment dates.

- A clause stating which state's laws apply in the case of a dispute. In addition, the contract should deal with how disputes, if any, are to be resolved (e.g. through arbitration).

- A mention that products may be altered in some way from how they are outlined in the agreement, with the licensor's permission, but that royalties and other provisions of the contract continue to apply to the altered merchandise.

- A provision stating that the licensee acknowledges that the property has its own "good will" value, which is owned by the licensor.

- A statement summarizing the licensee's agreement that the brand has acquired "secondary meaning." This is applicable to descriptive brand names; that is, where the name suggests the product (as opposed to a made-up name). Descriptive names cannot normally be trademarked. If a name has "secondary meaning," however, it is considered more than a mere description, but rather is distinctive to the merchandise with which it is associated. Such a brand can be registered as a trademark.

- A provision known as "licensee estoppel," which states that the licensee agrees that the licensor's properties are valid trademarks, and bars the licensee from disputing this fact.

- A provision that the licensee cannot assign any of the rights granted in the agreement to other parties.

The list of provisions outlined in this chapter is not exhaustive. Both licensees and licensors, in association with their attorneys, may require further points to be included in the contract, depending on the particulars of the situation.

## EXPANDING A LICENSING CONTRACT

Expansion or extension of a licensing agreement may occur for a number of reasons. For example, a successful licensee may, before the original contract period is over, add distribution channels, increase the number of products in its line or the range of sizes, expand into new geographic areas as yet unfilled by the licensor, and so on. In some cases these changes may be incorporated as an amendment to the original contract, or they may be the subject of an entirely new agreement. The former situation usually allows new products to get into the marketplace more quickly, but may not always be practical.

Another expansion situation occurs when a licensor offers a related, but separate, property to an existing licensee. For example, a licensee of Bugs Bunny may want to make products based on Marvin the Martian (both part of the Looney Tunes family of characters), or a Thomas the Tank Engine licensee may wish to also license Shining Time Station (two separate licensing programs based on the same PBS series). A manufacturer who licensed the original USA Basketball "Dream Team" that played in the 1992 Olympics may want to also produce merchandise based on "Dream Team II," which played in the World Basketball Championship in 1994, and subsequent "Dream Teams." Such situations are usually subject to a new contract negotiation.

In some cases, the licensee may reserve the right in the original contract to expand into new areas if the first products are successful. This means that if the licensee decides to extend its agreement later, with the licensor's okay, those categories or geographic areas will remain open rather than having been spoken for by another licensee. Because this bars the licensor from signing other manufacturers, however, licensees would be expected to pay a premium for such a contractual bonus.

## CONTRACTS BETWEEN LICENSING AGENT AND LICENSOR

Another type of contract is the bargain forged between a licensor and its agent, if it chooses to retain one. Many of the provisions are analogous to those found in the licensor-licensee agreement. Following is a brief synopsis of some of the important elements in a licensor-agent accord.

The contract specifies the term of the agreement — often two years, frequently with the option to renew if certain performance goals are met. It also outlines the agent's compensation, including its cut of licensing royalties, advances and guarantees, as well as other compensation, if any. For example, fees may be charged for certain duties outside the scope of the basic agreement, or an upfront fee may be required to show good faith, particularly for corporate trademarks. The agent's commission may decrease as a licensing program becomes established, since an ongoing program takes less work to maintain. Reporting and payment schedules and procedures should also be included, as should auditing provisions.

Which properties the agent will handle should be outlined, along with a statement that the licensor is and will remain the owner of those properties. The contract should also specify if the relationship is an exclusive one.

The contract should itemize the agent's duties; most licensors retain the right to approve all agreements negotiated by the agent. It should also summarize the division of costs and expenses that accrue in the context of the agreement. For example, the licensor will probably bear the cost of registering the trademarks, while day-to-day costs of administering the licensing effort will be the agent's responsibility.

The pact should stipulate what situations constitute grounds for termination, and what happens after the contract ends. For example, most agents are compensated for sales of licensed products accruing for a certain period after the contract is terminated, since their work led to many of these sales.

CHAPTER 10:
# COUNTERFEITING

Counterfeiting is a big problem for licensors and licensees. For licensors, infringement devalues their trademarks and copyrights, and for licensees, it contributes to lost sales. From fake Calvin Klein purses sold on the streets of New York to counterfeit Chicago Bulls caps hawked outside the arena during playoffs to unofficial Mickey Mouse t-shirts found at flea markets, the problem is large and growing.

The terms "infringement," "knockoffs," "piracy" and "counterfeiting" are usually used interchangeably, although there are subtle differences among them. Counterfeiting and piracy both refer to fraudulently copying an item, while infringement refers to the act of encroaching on a property owner's rights. Knock-offs also refer to making unauthorized copies; however, they imply cases where items are similar, but where a trademark is not necessarily violated. For instance, a knock-off artist might copy a jewelry design but not attach a specific designer's name to it.

## HOW BIG A PROBLEM IS COUNTERFEITING?

No one can accurately estimate the amount of counterfeit goods sold each year in the U.S. or worldwide, largely because it is difficult to find all the counterfeit merchandise and all the counterfeiters. Some infringers are legitimate businesses by day who illegally produce unlicensed merchandise at night. Many others are capable of shutting down or moving at a moment's notice. Several are located overseas, where regulations against such activities are either not in place or not enforced aggressively.

The fact that published estimates of the amount of counterfeit licensed merchandise sold each year range from $1 billion to more than $80 billion suggests the difficulty of getting a handle on the numbers associated with the problem. It is, however, universally agreed that counterfeiting is a major concern, especially for licensors and manufacturers associated with top-selling properties. It does not matter whether the property is short- or long-term in nature; if it is popular, it will be ripped off. The source of a property is also irrelevant; fashion, character, entertainment, sports, corporate trademark, music and all other types of properties are ripe opportunities for counterfeiters.

The Licensing Letter estimates that, as a rule of thumb, the street value of counterfeit goods sold associated with a particular property is equivalent to about 10% to 15% of the total retail sales value of all officially licensed merchandise based on that property. Of course, the percentage can be much higher for very hot properties or for programs without aggressive anti-infringement activities; some observers estimate that for certain licensing efforts, counterfeit sales can equal or surpass the retail value of official merchandise. Less popular properties, naturally, have less of a problem with counterfeiting, since merchandise based on these properties — both official and unofficial — is less in demand. As a specific example of the detrimental impact of counterfeiting, the 1989 *Batman* movie reportedly lost $100-$200 million in sales to counterfeit merchandise (vs. $1.3 billion in legitimate retail sales worldwide).

Licensors spend significant time, effort and money combatting the manufacture and sale of knock-offs. Administering an anti-counterfeiting program for the purpose of finding unlicensed merchandise, taking action against its manufacturers and preventing its occurrence, if possible, is an ongoing process requiring significant human resources and large financial outlays. The National Football League, for example, is estimated to have spent about $750,000 in 1991 to protect its Super Bowl marks, or the equivalent of 30% to 50% of its licensing royalties from that event.

## TRENDS IN COUNTERFEITING

Unfortunately, a major trend in the counterfeiting business is the increasing sophistication of infringers. Their production methods and packaging are becoming better than in the past, making it difficult for licensors and licensees — not to mention consumers (who probably do not care if they are purchasing legitimate merchandise or not, as discussed below) — to spot a piece of counterfeit merchandise or to distinguish it from the real thing. Five to 10 years ago it was fairly easy to detect counterfeit merchandise. No hangtag (an identifying tag attached to a garment or other product) or sewn-in labeling was used, or if one did appear it was vastly inferior to those on legitimate merchandise. Misspellings on logos, poor color reproduction, cheesy designs and cheap materials all made unofficial merchandise obvious.

Now, however, counterfeiters are able to produce high-quality merchandise with accurate color, reproduce designs and logos very similar to legitimate goods, and they use materials close or identical to what licensees use. They are able to accurately replicate hangtags and packaging. Infringers invest in expensive equipment; in fact, many use the same equipment as authorized licensees do. Computers make it possible for actual designs and product specifications to be stolen by counterfeiters without detection, and also eliminate a paper trail, making it harder to find the infringers. Counterfeiters are able to have knock-offs on the market within a few months of an announcement by a legitimate licensee about its new product line.

In spite of all this bad news, some progress is being made in the fight against counterfeiting. The judicial system is becoming more knowledgeable about the scope of the problem and law enforcement more aggressive against it. Additional legal means are also available to assist licensors in their anti-counterfeiting struggle. For example, retailers can now be held liable for selling counterfeit merchandise, even if they had nothing to do with its manufacture, whereas a few years ago only the hard-to-locate pirates could be prosecuted. Flea markets, local mom-and-pop stores and all other retailers now have an incentive to keep an eye out for licensed merchandise, and not only to avoid purchasing it, but also to alert licensors of its existence. Also, technological advances for hangtags and other labeling, to be discussed shortly, have the potential to help reduce counterfeiting.

## WHAT CAN BE DONE?

Enforcement against counterfeiting has two major objectives. First, licensors want to prevent counterfeiting from occurring in the first place, and second, they want to take some action against counterfeiters if illegal activity is discovered. Licensors also spend a great deal of time monitoring the marketplace for suspected counterfeiting activity.

## PREVENTION

The primary tool used in the attempt to prevent counterfeiting is education. Licensors try to educate manufacturers, retailers and even consumers on the existence of counterfeiting and to explain why it affects these constituencies negatively. For example, manufacturers need to be reminded that counterfeit merchandise cuts into their sales and that, since they know their markets and are among the most likely to run across unofficial merchandise, it benefits them to tell licensors of piracy so they can take action.

Consumers may not really care, frankly, if they are buying official licensed merchandise or not, as long as they like the item and feel it is fairly priced. Some may feel cheated, however, if they thought they were buying authentic merchandise but find out they were not. Many licensors, therefore, attempt to show consumers that counterfeit merchandise is available and that they may think they are purchasing authentic merchandise when they are really buyng a knock-off.

Furthermore, the cost to licensors of counteracting counterfeiting could, in the long run, be passed on to manufacturers in the form of increased royalties, subsequently to retailers in higher wholesale prices, and ultimately to consumers in higher retail prices. Thus, counterfeiting can eventually hit consumers in their pocketbooks. Some licensors are beginning to encourage consumers to report the existence of counterfeit merchandise if they think they spot some, providing 800 numbers to call with information.

As for retailers, the fact that they can become involved in litigation is a good reason to stop purchasing illegitimate merchandise. Higher prices, anger from consumers and the possibility of harming their relationships with licensees and licensors may also be deterrents.

### Publicity

The best way to educate all of these constituencies is through publicity and advertising. Ads in consumer and trade publications educate retailers, manufacturers and consumers about what officially licensed merchandise — particularly hangtags and packaging — looks like, and can encourage them to report suspected illegal activity to licensors. The NBA has run trade and consumer ads, as did MCA/Universal, the licensor of *Jurassic Park*. MCA/Universal provided a toll-free number — 1-800-DINO-COP — to make reporting easy.

Publicity releases sent to trade and consumer publications encourage the media to inform the business community and the public about seizures of illegal merchandise and anti-counterfeiting litigation and successes, as well as disseminating general information on counterfeiting and why it is a problem. Day-to-day contact with licensees and retailers also can be a good opportunity to stress the need to report suspected counterfeiting activity, and to reinforce how to spot such behavior.

All of this educational publicity and advertising is also directed at potential counterfeiters. Infringers read trade and consumer publications, too. The fact that retailers, licensees and consumers are all involved in the licensors' efforts may be a disincentive to potential pirates. When they see the dollars spent on publicity, and read about seizures and legal actions, theoretically they may feel that they are likely to be detected, and think twice before ripping off a trademark.

## Labeling

Another method of preventing knock-offs is to require licensees to use identical hangtags and labeling. These markings make merchandise easier to identify as authentic.

Hangtags can be duplicated by counterfeiters, of course. As a result, licensors are looking for ways to make hangtags and labels more difficult and more costly for counterfeiters to duplicate. Holograms, for example, are increasingly used on hangtags, as stickers on merchandise, or even incorporated into the product itself in some cases. Warner Bros. (with Batman), and the sports leagues, among others, have experimented with holographic labeling. Counterfeiters can learn to duplicate holographic labeling and packaging, but it is very expensive. Many infringers do not bother to copy them, since the costs prohibitively cut into their profit margins.

On the other hand, this technology can be prohibitively expensive for licensors — and licensees, who have to purchase the more expensive hangtags — as well. A master hologram can cost $1,500-$5,000, for example, with an additional cost of one-half to two cents per duplicate. Observers suggest that if a company is losing less than 5% of its business to counterfeiters, the cost of holographic labeling probably is not justified.

Many licensors who use holographic hangtags feel that investigators, retailers, manufacturers and consumers can detect legitimate merchandise more easily, and that the technology has a positive impact on anti-counterfeiting efforts, although exact results are hard to quantify. In fact, there are cases where licensees have been against the use of such devices when required by licensors, because of the added expense, but have become converts after seeing positive results.

Aside from education and using easy-to-recognize but hard-to-duplicate packaging or labeling, a couple of other important preventive measures against counterfeiting exist. First, licensors should ensure that their properties are adequately protected under trademark, copyright and other laws. These are the means that will be invoked when pursuing counterfeiters through legal channels. If a licensor's properties are not fully registered, it may still have grounds for a court case, but the better the legal protection the greater the chances of success in trying to remedy the problem through the court system.

Secondly, it is important to use common sense in terms of not allowing actual artwork or specifications to get into the wrong hands. For example, it is unwise to give detailed specs for logos or graphics to a company before that manufacturer becomes an official licensee.

## DETECTION

While tips from manufacturers and other informants are the major way of detecting counterfeiting activity, most major licensors maintain a network of private investigators throughout the world to help them verify the incidence of counterfeit merchandise. Licensors' employees also go out into the field to spot-check for unlicensed merchandise. They examine various retail outlets when they do their personal shopping and when they are on business in various cities and countries. They also systematically monitor likely areas at times when counterfeiting is expected. For example, if a big sports event is scheduled, licensors would want to specifically check the areas around the sports venue, including independent and larger retailers and street vendors. Similarly, Harley-Davidson patrols big get-togethers of Harley aficionados to be certain that illegal merchandise is not being sold.

In addition to investigators in the U.S. and abroad, most major licensors enlist the help of U.S. Customs. A lot of counterfeit merchandise is imported from countries outside the U.S., such as Southeast Asian nations, for sale in the U.S. market. With the assistance of Customs, unauthorized merchandise can be stopped upon entry into the U.S., before it reaches the street. Once a trademark is registered, it can be recorded with Customs, which can refuse importation of merchandise it believes to be counterfeit.

Other governmental bodies can be useful for helping to detect unlicensed merchandise and go after their producers. They include the U.S. Postal Service, U.S. Trade Commission, U.S. Embassies, the FBI, local law enforcement bodies, and the U.S. Marshall.

## LAWS

As mentioned earlier, trademark and copyright legislation are the primary tools to protect against and pursue counterfeiters. Federal trademark laws, applicable to products sold through interstate commerce, provide the best protection; individual states also offer trademark protection to various degrees. Both civil — pertaining to the rights of individuals — and criminal — pertaining to crime and its punishment — remedies are available under both trademark and copyright law.

In addition to copyright and trademark, other legal areas may apply. For example, a body of common law dealing with the right of publicity in various states may provide some protection when dealing with infringement of celebrity names and likenesses (see Chapter 8), while the concept of "trade dress" may apply when a knock-off product or packaging is confusingly similar to a licensed product, without being an exact duplicate. Trade dress is considered protectable, even though there is no mechanism through which to register the "look" of a product or its packaging. (Elements that are part of the whole can be registered as trademarks, of course.)

## REMEDIES

Based on the legal means roughly outlined above, licensors have a number of options in terms of possible remedies if their marks are infringed. The potential remedies vary depending on the situation, and this chapter does not attempt to sort out all the possibilities. It simply outlines some of the remedies that are available. The benefit of each should be weighed against its cost, in any case.

Many licensors first attempt to turn a counterfeiter into a legitimate licensee. Often a manufacturer uses a certain trademark or copyrighted entity without realizing that it needs permission. Either the manufacturer is not aware that it is infringing, or thinks that the property is in the public domain. If the counterfeiting is of this relatively innocent type, the licensor will usually try to iron out a contract with the manufacturer, allowing it to continue producing merchandise as a royalty-paying licensee. Many such manufacturers are willing to agree to this.

If the infringement is being done knowingly, or if the counterfeiter refuses to become a licensee, a cease-and-desist letter from an attorney is usually the next step. This action is relatively inexpensive, and can be effective against many infringers. The letter informs the counterfeiter that the licensor is aware of the situation, and that legal action will occur if the manufacturer does not immediately stop the production and sale of offending items.

If the cease-and-desist letter is ignored, several legal remedies are available through the courts. They can include seizures of counterfeit merchandise and manufacturing equipment; restraining orders or injunctions prohibiting the company from continuing its infringement; or the physical closure of the illegal operation. These actions can be costly and annoying to infringers, although in many cases they manage to set up shop again relatively quickly in a new location.

Ultimately, if a counterfeiter is convicted of a crime, jail time or fines are possible. Monetary damages can be awarded to the licensor as well, with amounts often based on estimates of lost sales or on the infringer's profits from the operation. Again, it is important to point out that the remedies need to be compared to costs. While receiving damages may seem attractive to a licensor, the costs of litigating may be prohibitively high. And, even if damages are received, the counterfeiter may be back in business in nearly no time.

It is critical that licensors keep records of all anti-infringement activities, including copies of cease-and-desist letters, records of efforts to police for counterfeiting activity and so on. This documentation will be used as evidence in the event that court proceedings are necessary against a counterfeiter. It demonstrates that the licensor is serious about protecting its marks, and has taken an active role in maintaining their value. Lack of such evidence could weigh against the licensor and for the infringer in a court proceeding; it could be argued that the mark is weak and that the infringer may have not been aware that it was legally protected.

## WORKING TOGETHER

Anti-counterfeiting activities are one instance where it benefits competing licensors to work together for the common good. When counterfeit merchandise based on one property is discovered, chances are that unofficial products based on other properties will be found as well. Therefore, licensors who pool their monetary and human resources in their efforts against counterfeiters can maximize the damage done to the counterfeiter's operation, making it more likely that the pirate will be prevented from infringing in the future. These licensors may also be able to enlarge the damages received. This concern is almost always secondary, however, to the objective of causing enough harm to the counterfeiter to prevent it from going back into business.

One association of licensors formed specifically to counteract infringement through education and enforcement is the Coalition to Advance the Protection of Sports Logos (C.A.P.S.). The organization's members include Major League Baseball, the National Football League, the National Basketball Association, the National Hockey League, the Collegiate Licensing Company (a licensing agent representing colleges and universities) and Starter, a major sports apparel licensee. During the 18 months ending in August 1994, C.A.P.S. participated in several civil and criminal seizures at flea markets, distributors and manufacturing plants, resulting in 200 arrests and seizures of $17 million in counterfeit goods.

In addition, informal confederations exist among competing licensors on a case-by-case basis as incidents come up that involve multiple properties. For example, if C.A.P.S. members uncover a counterfeiter who is making merchandise with Mickey Mouse on it, as well as knock-off sports products, the organization would alert Disney, which would be likely to join the action.

## EXAMPLES OF ENFORCEMENT ACTIVITY

The following examples illustrate various scenarios of enforcement activity typical in the licensing business, and show the types of results that can be expected:

- Major League Baseball Properties initiated litigation against Evans Sporting Goods in December 1993, centering on Evans manufacturing and selling unauthorized MLB replica and non-replica uniforms. The suit was resolved in September 1994 by Evans becoming an official licensee.

- In Spring 1993, Warner Bros. investigators served hundreds of cease-and-desist letters and seized more than 8,000 counterfeit garments illegally incorporating the Looney Tunes characters. In addition, a raid on a New York manufacturer led to the seizure of as many as 200,000 pieces of bogus Looney Tunes merchandise, 45 arrests and the closure of the building.
- In August 1991, King Features received more than $100,000 in a federal judgment against 34 New York retailers who were selling unauthorized Betty Boop merchandise. Six retailers were convicted of selling "lewd" Betty Boop buttons, and were fined $10,000 each plus King's attorneys' fees.
- In 1993, the University of North Carolina-Chapel Hill obtained a permanent injunction against Johnny T-Shirt, a retail and screen-printing business near the campus. This injunction, which permanently prohibited the company from producing or selling unlicensed UNC products, was awarded despite the fact that UNC had not had a licensing program or gone after infringers prior to 1992. The court ruled that UNC had not abandoned its trademark rights.
- In the last half of 1993, Body & Soul, a licensing agent, collected $50,000 in back royalties from two companies who had been selling unauthorized merchandise based on Bette Davis, Charlie Parker, Howlin' Wolf and Leadbelly, among other Body & Soul clients.

While each situations varies, these examples illustrate some of the remedies available to licensors in return for the time and resources they put into their anti-counterfeiting activities.

## CHAPTER 11:
# INTERNATIONAL LICENSING

International territories are considered by many to promise faster growth in coming years than the North American market. Licensors from the U.S. and Canada are eyeing international territories, while licensors based abroad are increasing their activities both in their own countries and in other regions. In the U.S. and Canada, as noted, the licensing market is maturing after significant growth over the last 10 to 15 years; thus, international areas, many of which are less developed as markets for licensed goods, promise greater rates of increase.

International territories currently account for less than about one-third of total worldwide retail sales of licensed merchandise (32% of the total $97.8 billion in 1993, according to *The Licensing Letter*), while the U.S. accounts for about 61%, and Canada approximately 7%. *Figure 13 (page 134)* shows worldwide sales of licensed merchandise by geographic region.

Rates of per-capita spending on licensed merchandise in the U.S. and Canada versus other regions also suggest that international territories have more room for growth. The spending rate per person in the U.S. and Canada is three times that in the next highest-spending market, Japan ($232 vs. $76 in 1993, according to *TLL*). Per-capita spending in foreign markets may never exceed U.S. levels — and many U.S. licensors currently view foreign territories as generating less business in return for more work than in North America — but it is reasonable to assume that greater increases are possible in areas with low current levels of spending. *Figure 14 (page 134)* shows per-capita spending rates on licensed merchandise worldwide.

Not only are U.S. consumers the dominant purchasers of licensed merchandise, but the U.S. is the dominant source of licensed properties as well. In fact, *TLL* estimates that 85% to 90% of properties originate in the U.S. That percentage should begin to decrease, however, as more international licensors enter the business or expand existing activities.

Many non-U.S. licensors are already beginning to do so. For example, British licensing agencies The Copyrights Group, Copyright Promotions and Winchester Entertainment all have set up subsidiaries to handle licensing activity in the U.S. and elsewhere, as have German agency EM-Entertainment and Japanese licensor Sanrio.

Meanwhile, some U.S. properties actually record greater sales overseas than in the U.S. "Beverly Hills 90210," for example, earned slightly more revenue from overseas licensing than in the U.S., while Tom & Jerry also witness more activity internationally. Some U.S. properties attribute as much as 65% to 70% of revenues to overseas territories.

## TRENDS IN LICENSING BY GEOGRAPHIC AREA

Following are some of the significant licensing trends in markets outside

## Figure 13
### 1993 WORLDWIDE RETAIL SALES OF LICENSED MERCHANDISE BY GEOGRAPHIC AREA

| TERRITORY | TOTAL RETAIL SALES | SHARE OF TOTAL |
|---|---|---|
| U.S./Canada | $66.6 billion | 68.1% |
| Western Europe | $19.4 billion | 19.8% |
| E. Europe/Commonwealth of Ind. States | $35.0 million | >0.1% |
| Australia/New Zealand | $1.3 billion | 1.3% |
| Japan | $9.5 billion | 9.7% |
| S.E. Asia | $385.0 million | 0.4% |
| South/Central America | $285.0 million | 0.3% |
| Other | $350.0 million | 0.2% |
| **TOTAL** | **$97.8 billion** | **100.0%** |

*Source*: The Licensing Letter; EPM Communications

## Figure 14
### 1993 PER-CAPITA SPENDING ON LICENSED MERCHANDISE BY GEOGRAPHIC AREA

| TERRITORY | SPENDING |
|---|---|
| U.S./Canada | $232.00 |
| Western Europe | $54.00 |
| E. Europe/Commonwealth of Ind. States | <$1.00 |
| Australia/New Zealand | $65.00 |
| Japan | $76.00 |
| S.E. Asia | <$1.00 |
| South/Central America | <$1.00 |
| Other | N/A |
| **TOTAL** | |

*Source*: The Licensing Letter; EPM Communications

the U.S. These descriptions are admittedly brief; they are intended as an introduction to some key issues.

## CANADA

The rights to the Canadian market are often granted along with those to the U.S. Canada is a relatively small country and is frequently considered too small by major licensees to be worth the high investment required to market to that country alone. Costs drop significantly when Canada is added to the U.S. territory, enough so that it becomes cost-effective to reach the additional market. (Some licensees, most of them Canadian, do service Canada alone, of course.) *TLL* estimates that about 10% of all sales of licensed merchandise occurring in the U.S. and Canada are attributable to the latter.

Many of the properties that do well in the U.S. sell in Canada also, although the nation should not be considered identical to the U.S. Tastes vary, and many Canadians are offended by being considered "part of the U.S." Still, the market parallels the U.S. in many ways, and several trends that occur south of the border also are evident to the north. For example, retail consolidation has occurred in Canada as it has in the U.S. The market for licensed goods is weighted heavily toward mass-market chains, while the high-end market is quite small.

It should be remembered that Canada has two official languages — English and French — requiring bilingual packaging. Tastes in French-speaking Quebec may differ from those in the rest of Canada, as well.

Several properties have originated in Canada and then moved south. For example, the entertainment properties Rupert and Dudley the Dragon are imports from Canada, as are several beer brands including Molsen, LaBatt's and so on. Beer licensing has been a big business in Canada for many years; beer brands are equated with an active lifestyle and merchandise is acceptable in many distribution channels, unlike the U.S. where it is considered too controversial for most retailers.

## WESTERN EUROPE

Licensors are increasingly adopting a pan-European outlook toward the continent. In fact, three pan-European licensing agencies have been launched as of this writing, and most regional agents are becoming part of loose confederations to better serve a one-market Europe. Still, it is important to remember that Europe is composed of many distinct markets within the larger economic community. Although it is legal for any licensee to sell to all markets within the European Community, each region differs and must be looked at as a separate territory.

For example, languages vary from country to country, affecting a licensee's packaging as well as the products themselves. Tastes are also diverse. A licensed product that sells well in Scandinavia may not sell at all in Italy, while a property that is popular in France may never cross the border into England, at least without significant changes. The comic book character

Asterix, for example, is among the most popular in France, but has little licensing activity elsewhere, with the exception of publishing. The Benelux countries — Belgium, the Netherlands and Luxembourg — are often an entry point for U.S. properties into Europe, because tastes there tend to be similar to those of North Americans in terms of the properties they embrace.

Product specifications also vary from territory to territory, as do typical retail structures. A large percentage of licensed merchandise is sold in hypermarts in France, for example, while department stores are the prime channel in the Scandinavian countries of Sweden, Norway and Denmark. Mom-and-pop stores dominate in Italy, while Germany witnesses very strong mail-order sales. Manufacturing capabilities vary from country to country, as well. The Benelux has little manufacturing infrastructure and must rely primarily on imports, for example, while the European toy industry is concentrated heavily in the U.K. and France.

In spite of the fact that licensors cannot technically prevent licensees from exporting their products to European countries not covered in their licensing agreements, licensors do in effect restrict their licensees to one market by dictating language, specifications and so on. Parallel imports — products imported from a foreign manufacturer that are similar or identical to those produced by a domestic licensee — are unattractive to licensors and to many licensees, because they cause multiple manufacturers of the same property to compete with each other in selling the same products. (Pan-European deals prevent such an occurrence.) While licensors cannot legally restrict their licensees' territory within Europe, they can effectively prevent parallel imports through the threat of choosing a new licensee at the end of the contract period. If a licensee wants to work with the same licensor in the future, it will abide by the licensor's wishes.

Western European countries accounting for the greatest sales of licensed merchandise are Germany, France and the U.K.

## EASTERN EUROPE AND COMMONWEALTH OF INDEPENDENT STATES

Eastern Europe and the former Soviet Union are truly in their infancy as a licensing market. Capitalism is just taking hold, and the manufacturing infrastructure is underdeveloped. Potential licensees lack capital, modern equipment and know-how. Furthermore, inadequate legal protection, monetary, economic and political concerns, lack of discretionary income and a large black market all contribute to difficulties for licensors there. Many licensors from Europe and the U.S. are beginning to enter the Eastern European market, but most are setting up a foundation for future sales rather than expecting large immediate returns. In fact, significant growth in Eastern Europe will probably not occur until after the turn of the century.

In spite of all these challenges, steady sales of counterfeit merchandise indicate that demand exists for licensed products, and that the territory is potentially lucrative once an adequate licensing and business infrastructure is set up and disposable income rises.

There are a number of ways to approach the Eastern European and former Soviet markets. Some licensors have set up subsidiaries there, some approach the market through joint ventures with local companies, some look for local licensees and use the services of local licensing agents, and some prefer to begin by exporting merchandise into Eastern Europe from the west.

The changeability of the Eastern European situation is illustrated by the fact that just three years prior to this writing, it was thought that then-Yugoslavia and the former Soviet Union had among the most potential to be developed as markets for licensed products. What happened since then, however, is that wars, crime, a strong black market and economic disintegration have significantly reduced the chances for immediate success in these territories.

## JAPAN

Japanese consumers have a significant appetite for character, fashion, sports and trademark merchandise. Domestic properties such as Sanrio's Hello Kitty, Japanese designers and the J-League, a new professional soccer league, do very well there, as do imported properties from the U.S. and Europe. Classic characters such as Peanuts and Betty Boop, corporate trademarks such as Pepsi and Jeep, museums and art-related properties from Europe and the U.S., American celebrities such as James Dean and Marilyn Monroe, and European and American fashion labels have all had success in Japan.

No matter what the source of a property, a branded approach is most successful in Japan. A strong brand identity is apparent on all products through hangtags, packaging and in-store signage; a strong emphasis on design and quality is important; and a retail presence through concept shops or freestanding stores based on one property is common.

Short-term entertainment properties usually do not do as well in Japan. Very little movie licensing exists, and children's animated series are difficult to license. TV animation tends to air for six months and then products disappear from stores (although there are licensing successes, including "Sailor Moon" and "Dragonball"). Furthermore, non-Japanese shows usually have a tough time getting on the air at all. Tastes are very different from the West as well. For example, while the Japanese comic book market is among the most active anywhere, U.S. comic book companies have not been able penetrate the market to a great extent so far.

Properties that originate outside Japan sometimes need to be altered to appeal to Japanese consumers. For instance, Blondie, the comic strip, is marketed as an apparel and accessory brand to adult women in Japan, while Holly Hobbie, a girls' doll in the U.S., has done well as an upscale design brand — products reflect a country lifestyle and the personality of the artist, but have nothing to do with the U.S. character.

Other traits of the Japanese market include a very strong system for legal protection of properties, but one that takes a long time to complete; a focus on long-term licensing for all property types; a slow decision-making process within businesses; and an emphasis on exclusive licensing agreements.

Most licensors who have done business in Japan agree that it is essential to work with a local partner, whether a retailer, a strong master licensee or a local agent. Business practices, local customs and tastes differ greatly from those in the west. Westerners who go in alone without local assistance run the risk of making mistakes.

## AUSTRALIA AND NEW ZEALAND

Australia and New Zealand together form a small territory in terms of total population, but they make up for their small size with their enthusiasm for licensed products. Culturally, they have similar customs and tastes to those in the U.S. and the U.K. Sports and entertainment properties are popular. For example, the NBA launched a licensing program there in 1993, which opened with very strong sales and large attendance at promotional events.

Australia and New Zealand are dominated by two major retail chains, which account for a significant proportion of retail sales of licensed merchandise. Some of the properties that originate in Australia and New Zealand include "Blinky Bill," Love Is..., Viva La Wombat, artist Ken Done, "Bananas in Pajamas" and "Johnson & Friends," all of which have made the jump to the U.S. and other countries.

## SOUTHEAST ASIA

Classic characters such as Garfield and Mickey Mouse, upscale trademarks and brands, fashion designers and labels, and international sporting events such as the World Cup tend to drive much of the licensing business in Southeast Asia. Conversely, short-term properties, such as films, tend to do less well there.

Southeast Asia is a fast-growing area for licensed merchandise, but there are some barriers. Many diverse countries make up the region, some of which find licensed merchandise appealing and some less so. Some of the countries have relatively small populations, and imports can be costly. Economic and political environments vary from country to country as well. In addition, counterfeiting is rampant. Many infringers operate in these territories, selling their pirated merchandise in local markets as well as exporting them to the U.S. and other regions.

Overall, however, Southeast Asia is generally thought to be underdeveloped as a market for licensed merchandise, and is viewed as having growth potential.

## SOUTH AND CENTRAL AMERICA

The countries of South and Central America (including Mexico, which is part of North America but in terms of licensing has similarities with the rest of the Latin countries) are in an early stage of development as markets for licensed merchandise. Brazil and Mexico are among the countries poised for growth. Mexico is being targeted by several U.S. licensors, including the major sports leagues (except hockey). Its proximity to the U.S. and the fact that it receives U.S. television broadcasts in northern regions, as well as what many view as the positive impact of NAFTA, all lead many licensors to view Mexico as a growth area. Current economic instability affects licensing in the short term, however.

Among the obstacles to overcome before Mexico and the rest of Central and South America reach their full potential: Economic and monetary conditions are very unstable in many Latin countries; currencies fluctuate rapidly and, in the early '90s, inflation is as high as 300% per month in some regions; import and export regulations can be prohibitive; a great deal of counterfeiting occurs; many potential licensees and some agents are inexperienced; and royalty revenues can be difficult to get back into the U.S.

Properties of local origin include Xuxa, the children's entertainer; Senninha, a cartoon character based on the late Formula One driver Ayrton Senna; and Monica's Gang, created by Brazilian animator Mauricio de Sousa.

## OTHER TERRITORIES

By far the majority of all licensing activity occurs in the territories discussed above. The rest of the world currently accounts for only .2% of the worldwide total, according to estimates by *The Licensing Letter*. Yet sales of licensed merchandise do exist outside of the major territories listed above. Israel, for example, is a small nation, but still has an appetitite for licensed merchandise, with retail sales totaling approximately $3 million, according to those doing business there. South Africa also witnesses some licensing activity, and should be a growing market thanks to political changes and the elimination of economic sanctions against the country. India and the Middle East are being considered as a market by some licensors, although licensing activity is minimal now.

China, with its 1 billion-plus population, has significant potential for sales of licensed merchandise, and is being targeted by many western licensors. Fashion designers, especially of the upscale variety, have begun to sell merchandise and even launch retail boutiques there. Other licensors such as Pepsi, fashion brand Lightning Bolt and the NBA are already marketing merchandise or are paving the way for licensing activity in China. Still, because of the Communist government, potential economic and trade sanctions, improving but not perfect intellectual property enforcement and the fact that capitalism is in early stages, China is not likely to become a major market for licensed products until after the turn of the century.

*Figure 15 (page 140)* shows a selection of properties that originate in various international territories.

## CHARACTERISTICS OF INTERNATIONAL LICENSING

Licensors should keep a number of key issues in mind when expanding internationally.

First, trademarks and copyrights must be registered in all countries where the licensor plans to do business. Copyrights registered in the U.S. apply in

## Figure 15
# SELECTED PROPERTIES WITH WORLDWIDE APPEAL, BY TERRITORY OF ORIGIN

**CANADA**
Big Comfy Couch
Canadian Football League
Dudley the Dragon
Labatt's
Mistle Toad
Molson Golden
Moosehead Beer
Rupert Bear

**GREAT BRITAIN**
Beatrix Potter
Budgie the Little Helicopter
Dr. Who
Magic Roundabout
Mr. Blobby
Mr. Men & Little Miss
Noddy
Paddington Bear
Postman Pat
Shoe People
Teddy Tum Tum
Thomas the Tank Engine
Thunderbirds

**CONTINENTAL EUROPE**
Armani
Asterix
Babar and Celeste
Benetton
Dick Bruna art
Gnomes
Gucci
Italian Football League
Krizia

Lucky Luke
Marimekko
Moomin
Pierre Cardin
Pumuckl
Smurfs
Spirou
Tintin

**ASIA**
Akira
Astro Boy
Dragonball
Gigantor
Godzilla
Hello Kitty
J-League
Keroppi
Kimba
Sailor Moon
Speed Racer
Tenko and the Guardians of Magic
Ultraman

**AUSTRALIA/NEW ZEALAND**
Bananas in Pajamas
Blinky Bill
Foster's Lager
Hafta, Just Hafta
Johnson & Friends
Ken Done
Love Is...
Ozzy
Viva La Wombat

*Note:* This list is not exhaustive.
*Source:* The Licensing Letter;
EPM Communications

most countries worldwide. Trademarks must be registered separately in all countries where licensed products will be sold, as well as in the major counterfeiting countries.

Secondly, most licensors agree that it is preferable to utilize the expertise of someone in each country or region where expansion is planned. The regional expert could be a local partner, an agent, a licensee or a retailer. Some companies set up joint ventures with partners abroad, or launch subsidiaries in various countries, staffed by locals. As noted earlier in the regional synopsis, local expertise is necessary since business practices, consumer tastes, local customs and retail structures, among other things, differ between the U.S. and international markets, and also vary from territory to territory within one geographic region.

Royalties overseas tend to be similar to or somewhat higher than those charged in the U.S., and in many areas guarantees can approach those for similar domestic agreements. Advances tend to be lower in many regions, however, since licensees and licensors would rather have the money spent on product development than high advances. In a multi-territory licensing agreement, separate guarantees are often required for each territory, to prevent an undue focus on certain regions where sales are high, while other regions are ignored.

Licensees and agents in small territories such as Italy, Israel or Scandinavia sometimes complain of a lack of interest in their regions from U.S. licensors. The total volume of merchandise sold is lower in these locales and thus the royalty revenues are less, while the cost of entering these markets can be high. Some U.S. licensors may not take the same care in choosing local agents or licensees in such regions, looking at the sales as extra, but not integral.

Another factor for licensors to consider is whether to sign local licensees in various countries, or to sign one master licensee to distribute in a broad region or even worldwide. Local licensees have expertise in their respective territories and relationships in place with local retailers; they will also treat the region as more important than a non-domestic licensee might, because it accounts for all or most of their business. On the other hand, some licensees are capable of worldwide distribution, and because they have local offices around the world they have expertise in various markets. They may prefer to sign worldwide agreements with licensors, particularly if they are in an industry where a large investment in product development or retooling is required.

Finally, no matter what territories are involved, licensing internationally requires patience and flexibility.

## FACTORS TO CONSIDER BEFORE ENTERING A NEW REGION

Before a licensor enters any new territory, it should learn as much as possible about that region. Each country differs in its specifics, and licensors should be aware of those particulars *before* they begin to do business. A region may not be worth it if too many factors point to difficulty in licensing there. Some important points to look into include:

- The political situation. Wars, governmental factors — including elections or coups — that may lead to amendments in business regulations, and changing borders all affect licensing.

- Economic factors. These include disposable income levels, inflation rates, currency fluctuations and so on. Average disposable income affects the types of products that can be introduced, while currency and inflation affect the revenues that are possible (and their U.S. currency equivalents).

- Trade considerations. Trade agreements such as NAFTA (North American Free Trade Agreement) or pacts within the European Community affect licensing decisions. Whether to license local companies or to allow licensees in other regions to distribute there, for example, is partially determined by import regulations and tariffs.

- Retail structure. Distribution methods vary among territories. Finding out what types of retailers dominate within a region and how those retailers buy merchandise is critical. Western distribution methods are not feasible everywhere, although the expansion of Toys R Us, Foot Locker and other U.S. retailers may make western practices more prevalent on a worldwide basis. The strength of the black market in a particular territory, syphoning sales from legitimate retailers, is also an important consideration.

- Tastes and culture. Regional tastes vary, and affect both what types of properties will do well in a country as well as what sorts of merchandise will sell there. For example, Mickey Mouse is known as Topolino in Italy, and many of the country's inhabitants feel almost as if the rodent is a native Italian. As for tastes in products, comic books are a booming industry in Japan, while that industry is virtually non-existent in Israel. Publishing is very important in Europe — it accounts for more licensing revenues than all other merchandise categories combined for some licensors — but is of less importance elsewhere.

- Size. The number of inhabitants of a region affects potential sales levels, of course, and population density may affect how cost-efficient it is to reach those people. Geographic size also affects licensing decisions; larger regions are more likely to vary culturally within a single territory, for example.

- Media. The status of the publishing, television and film industries within a region affect the marketing of a property within that area. Specific considerations include the total number of media outlets, the amount of advertising, whether media outlets are privatized or government-owned and whether global media — such as some cable networks — reach the population.

- Trademarks and other legal aspects. Some countries have very good systems in place for legally protecting properties and some do not. Some have adequate procedures in theory but do not enforce them. Legal processes in some countries are time-consuming. All of these considerations affect licensing in various ways, such as determining the likelihood of counterfeiting and the time frame necessary for introducing a property.

- Infrastructure. The status of manufacturing within a region affects a licensor's ability to grant rights to local licensees. If facilities and technological capabilities are outdated and manufacturing know-how is lacking, it may be worthwhile to consider imports rather than domestic licensees. Other infrastructure questions such as the condition of transportation systems also may affect distribution of licensed merchandise.

## INTERNATIONAL LICENSING AGENTS

The question of whether to set up a local office staffed by local employees or use an international licensing agent is similar to the question of whether to handle licensing in-house or hire an agent for a domestic licensing business. An agent based in an international territory has the advantage of expertise in that geographic area, contacts in the region and knowledge of local customs and tastes. In spite of the fees they require, they are often, at least initially, more cost-effective than launching a local subsidiary. On the other hand, a local office gives the licensor more control over the licensing program, and may be more cost-efficient in the long run. Hiring experienced local personnel brings many of the benefits of an agent in-house.

Criteria for selecting a foreign agent are similar to those for choosing a domestic licensing agent. The level of trust between licensor and agent, the agent's history with certain property types, the experiences of licensors who have worked with the agent in the past, the typical strategies the agent implements, the agent's ability to cover certain geographic areas itself or via a network of colleagues, the number of properties represented, costs and services offered, all affect the final decision.

Several licensing agents exist in each territory, with the most active regions boasting the greatest number of agents. For example, several agencies operate in the U.K., while there are few South American agents.

A U.S. licensor can work with an agent in each territory, or with one master agent for each large region (e.g. Western Europe). The master agent will often retain sub-agents in each country or region within the greater area (e.g. France or the Benelux within Western Europe). In some instances, a licensor's U.S. agent may act as a worldwide master agent, retaining international sub-agents. Some properties may be handled by a total of 10 to 20 agents worldwide. The more levels of agents, however, the lower the licensor's remaining royalties after commissions.

When a licensor signs a worldwide deal with a licensee in a particular category, systems should be in place so that all the agents worldwide are compensated for that licensee's sales. If the U.S. agent, for example, signs an eyewear licensee for exclusive worldwide distribution, that deal precludes any foreign agents from targeting that category in their regions. If the U.S. agent who closed the deal is the only one compensated, relationships with local licensees around the world will be damaged.

International agents usually get a commission of 20% to 33% of licensing revenues.

# CHAPTER 12
# PROMOTIONAL LICENSING

Most licensors support their licensing efforts with promotional activity, as noted in Chapter 5. Similarly, individual licensees often promote their licensed lines, either individually or in conjunction with one or more other licensees of the same property. The term "promotional licensing" includes a number of different types of non-retail licensing agreements, including:

- The use of a property for advertising, such as Peanuts characters in a long-term agreement with Met Life.
- Tie-ins with fast food companies, such as a USA Basketball/ McDonald's effort in the summer of 1994.
- Promotions with packaged goods companies, such as Disney's long-term alliance with Nestle for use of all of its characters and films on a variety of food products across all of Nestle's brands.
- Retail promotions including in-store concept shops, such as Barbie Boutiques at FAO Schwartz toy stores.
- Premiums such as a plush Totorro doll as part of FoxVideo's promotion for the children's video *My Neighbor Totorro* in 1994.
- Contests and sweepstakes, such as fashion label Bonjour's 1994 retail promotion offering a trip to Paris.

The list of possibilities is growing as companies look for new ways to participate in innovative promotions.

Promotional tie-ins can be appropriate for both long- and short-term properties, and for properties of every type, from trademarks to musical acts to book characters. They can vary in scope from a $60 million, multi-partner effort, such as Disney's activities supporting the lauch of its home videos of *Aladdin* or *Beauty & the Beast*, to a simpler promotion such as the use of Gumby in ads for Olsten Temporary Services to suggest the company's flexibility.

A single multi-tier, multi-partner promotion may involve premiums; radio, TV and print advertising; rebates; cross-promotions; packaged goods and retail tie-ins; contests involving mail-in responses or interactive phone technology; and/or personal appearances. The promotion will often target both consumers and the trade (the latter referring to retailers and distributors.)

Promotional licensing has two major benefits for the licensor: to generate income and to provide the property with additional exposure. For licensees, promotions add value to a property by generating awareness and boosting sales (as long as no competitors are involved in any way, such as providing premiums, which would draw business away). They can also help enhance loyalty toward the licensee's brand, and make that brand more attractive to consumers. Finally, promotions may encourage new customers to sample a licensee's product.

Even if a licensee is not a primary promotional partner that has its name associated with the tie-in, it still may be able to increase sales by providing premiums for a promotion. Comic books, trading cards, plastic cups, pre-paid phone cards, squeeze bottles, plush figures, PVC figurines and small toys are particularly popular. In fact, the provision of premiums can be a low-risk way for authorized manufacturers to sell large quantities of merchandise.

The fit between the partners, the property and the promotional elements must be sound, of course, just as the fit between property and product must be reasonable in retail licensing.

Promotions can occur at any time during the life cycle of the property. An anniversary, the launch of a new fashion collection, a video release or the introduction of a brand extension can all be reasons to promote a property. In addition, a good fit between a property and a tie-in partner can engender a promotion, regardless of whether it is timed to coincide with any significant property milestones.

## TIE-IN PARTNERS

In addition to licensees and licensors, there are several other groups that can participate in a licensed promotion. Entertainment companies — outside of the licensor, if the property is in the entertainment area — are frequent tie-in partners, for example. Theater chains, home video distributors, music companies, film studios, and cable and broadcast networks participate in promotions with all types of properties to increase awareness and generate increased sales or viewership.

Retailers, also frequent partners, benefit from participating in licensed tie-ins by increasing store traffic during the time period of the tie-in and by generating additional sales for licensed products based on the property. Other merchandise that has nothing to do with the promotion may also see greater sales during the tie-in period due to the increased store traffic. Retail partners can raise awareness for their company by associating with a high-profile property, and reinforce their image as a fun place to shop. A licensed tie-in may also have an element of exclusivity, causing the retailer to become a destination for a certain property or product line, at least for a limited time. Many types of retail outlets utilize licensed tie-ins. Aside from mass market, department and all kinds of specialty stores, they include fast food restaurants, grocery stores, video retailers and others.

Packaged goods companies and other product manufacturers who are not retail licensees also are frequent promotional partners. A promotional partner's participation usually does not alter the product itself, as would happen if it were a retail licensee. In other words, Nestle, whose Butterfinger candy bars are involved in a promotion with "The Simpsons," uses the characters in advertising and promotional materials but does not reshape the snacks into the image of Bart Simpson. On the other hand, in the case of "Where's Waldo?" Spaghetti-O's, a licensed product, the pasta is shaped like little Waldos and other characters. (Promotional alliances occasionally involve licensed products as part of the tie-in, in addition to other elements.)

A tie-in partner's involvement often incorporates on-pack ads or the use of the property in product packaging to support the tie-in. A promotion can also include other elements, such as cents-off coupons or cross-promotions with licensed products or with other manufacturers involved in the same tie-in. The partner may also mention the promotion in advertising within their regular media schedules.

These companies hope their participation will lead to increased sales because of the excitement of their association with the property. In addition, they often receive increased advertising exposure through being mentioned in ads by other partners. Food and beverage companies, apparel, accessory and footwear manufacturers, health and beauty firms and many others are frequent participants in licensed promotions.

Media partners — including radio stations, television stations and national networks, magazines and newspapers — are also involved in licensed promotions. Their participation may be national or in specific local markets; it allows the other partners further opportunity to promote the tie-in at a lower cost. The media partners usually provide space or air time; in return, they benefit from being associated with a highly visible property.

The involvement of more partners in a given promotion spreads its cost over more participants, making it more cost-effective for each partner. It also maximizes consumers' exposure to the tie-in, and brings the promotion into as many outlets as possible. Thus, licensors often seek a partner of each of the various types — fast food, retail, packaged goods and so on. Each has exclusivity in its category, of course, but is just one of several partners in the total effort.

On the other hand, the more partners there are, the more problems are likely to arise. Coordination among partners becomes more difficult, as does the timing of the tie-in, with lead times varying from partner to partner.

## AN OVERVIEW OF PROMOTIONAL TECHNIQUES

The main element of a licensed tie-in is the property itself. It is prominently displayed in the various elements of the promotion, such as in broadcast or print advertising, in newspaper inserts, on packaging or on hangtags. Personal appearances by a celebrity endorser or a costumed character at stores, promotional events and press functions are also often included as tie-in components to maximize the visibility of the property. The property is stressed within the trade elements of the promotion, as well. For instance, retailers and distributors may have a chance to meet key personalities associated with the property, see behind-the-scenes action such as a sports locker room or TV production set, or attend an event such as a film opening or a concert.

While incorporating the property itself into all promotional elements is key to any licensed promotion, other elements of the tie-in vary dramatically depending on the capabilities of the partners, the objectives of the promotion and the budget.

Every promotion is different — in fact, that is the point of a tie-in, "to cut through the clutter" — but there are certain promotional elements that are frequently utilized. Some have been touched upon earlier in this chapter, but here is a checklist of possibilities:

- Premiums. These are usually fairly inexpensive items sporting the property's likeness — whether a logo, character or personality — and are sold as a purchase-with-purchase, or are given away. Often premiums are exclusive; their design is unlike any retail products available.

- Rebates. One or more of the products involved in a promotion — licensed or not — may be tied to a rebate. Sometimes several promotional partners offer rebates through a bounce-back mechanism, where the purchase of one item entitles the consumer to rebates on other items.

- Contests. Sweepstakes or other types of contests get customers more involved in the promotion. Prizes can involve visits to sets or other locations, the chance to meet celebrities, or the opportunity to win merchandise. Contests can be aimed at the trade as well as consumers.

- Publicity directed at the trade and consumers. Publicity efforts support a promotion, cost-effectively increasing the number of impressions that the tie-in generates by having it covered in various publications and broadcast media.

- Events and personal appearances. Promotional events can be held in conjunction with contests or as a separate element. They tend to generate good feelings on the part of consumers and the trade alike.

- Non-profit overlays. Consumers often feel good about the fact that their participation in the promotion leads to some benefit for a non-profit organization. In addition, these overlays can drive licensed merchandise purchases, especially if a portion of the proceeds goes toward the non-profit group.

- In-store concept shops. Retail boutiques attract attention to the property at retail, increasing awareness and generating additional merchandise purchases.

- Changes to packaging and hangtags. Packaged goods companies and other participants often add the property's logo or a special promotional logo to their merchandise during the promotional period. The special packaging or labeling generates additional consumer impressions, and associates the partner's products with the property.

- In-store display materials. Point-of-purchase displays and other in-store signage help make a greater impact for the promotion throughout the store. Options include tabletop cards, banners and other signage, placemats in fast food restaurants, and posters.

- Exclusive products. Retailers or fast food companies may want to be the only place where exclusive merchandise based on the property can be purchased. The exclusive range could be a full line of products, such as a promotion undertaken by Target in 1990 with Alvin and the Chipmunks, or could be one product such as a plush toy or a Happy Meal toy.

All of these components can be used in various combinations, depending on the objectives of the promotion and the target audience. Most licensed promotions are more effective if they are targeted toward both trade and consumer constituencies.

The following examples illustrate the wide variety of promotions possible, and also show that properties of all types can be involved.

- In fall of 1992, Warner Bros. launched "The $10,000,000 Batman Collection Promotion." It included an eight-page merchandise catalog containing licensed products from 75 licensees bound into various consumer magazines with a combined circulation of 6.4 million; a promotional announcement in the catalogs for the animated Batman series and the video release of *Batman Returns*; a $2 mail-in rebate toward the purchase of $20 or more in Batman merchandise; a Fox Children's Network/Batman sweepstakes for a Batman birthday party and other merchandise prizes including Batman comic books; FCN on-air promotions; and a mini-comic in the Fox Kids Club magazine.

- World Wildlife Fund tied in with Kal Kan in 1991 with its Whiskas, Pedigree and Sheba pet food brands. The promotion included newspaper inserts containing coupons for free pet foods; Kal Kan made a donation to WWF based on the number of redeemed coupons. Another coupon enabled consumers to receive a free WWF licensed panda, with 15 proofs of purchase of Kal Kan products. The coupon also encouraged customers to join WWF.

- In 1993, the Harlem Globetrotters initiated a $1.5 million promotional campaign with Target Stores nationwide, which included television and print advertising for Target's "Extended Size" men's and boys' activewear brand, exclusive in-store Globetrotters merchandise and a four-city special event tour.

- The Major League Baseball Alumni Association tied in with Nabisco in 1993 and again in 1994. The promotion featured trading cards, baseballs and bats autographed by six Hall of Famers, which customers could receive by sending in two Nabisco proofs of purchase (for various brands) and $5 per trading card ordered. Mail-in certificates were on 60 million boxes of Oreo, Chips Ahoy!, Wheat Thins, Better Cheddars and Ritz products. Grocery stores could participate in a sweepstakes for signed balls and bats signed by two other Hall of Fame players. The promotion featured 600,000 pieces of autographed merchandise in total. Cents-off coupons for Nabisco products were included in Sunday newspaper free-standing inserts supporting the promotion, and point-of-purchase displays and ballot boxes were provided to stores for the sweepstakes.

- Children's book property *The Little Engine That Could* tied in with ShopKo stores during Holiday 1991. An instant-win game and exclusive purchase-with-purchase "Fun Kit" premium were part of the promotion.
- Marilyn Monroe was licensed for Chanel No. 5's television campaign in 1994. Monroe's image from *Some Like It Hot* is incorporated into the commercial, which is authorized for Christmas and Valentine's release for up to five years worldwide. Monroe is also shown in a theater eating popcorn (through the magic of special effects) and uttering the ad's tag line.
- French Toast, a children's apparel brand with several accessory and apparel licensees, tied in with Hasbro, Bantam Books and Super Club's Boscobel Beach (a Jamaican resort) in 1994 to co-promote its modeling contest. All the tie-in partners promoted the contest through their own marketing channels. (While it is difficult to define this as a "licensed" promotion as opposed to a corporate promotion, this example illustrates that corporate brands can be involved in tie-ins that promote their own and their licensees' products.)

## VALUING PROMOTIONS

Unlike retail licensing, which has a defined payment structure incorporating a royalty, guarantee and advance, promotional licensing varies in terms of payment structures. A licensing fee of some sort is usually involved, but sometimes advertising exposure, changes in packaging or other promotional elements are offered in lieu of cash.

The more complicated the promotion, the more creative the payment structure may be. For example, rights to use a licensed property appearing in a series of ads will probably be reimbursed with a flat fee or a percentage of the total media buy. On the other hand, in a complicated scenario incorporating all or most of the promotional elements discussed above, much of the payment may be in the form of tradeouts, with no cash changing hands. The elements that each partner has to offer are negotiated until all partners are satisfied that what they will get out of the promotion — in terms of increased sales, increased awareness, goodwill or whatever their goals may be — exceeds what they are putting into it, whether it be cash, added impressions or other components of value.

Promotional partners may contribute added value in various ways. For example, one participant may be responsible for providing premiums. Another could offer some type of advertising, perhaps in the form of mentioning the tie-in at the end of an existing TV ad, or by devoting one of its ads in an existing print schedule to the promotion. A manufacturer could change its packaging to promote the tie-in. A retailer may offer in-store support such as signage, flyers or point-of-sale materials. Media partners usually get involved because there is an incremental ad buy by one of the other participants. The media partner then provides additional space or air time, usually by tagging existing house ads with the tie-in theme and partner names.

Many of these costs are incremental ones to the provider; the company would need to print packaging or run ads anyway. However, they are contributing something of value to the promotion — added impressions — in return for being able to associate with the property.

Still, cash is involved in many cases. For a long-term promotion or a wide-ranging exclusive promotion, a fee to the licensor in excess of six figures would not be considered unreasonable. For a high-profile film, a major soft drink or fast food company would pay in the low- to mid-seven figures, in addition to being responsible for other costs such as committing to in-store promotional activities or signage, and/or being required to purchase premiums. Fees in the $10,000 to $50,000 range would be more in line with a short-term promotion. If premiums are involved, a royalty on the cost of each premium may be paid to licensors.

Generally, a licensing fee is required for associating with an established property or a new property with very high expections (e.g. *Jurassic Park*), whereas a new, relatively unknown property might be paid for through tradeouts alone. In some cases, each element of a promotion may require a separate fee, but licensees usually prefer one lump payment because it allows them to have more flexibility in implementation.

While the big promotions — those valued in the tens of millions of dollars — are the ones that receive the most attention, not all promotions have to be costly. A Thomas the Tank Engine promotion at Bloomingdale's in 1993, which attracted 25,000 people and generated a great deal of press coverage, cost a total of $42,000, according to Thomas's licensor, Britt Allcroft.

## MEASURING THE RESULTS OF A PROMOTION

It is often difficult to quantify the results of a licensed promotion. Increased awareness, for example, is hard to measure, as are goodwill generated by the promotion and "excitement" about a property or brand. Ironically, these are some of the major reasons for participating in a licensed tie-in.

It is also difficult to trace which results are attributable to which part of the promotion, especially for the more complex, multi-partner tie-ins. It is even hard to ascertain which results, if any, are traceable to the use of the property itself — the promotion's reason for being — rather than being attributable to other elements of the tie-in.

Certain measurable elements do exist. The number of coupon redemptions, the number of contest entries, the number of calls generated by interactive phone lines and the number of premiums sold or given away are among them. Other elements that are measurable, but not necessarily directly traceable to the promotion, include the box-office take for a film versus comparable films; store traffic or sales levels at a particular retailer during the promotion compared to nonpromotional periods or other tie-in periods; and awareness of the property and of the tie-in partners' brands, as measured through recall studies at periodic intervals during and after the tie-in.

Some examples of how results are measured include the following:

- A 1992 McDonald's/Batman promotion sold 48 million Happy Meals and 40 million promotional drink cups.
- A Barq's root beer promotion with a *Nightmare on Elm Street* film attracted 21,000 mail-in redemptions and increased sales of root beer 15% during the promotional period.
- A Pizza Hut promotion with "Eureeka's Castle," a Nickelodeon television program, increased traffic 70% and sold 4 million puppet premiums in 1990.
- A two-year Butterfinger candy bar promotion with "The Simpsons" increased sales 52%.

All of these are legitimate yardsticks by which to measure a promotion's success.

## PROMOTIONAL SUCCESS FACTORS

The major factors behind a successful licensed promotion parallel those that contribute to good retail licensing relationships. All partners need to be honest up front about their objectives and about what they are able to contribute to the promotion. This openness must continue throughout the promotional period. For example, when a film release date changes, a designer collection is delayed, deadlines cannot be met by one of the partners, the cast of a TV show changes, and so on, all partners should be informed immediately.

Honesty is also crucial when it comes to predicting results of a promotion. Excess inventory remaining at the end of a promotion is a problem; it wipes out any increased sales generated as a result of the tie-in. On the other hand, too little inventory can cause problems as well. For example, in a Muppets promotion a few years ago with Procter & Gamble, which offered Muppet dolls as premiums, a total of 150,000 doll redemptions was predicted; 1 million were redeemed. While the partners managed to meet demand in this situation, a similar occurrence could create bad feelings on the part of customers and the trade toward one or all partners.

All participants should be honest about the lead times required to maximize the impact of the promotion. Lead times vary depending on the partner. Packaged goods companies usually need eight to 12 months to prepare a promotion; retailers need six to seven months or more. On the other hand, entertainment companies sometimes try to put together promotional partnerships just two or three months prior to the release of a film. It is important for all companies involved in a tie-in to understand the needs of the other partners, and be flexible enough to meet those requirements while also maximizing the promotion's impact for themselves.

All partners should have compatible goals and target markets. As with retail licensing, a fit has to exist between the property and the partners, in terms of image, target demographics and timing. And the creative elements of the tie-in need to complement the property's attributes in order for it to work.

All partners should sign off on each promotional element so that everyone is happy with the total tie-in. All partners' businesses are reflected in the promotional elements, even if a particular aspect is not directly connected with one or another partner. Control over the whole promotion is especially important from the licensor's point of view, since the property is the central element and its reputation is at stake.

There must also be equality among partners in terms of what each contributes to the relationship and what each gets out of it. All should feel as if they have participated in a win-win situation.

# CHAPTER 13
# FINAL THOUGHTS

Awareness of licensing on the part of the general public is on the rise. Media coverage of the licensing business — particularly of sports and entertainment — is much more frequent than it was at the beginning of the decade. And, this publicity is not limited just to trade publications, but extends to every type of media outlet, from *The Wall Street Journal* to *Entertainment Tonight*.

Because of this increased exposure, more players are entering the licensing business, from small manufacturers hoping to boost awareness by associating with a well-known property, to large corporations analyzing their portfolio of brands to see if ancillary revenue streams from licensing are possible.

As more participants enter the business — and as overall growth in retail sales of licensed merchandise slows after a decade of fast-paced growth — competition among properties and among potential licensees becomes more acute. Every licensing program is unique, and there is really no one correct way to manage any individual effort. But in the face of increased competition, licensors and licensees who use a common sense approach to licensing will enhance their chances of being successful.

While each effort differs depending on the property's characteristics and its competitive situation, there are certain universal traits that are consistent among most successful licensing programs, no matter what their origination.

First, licensors and licensees should carefully consider the fit between product and property. The target demographics of each partner's customers should be compatible. And, the property should make sense in association with the product.

Secondly, successful licensing programs are those that manage to remain fresh throughout their lifetimes — whether short- or long-term — through promotional activity, new product introductions, and new media and/or entertainment vehicles. This holds true for any type of property.

Licensing participants who select right licensing partners — those whose objectives parallel theirs — also enhance their chances of success. In addition, maintaining these good relationships is critical. Honesty and open communication, fair treatment and an understanding of each other's businesses and goals are all important aspects of a strong partnership.

It helps to be realistic. An honest assessment of a property's characteristics will lead to a sound, common-sense licensing strategy and to appropriate deals. Hype is a large part of the licensing business, especially in the entertainment sector. But overstating a property's potential and promising things that it cannot achieve will hurt a company's reputation, not to mention leading to a lot of products that just sit on retail shelves.

Licensors and licensees who spend an adequate amount of time on planning will be rewarded, as suggested throughout this book. But it bears keeping in mind that flexibility is also a valuable trait for a licensing participant. Market conditions and consumer whims change quickly, and the ability to keep abreast of emerging trends and to react in a timely fashion to new developments is a key criterion for success. Yet, licensees and licensors who have invested the time and resources to thoroughly analyze their properties, products, markets and customers will be better poised to adapt to changes in an appropriate manner.

Members of the licensing community who are aware of their specific objectives *before* embarking on a licensing program will be ahead of the game. It is surprising how many people jump into licensing simply because "I know it's a way to increase my business." Yet they are unaware of what specific goals they expect licensing to help them achieve. Several possible objectives exist for entering the licensing field; determining which goals take priority is a prerequisite to creating a sound program.

While the licensing business is becoming more competitive, a growing number of opportunities are also evident. New product categories emerge continuously, especially with the rapid pace of technological change, leading to entirely new types of licensing deals. And new properties are springing up every day, it seems, tracing their origins to an extremely diverse group of industries. This situation creates new opportunities for licensees. Creativity, in addition to flexibility and planning, will drive many licensing relationships as we approach the next century.

For those of you considering licensing for the first time, and for those who already oversee established, successful businesses, good luck!

# PART 4:
# APPENDICES

# LICENSING BUSINESS GLOSSARY

*Note:* Phrases in **bold italics** signify cross-references. Please refer to individual listings.

# —A—

**Access.** The ability to acquire reproducible art based on a property. Mainly relates to art licensing, where a ***public-domain*** work can legally be used royalty- and permission-free, but where lack of access to the work may require a fee and permission to be paid to a third party (e.g. a museum).

**Added value.** A benefit that makes a product more attractive in the eyes of consumers. A premium, a discount or a license may all add value.

**Advance.** Part of the payment required for a license, usually due upon signing of a licensing contract. Often a portion of the ***guarantee*** rather than an additional payment.

**Advertising.** A method of promoting a property or licensed product line. The licensee, the licensor or both may advertise a licensed product or property.

**Advertising adjustments.** Variations on required royalty rates tied to advertising. An increase in royalties may be required for a general advertising fund controlled by the licensor, or a decrease in royalties may be allowed in return for advertising expenditures by the licensee.

**Allowable deductions.** Reductions in the sales figures upon which royalties are applied, authorized by the licensor. Usually limited to 2%-3% of the total. Very few such deductions are allowed; common examples include freight, cash/volume discounts and ***returns***.

**Ancillary merchandise.** Products related to a company's core product line; often licensed. For example, a magazine company would consider licensed videos or tote bags based on its titles as ancillary merchandise.

**Ancillary revenues.** Additional revenues coming from sources outside a company's core product lines. For the owner of a corporate trademark, royalties from licensing would often be considered ancillary revenues.

**Application.** 1) The way in which a property can be incorporated into a product. 2) The first step in registering a trademark or copyright.

**Arbitration.** A preferred means of dispute resolution in the event of a conflict between licensor and licensee.

**Auditing.** A means of verifying that correct royalty payments have been made. Licensing contracts usually contain a provision allowing the licensor to audit the licensee's books.

**Authors.** 1) Writers. Authors of licensed books are sometimes due a royalty in addition to the royalty paid to the trademark holder. 2) In copyright law, the creator of a work.

---

# – B –

**Behavioral characteristics.** Traits exhibited by a group of consumers, such as where they prefer to shop or what types of entertainment they enjoy. Knowing a target market's behavioral characteristics can be helpful in effectively reaching them.

**Big 3 discounters.** The three major national discount department store chains: Wal-Mart, Kmart and Target.

**Blockbuster.** A property that generates significant licensed merchandise sales, usually within a short time period.

**Boilerplate.** A contract containing standard provisions. Is often used as a basis for negotiating an individual licensing agreement.

**Bounceback mechanisms.** Promotional elements that tie various partners together. For example, a purchase of one product may lead to a discount on another product or service.

**Brand equity.** The value associated with a brand by consumers.

**Brand extension.** An additional product line under an existing brand umbrella. Brand extensions into related areas outside of a manufacturer's area of expertise are often licensed.

**Brand identity, Brand image.** The perception on the part of consumers of a single image that ties all products together under one brand name. Usually enhanced by the use of consistent packaging, labeling and point-of-purchase materials.

**Breach of contract.** A violation of one of the provisions in a licensing agreement. Often grounds for termination of the contract.

**Bridge.** A term in the apparel industry for mid- to higher-priced apparel. A level between mass market products and designer collections.

**Built-in audience.** A group of fans of a property who will become a primary target market for licensed merchandise associated with that property.

**Buyers.** Retailer personnel who are responsible for purchasing products for a given department. Responsibilities vary from retailer to retailer.

**By-products.** Products or ingredients that are created by a manufacturing process, but are not needed for the product being manufactured. By-products can sometimes be used as ingredients for other licensed merchandise associated with the original product.

# – C –

**© symbol.** A mark that is used to show copyright ownership. Can be used by the creator of a work of art or authorship even if the work is not registered with the Copyright Office.

**Cannibalization.** The process by which one distribution channel or manufacturer takes sales away from another distribution channel or manufacturer associated with similar products. For example, sales of a licensed product in a discount store may cannibalize sales of a similar, higher-priced product at a specialty store.

**Capital**. Financial assets or worth of a manufacturer or other company. The possession of adequate capital is a factor in the licensee selection process.

**Cartoon Q**. A survey conducted by Marketing Evaluations that measures the popularity of cartoon characters.

**Category killer**. A type of retailer known for a wide selection of products in a certain product category, as well as low prices. Compete with specialty stores and other retailers. Examples include Toys R Us; Bed, Bath and Beyond; and Sports Authority.

**Cease-and-desist letter**. A letter from an attorney sent to a counterfeiter asking it to immediately stop its illegal activity and threatening legal action. A cost-effective anti-infringement step taken before more expensive actions are initiated.

**Certificate of Registration**. A document from the Patent and Trademark Office signifying that a trademark is registered.

**Civil law**. Laws dealing with the rights of private citizens. Civil law provides protections and remedies against counterfeiting.

**Classic properties**. Properties that have a long life marked by strong, steady sales (with some cyclical ups and downs).

**Classifications, Classes**. In trademark law, categories of products. Trademarks must be registered in various classifications within which merchandise is to be marketed.

**Close-out**. The sale of merchandise at a very low price (sometimes below cost) in order to reduce inventory in a short time. After a licensing contract terminates, licensees are given a period to dispose of inventory, which is usually done at close-out prices.

**Co-insured**. An additional party named on an insurance policy. Licensors demand to be named as the co-insured on licensees' product liability, personal injury and/or property damage policies.

**Co-op money**. Financial contributions by licensees or licensors to a retailer's promotional or advertising efforts.

**Collateral materials**. Sales materials used to help promote a licensed product line; includes brochures, flyers, sales packets. Must be approved by the licensor if the licensed property is used in conjunction with the materials.

**Commitment**. A licensee's support of a property, outside of monetary compensation. Can include promising to market a large number of products or making the licensed line a major focus for a season. A greater licensee commitment may be agreed upon in lieu of a high guarantee.

**Common law**. The body of law based on legal precedent rather than on written laws. The *right of publicity* is based largely on common law.

**Concept shops**. In-store areas devoted to merchandise from various product categories based on one licensed property. Is accepted as one of the most effective ways to drive retail sales of licensed merchandise.

**Conceptual drawings or models**. Early representations of what licensed products will look like. Usually must be approved by the licensor before production of the licensed line can proceed.

**Concession stands**. Retail areas at theme parks, sports arenas or concert venues that sell merchandise related to the event. Concession stand merchandise can be licensed, but is often purchased by the licensor from a company for that purpose only rather being licensed.

**Consolidation**. The existence of fewer retailers or manufacturers or licensors within a given sector of the licensing business. Retail consolidation has been occurring among department stores, as has consolidation among sports apparel licensees and among entertainment licensors as larger ones purchase subsidiaries in related fields.

**Consumer awareness**. The level of recognition that a property has among its target market.

**Consumer backlash**. A negative perception by the public toward a property or product, due to a controversy or to the fact that licensed products are inappropriate for the property.

**Contract**. The agreement between licensee and licensor, licensor and licensing agent, or manufacturer and licensing consultant. Outlines the rights and responsibilities of each party in the scope of the agreement.

**Contract negotiations**. The process of agreeing upon the provisions contained in a licensing contract. Virtually every point in a deal is negotiable depending on the circumstances.

**Control**. The ability of the licensor to maintain the value of the brand, even when products associated with it are manufactured by licensees. The product approval and licensee selection processes are key components of maintaining control.

**Conversationals**. Apparel and accessories containing fun designs that encourage comment. Ties and socks, often licensed, are among the major conversational categories.

**Copyright**. The laws governing the protection of works of art, music or literature from *infringement*. A right of creative ownership.

**Core products**. A company's primary product line. Can be manufactured in-house or licensed to other manufacturers.

**Cost of goods sold**. The unit cost of each product sold. Royalties, which accrue upon sales of each unit, are usually considered a component of the cost of goods sold.

**Costumed characters**. Actors portraying licensed characters, logos or mascots. Usually present at live promotional events supporting a property.

**Counterfeiting**. The act of illegally copying a product. Counterfeiting is a major concern of licensors and licensees.

**Coverage**. In the syndicated television business, a measure of the number of households that can receive a syndicated television show. Measured in percentage of total U.S. television households.

**Criminal law**. Laws pertaining to crimes and their punishment. Criminal law provides protection and remedies against counterfeiters.

**Cross-licensing**. The combination of two or more properties on one licensed product.

**Cross-merchandising**. The joint retail display of two or more different licensed products based on the same property. Cross-merchandising tends to increase sales and is a growing phenomenon for properties of all types from designers to characters to sports to trademarks.

**Cross-packaging, Co-packaging**. The act of combining two or more licensed products based on the same property in the same package for one price. Examples include videos that come with plush toys and action figures that are packaged with comic books.

# – D –

**Deadline**. A target date at which a certain action must be completed. Deadlines such as product introduction dates and first shipping dates are often included in a licensing contract, because the meeting of these deadlines is crucial to the success of the licensing program.

**Dealer networks**. Wholesalers or retailers that sell a manufacturer's core products. Also provide opportunities for sales of related licensed products. Examples include automobile dealerships and soft drink distributors.

**Demand**. Consumers' desire for licensed products based on a given property. The ability to meet demand while it exists and to anticipate the decline of demand so as to prevent excess inventory are key factors in a licensing program.

**Demographic group**. Consumers with similar *demographic* characteristics. Can be targeted in the aggregate.

**Demographics**. Characteristics including sex, age and income levels. Demographic traits are a major criterion in determining the strategy for a licensing program.

**Department stores**. Upscale stores that sell a wide variety of merchandise grouped into different areas. Prices tend to be higher, volumes lower and customer service a greater focus than in *mass market* stores.

**Detection**. The process of seeking out and discovering counterfeit activities. Usually involves the cooperation of manufacturers, retailers and customers, as well as the use of private investigators.

**Developers**. In the electronic game industry, people who create videogames and the game architecture that makes play possible. Developers usually receive a royalty, in addition to the royalty earned by the trademark holder.

**Differentiation**. The act of distinguishing a manufacturer's product line or a retailer's store from those of their competitors. Associating with a licensed property is one method of differentiation.

**Dilution**. A decrease in the value of a brand. Product overproliferation, lack of quality, or entry into inappropriate distribution channels can all contribute to brand dilution.

**Direct market**. In the comic book industry, specialty comic book stores (as distinguished from mass market stores). The direct market accounts for most sales of comic books, except for those targeted at young children, and also provides an outlet for licensed merchandise based on comics, science fiction and other properties.

**Disposable income**. The amount of income that consumers have left over for purchases after required expenses. The disposable income of a property's target audience will determine appropriate types of licensed products and price points.

**Disposal period**. A period of about 30 days after contract termination, during which licensees are allowed, on a non-exclusive basis, to sell off remaining inventory produced under the terms of the agreement. Disposal usually occurs at *close-out* prices.

**Distribution channels**. The method by which licensed merchandise reaches the consumer. Distribution channels include traditional retailers of various types, mail order, tele-shopping and concession stands.

**Distribution license**. An agreement allowing a company to distribute products. Distinguished from retail product licensing agreements, which allow the manufacture or sale of newly created products based on a property. Distribution licenses are granted for home video distribution of theatrical films or television episodes, for example.

**Distribution tiers**. Levels of retail stores. Two major distribution tiers are upstairs, including department and specialty stores, and downstairs, including discount stores, category killers, convenience, variety and drug stores.

**Distributors**. Companies that represent or buy from manufacturers and sell to retailers. Licensors often wish to authorize the use of distributors by their licensees.

**Divisional merchandise managers**. Retail employees that supervise buyers of various product categories. Licensors seeking to put together *concept shops* must usually approach personnel at the DMM level or higher, since buyers are responsible for bottom lines within their departments only.

**Downstairs**. A distribution tier with low prices, high volume and low levels of customer service. Includes discount department stores, *category killers*, variety, convenience and drug stores.

# – E –

**Endorsement**. The association of a property (often a celebrity — live or deceased — but sometimes characters or other properties) with a product, implying use. An endorsed product does not involve altering the merchandise itself, as a licensed product would. Endorsements are usually compensated with a flat fee, or a fee with a percentage of merchandise sales.

**Entertainment vehicles.** Films, television shows, home videos, sequels, videogames, publishing and live events that serve to add excitement to a property. All are opportunities for additional merchandise sales and for promotions supporting the property.

**Estate.** The heirs of a deceased celebrity. Royalties from licensing the name, likeness, signature, etc., of a deceased celebrity usually go to his or her estate.

**Exclusivity.** An agreement that allows a licensee to be the only party granted rights to use a property in a particular product, territory or distribution channel. Exclusivity can be defined broadly or narrowly.

**Exploitation.** The commercial use of a trademark. *Trademarks* must be exploited in various classifications of products, or their validity in those classes could be questioned.

**Exposure.** The amount of opportunity consumers have to see or hear about a property. Advertising, publicity, entertainment and media vehicles, and live events can all enhance a property's exposure.

**Extension of contract.** The expansion of a licensing agreement to include additional properties, products, territories or distribution channels.

# – F –

**Fan shops.** Specialty stores that exclusively sell licensed merchandise, particularly sports apparel.

**First shipping date.** The date at which manufacturers must make their first shipment of a licensed product line to retailers. Usually written into the contract because of the importance of having merchandise in stores in time for key selling seasons.

**Fit.** The appropriateness of an association between product and property in terms of product application, target audience, licensee's and licensor's objectives and other criteria.

**Flat fee.** An alternate method of payment for a license; usually applies to promotional licensing. Sometimes applies to products, particularly when several licensors are involved, in which case a flat fee per unit may be charged in lieu of a royalty.

**Flea markets.** Retail environments at which counterfeit merchandise has been known to be discovered.

**Flexibility.** The ability to adapt to changing market conditions. While thoughtful strategic planning is important to the success of a licensing program, flexibility is also key.

**Flop.** A licensing program that fails to drive licensed merchandise sales. Licensing efforts that are considered flops may still have some successful product lines.

**Free goods**. Licensed products that are given away, such as samples. Usually are royalty-free, within limits.

**Free-standing stores**. Retail outlets focusing on one property or family of properties. Similar to a *concept shop*, except in its own retail location rather than within another retail store.

**Full-time licensor**. A property owner whose branded products are exclusively licensed rather than being manufactured in-house. Several fashion labels opt to become full-time licensors if royalty revenues for licensed lines exceed profit margins for products manufactured in-house.

# – G –

**Generic merchandise**. Non-licensed products.

**Goodwill**. Value associated with a property. Considered to be owned by the licensor; contracts contain a provision stating this fact.

**Grant of rights**. A major provision of a licensing contract, outlining what properties, products, territories and distribution channels are authorized under the agreement.

**Gross margin**. The difference between wholesale unit cost and *cost of goods sold*. In industries where licensed products do not command premium prices, royalties cut into manufacturers' gross margins.

**Grounds for termination**. Actions on the part of either the licensee or the licensor that would cause the contract to become invalid. Grounds for termination are outlined in the agreement.

**Guarantee**. A minimum royalty payment, usually based on expected sales. Actual royalty payments accrue against the guarantee amount; whatever remains of the guarantee after total royalties are tallied is due at the end of the contract period. If royalties exceed the minimum guarantee, no further money is owed. (In some non-exclusive licensing agreements, the guarantee can simply be a performance criterion, rather than a required minimum payment.)

# – H –

**Hangtags**. Hanging labels on licensed merchandise. Hangtags are usually consistent across all licensed merchandise in order to enhance the *brand identity*. Consistent hangtags also make spotting counterfeit merchandise easier.

**Hard goods**. A retail term referring to products not made of textiles, such as toys or furniture. The opposite of *soft goods*.

**Holograms**. An expensive-to-duplicate method of making labels or hangtags. Can also be incorporated into the products themselves. Often used as a means to counteract infringement, since they are easy to spot and costly to copy.

**Home runs**. Another name for *blockbusters*.

**Hot properties.** The most popular properties within a given year. Usually refers to *short-term* rather than *classic properties*.

**Hypermarts.** Very large retailers featuring low prices and large selections. A major distribution channel in France.

# — I —

**Impressions.** The cumulative number of times consumers see or hear of a property. The use of a property on packaging, in advertising and in live events all contribute to the total number of impressions generated.

**Impulse purchases.** Products bought by consumers on the spur of the moment, without prior planning. Many licensed products, especially those based on entertainment or character properties, are frequently impulse purchases.

**In-store boutiques.** Another name for *concept shops*.

**Incremental costs.** The difference between costs associated with a licensed tie-in and costs that would accrue anyway. For example, for a promotional partner, the cost of placing an ad mentioning the promotion specifically, within an existing advertising schedule, versus the costs for the ad originally planned within that schedule, would be an incremental cost.

**Indemnifications.** Protections against lawsuits by third parties. Licensees indemnify licensors against personal injury suits involving a licensed product, for example, while licensors indemnify the licensee against suits charging that the trademark infringes on other marks.

**Infrastructure.** The system in place for the manufacture and transportation of goods. The state of a particular territory's infrastructure — technology, manufacturing capability, transportation, etc. — is an important factor in the decision of whether a licensor should enter that territory.

**Infringement.** The unauthorized use of a trademark.

**Injunctions.** Court-ordered restrictions on a party's activities. A court can issue an injunction against an alleged counterfeiter, barring continued manufacture and sale of the goods.

**Installed base.** The number of consumers and/or businesses that already own the hardware necessary for a given technology to be used. Applies to electronic games and multimedia; the size of the installed base for a given platform determines the current potential market for software sales related to that platform, for example.

**Interactive multimedia.** A term referring to technologies that allow the user to input and manipulate information as well as receive it (interactive) and that combines sound, video, computer and other technogies (multimedia). A current question is whether there will ever be one standard for interactive multimedia.

**International copyright convention.** One of a number of international agreements, including the Berne Convention and others, dealing with copyright protection. Most countries subscribe to either Berne or to the provisions of another international copyright convention, or are parties to separate bilateral agreements covering copyrights. The existence of these copyright conventions and treaties means that a copyright registered in the U.S. is valid in many other countries as well.

**Interstate commerce.** The marketing and selling of products across state borders. Interstate commerce is required for federal trademark laws to apply.

**Inventors.** Creators of games or toys. Inventors usually require a royalty in addition to the royalty owed to trademark holders.

**Inventory control.** The process of maintaining adequate production levels to meet demand for a licensed product while it is high, and to prevent excess inventory after demand falls off. An important consideration for merchandise based on *short-term properties*.

**Invisible licensing.** The act of creating licensed products that are perceived by consumers to be manufactured by the licensor rather than the licensee. Brand extension licensing in food, fashion and other corporate trademark types is often "invisible."

# – J –

**Joint ventures.** 1) A type of business structure where two or more parties share ownership. 2) A common method of expanding into new geographic territories; an alternative to licensing or setting up a subsidiary. 3) A licensing agreement is not a joint venture; this fact is stated in the contract.

**Jurisdiction.** The state law under which a licensing agreement is valid and under which disputes will be resolved.

# – K –

**Key category.** An important product category. Its importance may relate to the awareness or advertising it generates (e.g. a master toy licensee for an entertainment property); to the way it enhances the core property and creates a connection between the consumer and the property (e.g. home video, videogames or publishing); or to the fact that it is the category for which a brand is known (e.g. sportswear for a fashion brand).

**Knock-offs.** Illegal products that are confusingly similar to legitimate licensed merchandise. May or may not be exact copies.

**Know-how.** Expertise in manufacturing or marketing. The level of know-how in certain geographic territories where capitalism is in its infancy may be an important criteria in the decision of whether to expand there.

# – L –

**Labeling.** Identifying marks on licensed products, including *hangtags*, sewn-in labels and packaging. Consistency in labeling enhances brand image and assists in spotting counterfeit merchandise.

**Launch date**. The date at which licensed products will appear at retail. Launch dates may vary from product to product, depending on the *rollout* strategy for the property.

**Lead times**. The amount of time required for products to arrive at retail. Lead times vary from licensee to licensee, between licensee and licensor and among promotional partners. Factors affecting lead times include length of contract negotiation, product development time, re-tooling requirements, time lags related to importing, etc.

**Legal marking**. Placing notices on labels, printed matter, etc. that contain depictions of trademarks and copyrights. The act of legal marking prevents infringers from claiming ignorance of the existence of the mark, and proves to the courts that the licensor is serious about protecting its trademarks and copyrights.

**Legal protection**. The act of registering appropriate *trademarks* and *copyrights* in order to have a legal means to counteract *counterfeiting* and *infringement*.

**Legal remedies**. Rewards a licensor can receive and/or punishments required for a counterfeiter when the licensor's marks are infringed, if those marks are adequately protected. Remedies can include injunctions, damages, fines and jail time.

**License acquisition**. The process the licensee goes through to seek appropriate properties with which to associate and to negotiate acceptable terms for a licensing agreement.

**Licensed promotions**. Events that generate awareness for the promotional partners, of which a licensed property is the focus.

**Licensee**. The party that acquires the rights to utilize a property, usually for a retail product but sometimes for promotional use.

**Licensee estoppel**. A contractual provision that prevents a licensee from questioning the validity of a licensor's trademarks during the term of the agreement.

**Licensee evaluation form**. A method licensors use to screen potential licensees. Licensees must provide sales, marketing and financial information regarding their company and their plans for the property.

**Licensing**. A lease agreement in which a *licensor* rents the rights to a legally protected property to a *licensee* for use in conjunction with a product or service.

**Licensing agent**. A company or individual that acts on behalf of the licensor in launching, administering and/or evaluating a licensing program. The agent takes over many of the licensor's duties, with approval by the licensor, in return for a commission.

**Licensing consultant**. A company that represents the interests of a licensor in launching or administering a licensing program, or that represents the interests of the licensee in seeking and acquiring licenses. Several licensing consultants specialize in serving manufacturers only. Usually paid with a retainer or some combination of retainer and commission.

**Licensing in**. The act of acquiring a license. Licensees license in.

**Licensing fee**. A flat fee required as payment for the use of a license. An alternative to a royalty, generally for promotional or advertising uses rather than for retail products.

**Licensing out**. The act of leasing rights to other parties. The licensor licenses out.

**Licensor**. The *property* owner.

**Life span**. The time period starting with the launch of a property and ending when demand for licensed products based on the property ends. Classic properties have long, even unlimited, life spans, while short-term properties have life spans of about three to five years or less.

**Likenesses**. Depictions of celebrities. Celebrities or their *estates* usually retain the right to approve the use of their likenesses, whether these likenesses are the central property or a component of another property (such as actors in a film).

**Litigation**. Taking legal action against another party. Contract disputes and anti-counterfeiting activities may lead to litigation.

**Logo**. A graphic representation of a trademark or brand. Logos are usually one element of a property that can be used by a licensee. Special logos are often created for special events, for sub-brands based on a property, or as an umbrella to tie diverse properties together.

**Long-term properties**. Properties that have long life spans, stretching over several decades. The strategy behind managing a long-term property is much different from that for a *short-term property*.

**Low-end merchandise**. Low-priced products such as key chains, buttons and pencils. Sales are primarily *impulse purchases*.

# – M –

**Manufacturer's representative**. 1) In licensing, a consultant exclusively representing the interests of licensees in seeking licenses, managing licensing programs and negotiating contracts. 2) In sales, a company that serves as a middleman in selling a manufacturer's products to retail.

**Markup**. The difference between the retail and the wholesale price, divided by the retail price.

**Mass market**. Distribution channels with high volume, low prices and little customer service. Includes discounters and *category killers*.

**Master licensee**. The major licensee in a given category, with rights to several products within that category. May *sub-license* certain products out to other manufacturers with expertise in those areas, within the context of their agreement with the licensor.

**Maturing market**. A market in which annual sales growth is slowing or leveling off after several years of very large increases. Part of the natural business cycle. Many observers believe that the licensing business, at least in the U.S. and Canada, is a maturing market.

**Measureability**. The ability of a promotional element to be measured for success. Coupon redemptions, calls to an interactive phone line, number of uses of an online system are all measurable.

**Media buy**. The total amount spent on print, television, radio and other forms of advertising.

**Media vehicles**. Book and comic book publishing, television shows, films, videogames and home video, all of which add to the awareness of the property and keep it fresh, as well as offering promotional opportunities.

**Merchandise mix**. The relative shares of various types of products stocked by a retailer. A store's merchandise mix helps determine if it is an appropriate outlet for a licensed product line.

**Merchandising**. 1) The placement of goods at retail so as to maximize sales levels. 2) Promoting the sale of products through advertising, promotion or point of sale materials. 3) Sometimes used as a synonym for retail product *licensing*.

**Milestones**. Measurable performance benchmarks that, when achieved, can affect payment or other aspects of a licensing relationship.

**Monetary damages**. Financial payments that may come due to a licensor when a party is convicted of counterfeiting or infringement. The amount of damages may be based on lost sales by legitimate parties (licensors and licensees) or on the counterfeiter's profits.

**Multi-partner promotions**. Promotional tie-ins that involve several parties, such as a retailer, a packaged goods company, a licensor, a media partner, etc. More partners help reduce costs to each partner, but create difficulties in terms of logistics.

**Multi-tiered distribution**. A strategy by licensors in which licensed merchandise is distributed through both *upstairs* and *downstairs* retail channels. Care must be taken to differentiate merchandise in each respective tier, however, so that one channel does not *cannibalize* sales in the other.

**Music merchandising**. The method by which products are sold at concert venues. Music merchandisers act as licensees for the musical acts, producing most merchandise, and *sub-license* other companies for certain categories. In addition, music merchandisers sometimes (increasingly) act as licensing agents, arranging deals for merchandise sold in traditional retail channels.

# – N –

**Net sales**. The sales amount to which royalties are applied. Usually is the wholesale price to retailers less certain *allowable deductions*.

**Niche**. A small, reachable target market. Niche licensing programs are narrow in scope — aiming at a small but avid market with a few products — but can be lucrative for licensees who participate.

**Nielsen ratings**. A measurement of television viewership. Used by licensors to demonstrate awareness for the property.

**Non-exclusives**. Licensing agreements allowing several licensees to produce merchandise that overlaps in distribution level and/or territory, and/or where the products themselves are similar or identical.

**Non-profit overlay**. Adding a non-profit organization as a promotional partner. Some of the proceeds from merchandise purchases within the context of the promotion go to the non-profit group, providing a purchase incentive for many consumers.

**Non-traditional outlets**. Distribution channels for licensed merchandise where such products are not usually sold. For example, selling licensed entertainment merchandise in video rental stores, selling plush toys in housewares departments in conjunction with related licensed housewares, or selling t-shirts in bookstores would all be examples of exploiting non-traditional outlets. Tele-shopping is also considered a non-traditional outlet, although it is becoming more common.

**North American Free Trade Agreement (NAFTA)**. An agreement among the U.S., Canada and Mexico reducing restrictions on trade. It is an example of a trade agreement that will affect international licensing programs.

**Notice of Allowance**. A communication from the Patent and Trademark Office stating that no third parties oppose the use of a trademark. Part of the trademark registration process. The licensor has six months to exploit the mark in interstate commerce or file an extension once it has received its Notice of Allowance.

**Novelization**. A book that tells the story contained in a film or television show, following the plot closely. A common licensed product for entertainment properties.

# – O –

**Objectives**. The specific goals of a licensing strategy. Identifying objectives should be the first step in a licensing program, and the objectives of the licensor and its licensees should be compatible.

**Official Gazette**. A monthly Patent and Trademark Office publication that posts trademark applications so that parties who feel they will be hurt by a mark have the opportunity to oppose its registration.

**Opposition**. The act of alerting the Patent and Trademark Office that a proposed trademark will hurt an existing trademark.

**Option to renew**. A provision sometimes included in a licensing contract that allows existing licensees to renew the contract at the end of the term, if certain performance benchmarks are met.

**Outright sale**. For artists and designers, an alternative to licensing. The outright sale of a design for a flat fee means that the artist loses control over and ownership of the design, and is not authorized to make agreements for its use in other product categories.

**Overproliferation, Oversaturation.** The existence of so many similar properties or products that supply exceeds demand. One successful licensed property or product often breeds several similar properties or products, leading to oversaturation and ultimately to a *shakeout*.

# – P –

**Packaging.** The container or wrapping surrounding a licensed product. Consistency in packaging helps enhance brand image and assists in spotting counterfeit products.

**Pan-European licensing.** The act of granting one license for all European territories rather than separate licenses for each territory. Not all manufacturers are equipped to become pan-European licensees because of differences in distribution structures and tastes among European countries.

**Paper trail.** The paperwork associated with anti-counterfeiting efforts, including copies of *cease-and-desist* letters and records of anti-infringement activities. A paper trail will help convince a court that a licensor is serious about protecting its trademarks and that an alleged infringer should have known of the existence of such trademarks.

**Parallel imports.** The ability to import licensed products into one European country from another, in spite of the fact that a local licensee has been granted rights for similar or identical products in that territory. Parallel imports are legal within the European Community, but are discouraged by licensors.

**Penalties.** Additional payments required for late royalty payments, missed deadlines or other violations of contractual provisions.

**Per-capita spending.** In licensing, the amount spent per person on licensed merchandise in a given geographic territory. Regions with lower per-capita spending are often perceived as having more room for growth than markets with high current per-capita spending rates.

**Performance criteria.** Benchmarks written into a licensing contract or a licensor-agency contract that determine whether or not the contract can be renewed. Not meeting these benchmarks may also be grounds for termination, depending on the situation.

**Permissions.** The act of authorizing the use of a property, usually for editorial purposes. May require a fee.

**Pilferage.** The theft of merchandise from retail outlets. Fear of pilferage is one reason behind the reluctance of some independent specialty stores to sell licensed products.

**Piracy.** The unauthorized copying of merchandise. Piracy includes merchandise sporting unauthorized logos as well as copies of product designs (patent infringement).

**Platform.** A type of videogame hardware or computer operating system. Each platform is distinct, meaning that only software made for it can be used on it. In licensing, property owners often authorize several licensees to produce software, each for one or a few platforms.

**Play value.** How fun it is to play with a given toy. A license applied to a toy does not add value or drive sales unless it enhances the play value of that toy.

**Plush.** Stuffed toys or figures.

**Point-of-purchase materials.** Display items used in stores to attract attention to licensed merchandise. POP materials include countertop displays, pre-fabricated merchandise racks, posters and banners.

**Policing.** The process of detecting incidences of counterfeiting, finding counterfeiters and taking action against them. The amount of policing done by a licensor depends on its properties' popularity and the amount of counterfeiting activity associated with them, as well as the resources it is willing to spend.

**Pre-production samples.** Product prototypes that indicate how the product will look when it is manufactured. Licensors must approve pre-production samples before manufacturing can begin.

**Premium.** 1) A promotional item that is purchased or given away to consumers and members of the *trade*. A good sales outlet for authorized licensees. 2) A higher price. Licensed products in some industries can command premiums over generic products, allowing licensees to pass the royalty cost on to consumers.

**Price point.** A pre-established retail price within a product category.

**Private investigators.** Independent contractors retained to help in the detection of counterfeiting activity.

**Private label.** A brand that is exclusive to one retailer. Private labels can be licensed, such as Wal-Mart's *Popular Mechanics* hardware brand.

**Privatization.** The transformation of industry or media from government to private ownership. Privatization within a geographic region usually makes that territory more attractive to licensors in the long run.

**Product approvals.** The quality control process by which the licensor monitors the manufacture of licensed products based on its properties. Approvals are generally required for *conceptual drawings or models, pre-production samples* and *production samples*.

**Product category.** A group of related products. For example, toys and games is a product category containing dolls, plush, board games, activity toys, action figures, etc.

**Product introduction date.** The date at which licensed merchandise is first introduced to retailers, usually at a trade show. Product introduction dates are important milestones, since late products can damage overall sales for the property.

**Product liability insurance.** A type of insurance that can be required contractually by licensors to financially back up the licensees' *indemnifications*.

**Product line**. A range of related products manufactured by one licensee.

**Production samples**. Manufactured products that must be approved by the licensor before selling can occur.

**Profit margins**. The difference between revenues and expenses, divided by revenues. If profit margins for a product line are less than royalty revenues would be for the same line if licensed out, licensors would consider licensing over in-house manufacturing.

**Promotional licensing**. The act of licensing for advertising, premiums or other marketing purposes, rather than for a retail product.

**Promotions**. Events that support a licensing program by generating awareness. Can include sweepstakes or contests, discounted merchandise, live appearances, *cross-merchandising*, exclusive product lines at retailers, or other elements.

**Property**. A legally protected entity that forms the core of a licensing agreement. The property is what is leased by the licensee from the licensor.

**Property-specific catalogs**. Mail-order catalogs containing a selection of merchandise based on a given property. The merchandise may be licensed, or it may be purchased instead by the licensor from a manufacturer specifically for this purpose. Products may be exclusive or similar to those found at retail.

**Property-specific stores**. Retail outlets that focus on one property or family of licensed properties. Merchandise may be manufactured by licensees or may be contracted specifically for the stores. Products are often exclusive, to prevent cannibalization of sales of similar licensed merchandise in other retail stores.

**Property type**. A method of classifying properties by origin.

**Prototypes**. Pre-production samples of products, used to pre-sell to retailers before manufacturing begins. While prototypes look like the finished product, they are often flimsy, since they are generally handmade.

**Psychographic characteristics**. A psychological profile of a group of people. Examining psychographic traits of a property's target market can help determine the best way to reach them.

**Public domain**. The collection of properties that are, in effect, owned by the public and therefore can be used commercially by anyone. Examples include properties whose copyrights have expired, trademarks that have expired due to lack of exploitation or lack of monitoring, and government-sponsored events.

**Publicity**. A method of generating awareness of the property through coverage in the media. Events and press releases outlining activities surrounding the property are typical publicity tactics.

**Purchasing habits**. Characteristics of a certain target market in terms of where they shop, whether their purchases are planned or *impulse*, whether they prefer mail or tele-shopping over shopping in person and so on. Helpful in determining how that target market can best be reached.

# – Q –

**Quality control.** The process by which licensors (and licensees) ensure that the products on the market meet the product specifications set up for them. The *product approval* and licensee selection processes are the major tools the licensor uses for quality control.

# – R –

**® symbol.** The legal marking placed next to trademarked names, images, etc., to demonstrate that they are registered marks.

**Re-tooling.** The process necessary to make existing machinery able to produce a new line of merchandise. In some industries, such as toys, retooling is a major cost and may prevent some companies from considering risky, short-term properties where they are not reasonably certain that their re-tooling investment will be re-couped.

**Rebates.** Promotional tools in which customers receive discounts on merchandise. The consumer purchases the merchandise, then redeems a coupon entitling him or her to money back.

**Redemptions.** The number of coupons returned within the context of a promotion. A method of measuring the effectiveness of a tie-in.

**Registration.** The process by which a trademark or copyright becomes fully protected under the law.

**Release date.** The date at which a home video, musical recording or videogame first appears at retail.

**Repositioning.** The process of changing a brand image. Licensed merchandise can help reinforce other marketing activities undertaken to reposition a brand.

**Reproduction programs.** Licensing programs where licensees manufacture exact replicas of objects in a licensor's collection. Generally applies to museum licensing efforts, where art objects or historical furniture are reproduced for sale at retail.

**Reserve for returns.** A portion of royalty payments withheld for a time to account for merchandise that is likely to be returned later. In industries where merchandise is fully returnable and a certain percentage of sales are expected to come back as returns (such as book publishing), a reserve for returns (e.g. 10%-15% of sales) makes accounting simpler.

**Restraining orders.** Court orders barring a company from continuing an illegal activity. One method of preventing alleged counterfeiters from continuing to infringe on a mark.

**Retail sales.** Sales of merchandise, measured in terms of the price paid by consumers.

**Retailers.** Sellers of merchandise. An increasingly important player in the licensor-licensee-retailer partnership, since retailers are best able to assess consumer demand. Licensors and licensees must sell concepts and merchandise, respectively, to retailers before consumers have access to their property.

**Retainer**. A payment for ongoing services. Licensing consultants are often paid by retainer, sometimes in combination with a commission.

**Returns**. 1) Merchandise that is sold to consumers and then brought back to the store for a refund. 2) Merchandise that is sold (sometimes on consignment) to retailers and then returned to the manufacturer if not sold to consumers. In industries where merchandise is fully returnable, such as book publishing, a *reserve for returns* is withheld from royalty payments.

**Right of publicity**. The legal notion that a celebrity or his or her estate has the sole right to exploit that celebrity's image and name for commercial use. No federal right of publicity exists, but some states do recognize it. It is based for the most part on *common*, rather than *statutory law*.

**Risk management policy**. A financial strategy that ensures money will be available to defend against lawsuits. Takes the place of insurance in industries where insurance is prohibitively expensive.

**Rollout**. The systematic expansion of a licensing program into new product categories, new distribution channels or new geographic territories. A program's proposed rollout is a strategic consideration that varies depending on the property.

**Royalty**. The basic form of payment in a licensing agreement; usually a percentage of the *net sales* price of each unit of licensed merchandise sold.

**Royalty compliance**. The timely and accurate reporting and payment of royalties. Auditing provisions are included in licensing contracts to ensure royalty compliance.

**Royalty reporting**. The act of providing licensors with accurate and fairly detailed information on the sales results and associated royalties due over a period of time (usually three months).

## – S –

**Samples**. 1) Units of licensed merchandise used in the selling process rather than being sold to consumers. 2) Representations of licensed merchandise at various stages of the manufacturing process, given to licensors for their approval.

**Secondary meaning**. A legal term that applies to descriptive trademarks (e.g. a brand name that describes the product rather than being made up). While such marks cannot normally be registered as trademarks, they can be if they acquire secondary meaning; that is, consumers associate that name with that product alone. Contractually, licensees may be required to state that a descriptive mark has acquired secondary meaning, thus preventing them from later claiming that a mark is descriptive and unregistrable or unenforceable.

**Seizures**. The act of legally confiscating goods or machinery. Seizures of merchandise are common remedies for illegal counterfeiting activity.

**Sell-off period.** A period of about one month after the termination of a licensing agreement during which licensees have the opportunity to dispose of excess inventories of licensed merchandise on a non-exclusive basis. After the sell-off period, the licensee is not allowed to let any of the merchandise reach the market.

**Selling seasons.** 1) The traditional time period in which manufacturers sell to retailers. 2) The traditional time period in which retailers sell to consumers. The latter is generally six to nine months after the former. For example, the major selling season for the toy business is in the fourth quarter, but manufacturers sell to retailers in February. For apparel, the two major seasons are Fall and Spring; selling seasons to retailers are about six months prior.

**Separate guarantees.** Individual *guarantees* tied to different product categories, distribution channels or territories within the same licensing agreement. Separate guarantees ensure that no single part of an overall agreement will be ignored.

**Shakeout.** A reduction in the number of companies doing business in a particular field, or in the number of properties of a similar type. Usually follows a period of *oversaturation*.

**Short-term properties.** Licensed properties with a natural life span of as little as one year and as much as five years. Such properties may be very lucrative during that short window.

**Sidelines.** A term in the bookselling industry for non-book products sold in bookstores. Many of these products are licensed.

**Soft goods.** A retail term meaning merchandise made of textiles, such as apparel and domestics. The opposite of *hard goods*.

**Specialty stores.** Retailers that focus on one or a few product categories. Stores are usually relatively small in square footage and can be independently owned or part of a chain. Prices are in the middle to high range, product selection is limited and volume is relatively low. Customer service and product differentiation are the major competitive advantages over other stores.

**Specifications.** The details of what a given product should look like and how it should be manufactured. Specifications include materials, colors and allowable depictions of a property.

**Spokescharacter.** A licensed character used in an advertisement or promotion, implying endorsement of the product.

**Spot checks.** A method of detecting sales of counterfeit merchandise at retailers, flea markets or on the street. Licensor personnel conduct spot checks regularly, with particular emphasis on times when the appearance of counterfeit merchandise is likely.

**Statement of Use.** A part of the trademark registration procedure in which the licensor states that its marks are being exploited in interstate commerce.

**Statutory law.** The body of written state and federal laws.

**Stock-keeping units (SKUs)**. Unique numbers assigned to each different product to allow retailers and manufacturers to keep track of sales on a product-by-product basis and to help in the reordering process.

**Stockpiling**. The act of acquiring several licenses and paying required advances and minimum guarantees, but not bringing all the properties to the marketplace.

**Store traffic**. The number of people who shop at a store or eat at a restaurant during a given period. Assessing changes in store traffic is one method of measuring the success of a licensed promotion.

**Strategy**. The plan behind the implementation of a licensing program. A strategy should be based on the program's objectives, and should allow flexibility in the face of a changing marketplace.

**Street value**. The value of counterfeit merchandise, as measured by what customers pay for it.

**Style book**. A guide created by licensors to illustrate to licensees the allowable uses of a property, product specifications and required legal markings.

**Sub-agents**. Licensing agents specializing in one territory or one product category, who are retained by a master licensing agent rather than directly by the licensor.

**Sub-brands**. Identities that pull together certain types of merchandise within the context of a larger brand. Major League Baseball's Rookie League sub-brand for children's merchandise and Walt Disney's Princess Collection sub-brand for girls' merchandise incorporating various Disney animated princesses are examples.

**Sub-contracting**. The act of purchasing merchandise from a third party within the scope of a licensing agreement. The licensee has the right to market and sell the merchandise, but another company, approved by the licensor, actually manufactures it to the licensee's and licensor's specifications.

**Subsidiaries**. A company owned by another company. Setting up a subsidiary in a foreign country is an alternative to seeking licensees or retaining a licensing agent there.

**Sunk costs**. Financial investments relating to a product line that are lost if the product does not do well. Different from variable or unit costs, which accrue as each unit of product is manufactured. For a licensee, sunk costs include advances and guarantees, re-tooling and product development costs.

**Syndication**. A method of distributing television shows whereby individual stations purchase the rights to air a program in their market at a time of their choosing. Different from a network show, where a program is purchased by a network for airing on all of its affiliates at the same time.

# –T–

**Target market**. The group of consumers likely to purchase a given licensed product.

**Tariffs.** Payments required in order to import or export goods. A consideration in the decision of whether to use local licensees or import licensed goods into a particular country from another region.

**Tele-shopping.** A distribution channel where consumers view merchandise on television and order by telephone. Includes home shopping networks, *transactional television shows*, infomercials and short advertisements.

**Term.** The duration of a licensing agreement. Varies, but most commonly two to three years for sports and entertainment properties, longer for fashion and corporate trademarks.

**Territory.** A geographic region. One of the key elements in the *grant of rights*.

**Third-party catalogs.** Mail-order catalogs that sell licensed merchandise, but are not owned or licensed by a particular licensor.

**Tie-ins.** Promotions in which one or more partners associate themselves with a licensed property.

**Timing.** A key strategic consideration in setting up a licensing program. Timing issues include *launch dates, selling seasons, lead times* and *rollout*.

**™ symbol.** A marking used by property owners to signify that they consider their mark a brand not to be infringed. Does not mean that the trademark is registered.

**Traceability.** In a promotion, the ability to not only measure the success of a promotion, but to attribute that success to one promotional element.

**Trade, the.** Term used to describe retailers, wholesalers, distributors, manufacturers and licensors, as distinguished from consumers.

**Trade dress.** The total look of a product or packaging. Considered legally protectable, although not specifically referred to in trademark law. Individual elements within the total image may be trademarked, but trade dress is considered protectable regardless of whether elements incorporated in it are registered.

**Trade shows.** Industry conventions in which manufacturers or licensors can exhibit their products or properties to other members of *the trade*. An important selling tool.

**Tradeouts.** In a promotion, the barter of various promotional elements in lieu of cash payments.

**Trademark.** 1) A method of legal protection; the most common and effective method for licensors to legally protect their properties. 2) A type of property. Refers to corporate trademarks and brands, as opposed to trademarks originating in fashion, entertainment, publishing, sports or other areas.

**Transactional television programs.** Television shows in which entertainment or talk is combined with a sales message; viewers are able to order merchandise over the phone during the show.

**TRSTS.** A survey of toy sales conducted by the NPD Group. Used by licensors as evidence that a particular property is popular with children.

# — U —

**U.S. Customs.** An arm of the U.S. government that oversees imports. Trademarks registered with the Patent & Trademark Office can also be registered with Customs, so that counterfeit merchandise can be spotted and seized at the border. An important partner in anti-infringement efforts.

**Untapped market.** A product category or audience/consumer group that has not been targeted heavily by a given group of marketers, and that shows potential for sales growth. Untapped markets provide opportunities for the sales of licensed merchandise.

**Upscale products.** High-priced, high-quality merchandise targeted at consumers with large disposable incomes. Volumes are low, but per-unit profits can be large.

**Upstairs.** The *distribution tier* that contains department and specialty stores.

# — V —

**Vendor.** A retailer's term for a manufacturer or wholesaler that sells it merchandise.

**Volume.** The amount of merchandise sold by a retailer or manufacturer, usually measured in units or *wholesale* revenues.

# — W —

**Warranties.** Contractual guarantees that each party is able to deliver on its promises.

**Wholesale sales.** Sales of merchandise, as measured by the invoice amount to retailers.

**Worst-case scenario.** The worst thing that could happen as a result of a licensing agreement. Since the financial ramifications of a licensing agreement are difficult to predict, one criterion in a licensee's decision would be to look at the worst-case scenario and determine whether the company could withstand it.

# FREQUENTLY ASKED QUESTIONS ABOUT LICENSING

## GENERAL QUESTIONS

### What is the definition of licensing?

Licensing is the act of leasing the rights to a trademarked and/or copyrighted entity (the property) for use in conjunction with products or services. The owner of the rights is known as the licensor; the licensee rents the rights from the licensor. *See Chapter 1.*

### How do you pay for a license?

The primary form of payment for a retail licensing agreement is a royalty, or a percentage of the wholesale price of each unit of product sold, paid by the licensee to the licensor. A minimum guaranteed royalty is usually required, a portion of which is paid as an advance. *See Chapter 7.*

### What is the average royalty, advance and guarantee?

It is hard to talk about average payment for licensing agreements, since they vary widely depending on a number of factors. While royalties are commonly in the 5%-12% range, they can be as low as 1% and as high as 20%. Similarly, while the majority of guarantees are probably in the $10,000 to $50,000 range, they vary from as low as $1,000 or less to several million dollars. Advances also vary. *See Chapter 7.*

### What are the risks of licensing?

For the licensor, the major risk of a licensing program occurs if control over the property is lost. For the licensee, the major risk is a financial one, since minimum guaranteed royalties and investments in product development and tooling are sunk costs regardless of the performance of the property. *See Chapter 1.*

### What are the responsibilities of the licensee and the licensor?

In general, the licensor is responsible for maintaining the value of the property, through adequately protecting it legally and through monitoring and counteracting infringement by unauthorized parties. The licensor also provides marketing support for the property. The licensee, in turn, is responsible for manufacturing, marketing and selling the licensed product line. *See Chapter 1.*

### What are the provisions in a licensing contract?

Licensing contracts vary depending on the situation, but some of the major provisions include the grant of rights, payment and auditing procedures, the approval process, warranties and indemnifications. *See Chapter 9.*

### Are concept shops effective ways to sell licensed merchandise, and how are they set up?

Concept shops, or in-store boutiques, are recognized by licensors, licensees and retailers as among the best ways to drive sales of licensed merchandise. Licensors take the initiative in setting up concept shops, meeting with appropriate retailer personnel and providing point-of-purchase materials. *See Chapter 4.*

### How do I forecast the financial impact of licensing on my business?

The financial impact of licensing is difficult to predict. One method for licensors is to look at comparable properties and assess the relative strength of the licensor's property versus the others over time (an inexact science at best). Licensees should consider whether their company can easily withstand a worst-case scenario given the investment required, look at the license's effect on their margins, and examine whether other marketing methods may achieve the same volume increases at less cost. *See Chapters 5 and 6.*

### Who initiates the licensing agreement?

Either the licensee or the licensor can make the first contact. Licensors usually offer a contract to the licensee (except in certain industries such as publishing), which is then virtually always negotiable. *See Chapter 9.*

### How big a problem is counterfeiting?

Counterfeiting is a huge problem, requiring significant human and financial resources to combat. The more popular a property, the more counterfeiting activity occurs. *See Chapter 10.*

### What are net sales?

Net sales are usually defined as wholesale sales (the amount invoiced to retailers), less certain allowable deductions (e.g. freight, cash/volume discounts, returns). Deductions are normally limited to 2%-3% of the invoice amount. *See Chapter 7.*

### What's the difference between a copyright and a trademark?

Trademark registration is the primary tool for legally protecting a property for purposes of commercially exploiting it. Trademarks can be renewed indefinitely if exploited in interstate commerce; for maximum protection, they must be registered separately in each geographic area and product classification where the marks are intended to be used. Names, graphics and other elements that serve to differentiate one product line from another can be registered as trademarks. Copyright is an automatic right that begins with the creation of a work of art, literature or music; it expires 50 years after the death of the creator. Registration is effective on virtually a worldwide basis, and is suggested for full protection, but not required. For most retail product licensing, copyrights are a secondary method of protecting logo and character designs. *See Chapter 8.*

### Can I use a property that is in the public domain for free? What does it mean when the property is in the public domain?

A public domain work is, in effect, owned by the public and can thus be exploited by anyone for commercial use. Public domain properties are generally copyrighted properties that have expired or trademarked properties that have gone into the public domain through inadequate exploitation by the trademark owner. Government-sponsored events are also usually in the public domain. A public domain property can be used by anyone, assuming that the user can gain access to reproducible depictions of the property. *See Chapter 8.*

**Are all licensing agreements exclusive?**

No. Exclusivity ranges from true exclusives for a whole product category or geographic region, to narrow definitions of exclusivity, to no exclusivity at all. *See Chapter 9.*

**How is compensation structured for promotional licensing?**

Compensation for promotions range from a flat fee (such as for advertising or endorsements), to a percentage of a media buy (such as for advertising), to a percentage of merchandise, food or ticket sales (such as for licensed restaurants, arcades, live event appearances), to no cash at all. Some of the payment may take the form of providing a promotional element of value, in lieu of a cash payment. The possibilities vary widely depending on the situation. *See Chapter 12.*

## QUESTIONS LICENSORS ASK ABOUT LICENSING

**How are licensing agents compensated?**

Licensing agents are generally paid by commission, often 25%-35% of all licensing revenues. This commission can be higher or lower, depending on the specifics of the situation. *See Chapter 5.*

**What is the step-by-step procedure for setting up a licensing program?**

There is really no step-by-step procedure, since every licensing program is unique. However, all licensors should know their objectives for the licensing effort and the characteristics of their property and its target audience. Based on these factors, several strategic decisions can be made. Some of the considerations include which product categories to select, which distribution channels to target, how much to require as payment, when to launch the program, and how fast to roll it out. *See Chapter 5.*

**Do I get to approve products made by my licensees?**

Yes. In fact, the product approval process — along with the licensee selection process — is the most important way to maintain control over the program and the property's image. *See Chapter 5.*

**How does the strategy for a "hot" property differ from the strategy for a classic property?**

The objective for a licensing program based on a "hot" property is usually to maximize revenues and/or awareness in a relatively short window of opportunity. Thus, the licensing strategy may include wide distribution, many products and many licensees. On the other hand, for a classic property, maintaining the property's value over time is of the essence; more emphasis will be placed on avoiding market oversaturation and on keeping the property and associated products fresh over time. *See Chapter 5.*

## How long does it take to get products into retail after the contract is signed?

Lead times vary, but a rule of thumb is about a year from contract signing to products at retail. Some product categories require at least a year and a half, while others can get to retail in as little as three months, if necessary. *See Chapter 5.*

## How do I sell my property to licensees and retailers?

The more concrete information you can provide, the better. Selling tools include marketing information (such as sales figures, viewership, attendance numbers, etc.), information about the property itself (stylebook and other art reference, story boards, character synopses, information about how consumers perceive the brand, etc.), information about the target audience and examples of how the property can be applied to merchandise. *See Chapter 5.*

## How do I decide which licensees to sign?

Licensee selection criteria include the licensee's existing retail customer base, what the licensee is willing to pay, the financial strength of the company, the design and quality of the licensee's products, etc. The relative importance of these criteria depend on the licensor's objectives. *See Chapter 5.*

## How do I decide if I should use a licensing agent?

Licensing agents offer expertise and licensing contacts to companies which lack in-house personnel with the same experience. Financial considerations also play a role: at what point does the agent's commission exceed what an in-house licensing department would cost? *See Chapter 5.*

## How do I prevent counterfeiting?

Licensors can take a number of steps to attempt to prevent counterfeiting, including educating licensees, retailers, consumers and potential counterfeiters on what counterfeiting is and what penalties will follow an occurrence; making product packaging and labeling consistent to make spotting counterfeit merchandise easier; and encouraging licensees, licensors and retailers to report incidences of counterfeiting. *See Chapter 10.*

## What remedies do I have against counterfeiters if counterfeiting should occur?

Civil and legal remedies against counterfeiting include restraining orders, seizures of merchandise and machinery, fines, monetary damages and jail time. The remedies sought should be balanced against the cost of pursuing them. *See Chapter 10.*

## How do I expand internationally?

There is no one way to expand internationally. While international territories are considered to have encouraging growth potential, individual licensors should examine various factors. They include how well known the property is in various countries; the political, economic and cultural characteristics of each territory; and the methods of doing business in each region. *See Chapter 11.*

### How do I know if I need a foreign agent?

Most observers recognize the need for a local partner in a foreign territory, whether it be an agent, a retailer, a master licensee, a joint venture or a subsidiary staffed by local personnel. Foreign agents have expertise in their regions and may be the most cost-effective option, especially initially. *See Chapter 11.*

### How do I keep a property fresh over time?

There are various methods of rejuvenating classic properties over time. They include creating new events or media vehicles, such as films, sporting activities, television shows, etc.; launching promotions to commemorate anniversaries, tie in with new events or just because there is a good fit between the property and a promotional partner's business; and introducing new product lines, either through expansion into new categories or through fresh designs of existing products. *See Chapter 5.*

## QUESTIONS LICENSEES ASK ABOUT LICENSING

### How do I, as a licensee, decide which properties I should license?

The best property for a given licensee will be one where the licensor's goals match the licensee's and where the fit between the property and product and their respective target audiences is appropriate. A number of properties may be appropriate for any given licensee, depending on its objectives. *See Chapter 6.*

### Where do I find out about properties that are available and who owns them?

Trade publications, trade shows and directories of the licensing business are all good sources of information. In addition, licensees can hire a licensing consultant to be their eyes and ears in the licensing business. *See Chapter 6.*

### What are the hottest licenses?

The hottest licenses vary from season to season. More important, however, is the fact that the hottest license is not always the best license for a given licensee. A smaller, less visible property may be much more lucrative than a blockbuster for an individual licensee, if the fit is more appropriate. *See Chapter 6.*

### If I am a small manufacturer with no prior experience in licensing, can I become a licensee?

Yes, although it may not be easy. Opportunities exist for licensees who have expertise in a certain niche distribution channel, who have an idea for a unique licensed product or who are willing to commit to an unproven license in its early stages. *See Chapter 6.*

## What do I have to do to become a licensee?

Licensors usually require licensees to fill out evaluation forms. They ask for the licensee's plans for the licensed product line, historical data about the licensee's business, financial status of the licensee and retail and credit references. In addition, they want to see samples of products similar to those the licensee proposes to manufacture under license. *See Chapter 6.*

## Is there anything like a licensing agent that represents the interests of manufacturers?

Yes. There are a number of licensing consultants who exclusively represent the interests of licensees in seeking appropriate properties to license. *See Chapter 6.*

## If I license a film do I automatically get to use actors' likenesses?

Not necessarily. Licensees should find out up front if there will be problems using actors' likenesses on products, or if the use of likenesses is allowed at all. Also, while the legal right to use an actor's likeness may exist, if the actor doesn't like the idea a studio often will choose not to risk alienating the person out of fear the individual won't help publicize the film or might not work with the studio in the future. *See Chapter 8.*

# TRADE PUBLICATIONS AND DIRECTORIES

## LICENSING PUBLICATIONS
We're obviously partial to The Licensing Letter, but here's a list of all the major licensing publications currently available:

*The Licensing Letter*, 718-469-9330

*The Licensing Book, The Licensing Report, The Licensing Book International*, 212-575-4510

*Licensing Today International, Licensing Reporter Europe*, 011-44-384-440591

*Index*, 212-630-4882

*Licensing Trends*, 212-630-4882

*Team Licensing Business*, 602-990-1101

*Sports Licensing International*, 212-779-5000

*The Licensing Journal*, 203-358-0848

## LICENSING DIRECTORIES
*The EPM Licensing Letter Sourcebook*, 718-469-9330

*Guide to the Licensing World*, 011-44-825-713611

*The International Licensing Directory*, 011-44-384-440591

*The Licensing Resource Directory*, 203-256-4700

## TRADE PUBLICATIONS
These trade publications are organized by the industries they cover; all occasionally feature some licensing-related information.

### TOYS
*Playthings*, 212-689-4411

*Toy & Hobby World*, 212-685-0404

*The Toy Book*, 212-575-4510

### CHILDREN'S PRODUCTS
*Children's Business*, 212-630-4693

*Earnshaw's*, 212-563-2742

### APPAREL
*Women's Wear Daily*, 212-630-4610

*Daily News Record* (men's apparel), 212-630-4000

### SPORTING GOODS
*Sporting Goods Dealer*, 212-779-5000

*Sporting Goods Business*, 212-869-1300

*Sports Trend*, 404-252-8831

## ENTERTAINMENT
*Entertainment Marketing Letter*, 718-469-9330
*Hollywood Reporter*, 213-525-2000
*Daily Variety*, 213-857-6600
*Broadcasting & Cable*, 202-659-2340

## MARKETING
*Brandweek*, 212-536-5336
*Promo*, 203-761-1510
*Advertising Age*, 312-649-5200

## PUBLISHING
*Publishers Weekly*, 212-463-6758
*Comics Retailer*, 715-445-2214

## GIFTS
*Gifts & Decorative Accessories*, 212-689-4411
*Gift Beat*, 201-358-6868
*Giftware News*, 312-849-2220
*Gift & Stationery Business*, 212-626-2272

## GENERAL RETAILING
*Discount Store News*, 212-756-5100
*Stores*, 212-244-8780
*Discount Merchandiser*, 212-889-6030

## HOME FURNISHINGS
*HFN - Home Furnishings Network*, 212-620-4779
*Home Textiles Today*, 212-337-6900

# TRADE SHOWS

## LICENSING TRADE SHOWS

**Licensing Show,** Licensing Industry Merchandisers Association, 212-244-1944; staged annually in June.

**Worldwide Licensing Exposition,** The Licensing Book, 212-545-4510; held in April.

## MAJOR U.S. CONSUMER PRODUCTS TRADE SHOWS

*JANUARY*

**International Winter Consumer Electronics Show,** Electronic Industries Association, 202-457-8700.

**International Housewares Show,** National Housewares Manufacturers Association, 800-553-0505.

**New York International Gift Fair,** George Little Management, 800-272-SHOW.

**NATPE,** NATPE, 310-453-4440.

*FEBRUARY*

**Super Show,** Super Show, 305-893-8771.

**MAGIC and WWD/MAGIC,** Magic International, 310-393-7757.

**American International Toy Fair,** Toy Manufacturers of America, 212-675-1141.

*MARCH*

**International Kids Fashion Show,** Larkin Group, 212-594-0880.

**National Association of Mens Sportswear Buyers Show,** NAMSB Show/Schimel, 212-986-1811.

*APRIL*

**DRTV,** Advanstar Expositions, 714-513-8400.

**National Association of College Stores Annual Meeting & Campus Market Expo,** NACS, 216-775-7777.

**Comdex/Spring,** Interface Group, 617-449-6600.

**International Home Furnishings Market,** International Home Furnishings Marketing Association, 919-889-0203.

*MAY*

**Premium Show,** Miller Freeman Trade Shows, 516-627-4000.

Electronic Entertainment Expo, Knowledge Industry Publications,
914-328-9157.

National Stationery Show, George Little Management,
800-272-SHOW.

Surtex, George Little Management, 800-272-SHOW.

VSDA Convention, Video Software Dealers Association, 818-385-1500.

## JUNE

American Booksellers Association Show, ABA, 914-591-2665.

National Association of Mens Sportswear Buyers (NAMSB) Show,
NAMSB Show/Schimel, 212-986-1811.

## JULY

NSGA World Sports Expo, National Sporting Goods Association,
708-439-4000.

## AUGUST

International Kids Fashion Show, Larkin Group, 212-594-0880.

New York International Gift Fair, George Little Management,
800-272-SHOW.

MAGIC and WWD/MAGIC, Magic International, 310-393-7757.

## SEPTEMBER

International Kids Fashion Show, Larkin Group, 212-594-0880.

National Association of Mens Sportswear Buyers (NAMSB) Show,
NAMSB Show/Schimel, 212-986-1811.

International Home Furnishings Market, International Home
Furnishings Marketing Association, 919-889-0203.

## NOVEMBER/DECEMBER

EPM Entertainment Marketing Conference, EPM, 718-469-9330.

International Juvenile Products Show, Juvenile Products
Manufacturers Association, 609-985-2878.

Comdex/Fall, Interface Group, 617-449-6600.

School & Home Office Products Association (SHOPA) Show,
SHOPA, 513-297-2250.

# INDEX

# — A —

# – B –

# – D –

# – E –

# – F –

# – G –

# – H –

# – I –

# –J–

# –K–

# – M –

# – P –

THE LICENSING BUSINESS HANDBOOK

# – S –

# – T –

# – U –

# – V –

# – W –

# –X–

# –Y–

# ABOUT THE AUTHOR

Karen Raugust has been Executive Editor of *The Licensing Letter* since January 1990, a position that includes writing and editing the monthly EPM Communications newsletter and compiling TLL's annual survey data on the licensing industry.

Ms. Raugust edits EPM's other licensing-related publications, including "The EPM Licensing Letter Sourcebook," "Licensing Business Profit and Opportunity Outlook," and "Licensing Business Databook," among others. She is also author of "Merchandise Licensing For The Television Industry," published by Focal Press (October 1995).

Through EPM's 60-Minute Consultant program and custom projects, Ms. Raugust serves as a consultant to the licensing community. She is frequently quoted in the trade and consumer press on licensing subjects, and has taught a course on sports licensing at New York University.

Prior to her work with EPM, Ms. Raugust held various positions in the publishing industry, including Managing Editor at Union Square Press and Advertising Production Manager at *Editor & Publisher* magazine. She holds a BA from Carleton College and an MBA from Columbia University.

# ABOUT EPM COMMUNICATIONS, INC.

EPM Communications, Inc. is a New York City-based publishing, research and consulting firm.

The privately held company publishes the newsletters *The Licensing Letter, Entertainment Marketing Letter, Research Alert, Minority Markets Alert* and *Youth Markets Alert*.

In addition to "The Licensing Letter Handbook," EPM publishes two annual directories, "The EPM Licensing Letter Sourcebook" and "The EPM Entertainment Marketing Sourcebook," along with research studies including "At Our Leisure," a landmark survey of how Americans spend their leisure time.

The company provides consulting services through its telephone-based "60-Minute Consultant" program, develops in-house seminars for subscriber corporations, conducts property evaluations for licensed properties, and produces the annual EPM Entertainment Marketing Conference.

The company was founded in 1988 by Ira Mayer, a prominent entertainment industry journalist and media analyst, and his wife and partner, Riva Bennett, who had been associated with LINK Resources, National Data Corp., and other research and finance institutions.